Toward an Aesthetic of Reception

Toward
an Aesthetic
of Reception

Hans Robert Jauss
Translation from German by Timothy Bahti
Introduction by Paul de Man

Theory and History of Literature, Volume 2

University of Minnesota Press
Minneapolis

Publication of this work has been made possible in part
by a grant from the Andrew W. Mellon Foundation.

The University of Minnesota Press gratefully acknowledges
the support of Inter Nationes for the translation of this book.

Published by the University of Minnesota Press,
111 Third Avenue South, Suite 290, Minneapolis, MN 55401-2520
Printed in the United States of America on acid-free paper.
Eighth printing, 2007

Library of Congress Cataloging in Publication Data

Jauss, Hans Robert.
    Toward an aesthetic of reception.
    (Theory and history of literature; v. 2)
    Includes index.
    Contents: Literary history as a challenge to literary
theory — History of art and pragmatic history — Theory
of genres and medieval literature — [etc.]
    1. Reader-response criticism — Addresses, essays,
lectures. I. Title. II. Series.
PN98.R38J38   801'.95   81-16260
ISBN 0-8166-1034-7   AACR2
ISBN 0-8166-1037-1 (pbk.)

The German texts of "Literary History as a Challenge to Literary Theory" and "History of Art and Pragmatic Theory" are © 1970 by Suhrkamp Verlag. They appear here in English by courtesy of Suhrkamp Verlag. A different English version of certain sections of "Literary History as a Challenge to Literary Theory" appeared in *New Literary History* I (1969). For permission to use the translation that appeared in *New Literary History* the publisher is grateful to that journal and its editor Ralph Cohen. The English translation of "History of Art and Pragmatic History" appears here through the courtesy of Princeton University Press, where it appeared in *New Perspectives in German Literary Criticism*, edited by Richard Amacher and Victor Lange (© 1979 by Princeton University Press). "Theory of Genres and Medieval Literature" originally appeared in German in *Grundriss der Romanischen Literaturen des Mittelalters*, volume six (© 1972 by Carl Winter Universitäts Verlag) and appears here by permission of Carl Winter Universitäts Verlag. "Goethe's and Valery's Faust: On the Hermeneutics of Question and Answer" originally appeared in German in *Comparative Literature* 28 (1976). The essay appears here through the courtesy of that journal and its editor Thomas Hart as well as through the courtesy of Wilhelm Fink Verlag. "The Poetic Text within the Change of Horizons of Reading: The Example of Baudelaire's 'Spleen II'" originally appeared in German in *Romantische Zeitschrift für Literaturgeschichte*, Heft 2/3 (1980), and appears here in English translation courtesy of the author.

The University of Minnesota
is an equal-opportunity
educator and employer.

Contents

Introduction
Paul de Man

By his own volition, the work of the German literary historian and theorist Hans Robert Jauss has been associated with a study group for which he is a spokesman and which practices a specific way of investigating and teaching literature. In the field of literary theory, the existence of such groups is not an unusual occurrence. They are, at times, centered on a single, dominating personality and take on all the exalted exclusiveness of a secret society, with its rituals of initiation, exclusion, and hero-worship. Nothing could be more remote from the spirit of the group of which Jauss is a prominent member. The Konstanz school of literary studies, so named because several of its members taught or are teaching at the newly founded University of Konstanz in Southern Germany, is a liberal association of scholars, informally united by methodological concerns that allow for considerable diversity. It has the character of a continuing research seminar that includes some constant members (of which H. R. Jauss is one) next to more casual participants; a somewhat comparable instance of such a group, in structure if not in content, would have been, in this country, the Chicago critics of the Forties and Fifties, who shared an interest in Aristotelian poetics. The concerns of such groups are methodological rather than, as in the case of the New Criticism or the Frankfurt School, cultural and ideological; their influence is didactic and "scientific" rather than critical. One has to bear this aspect of Jauss's work in mind in reading the essays included in this volume: it accounts for their programmatic and relatively impersonal tone. Whereas the "masters" of an earlier generation in Germany and elsewhere, literary scholars such as Vossler, Spitzer, Curtius, Auer-

bach, or even Lukács, wrote as individual talents engaged in specula-
tions of their own, Jauss sees himself as a participant in a team that
also is concerned with the professional aspects of literary instruction.
The attitude is typical for a generation whose approach to literature
has become more systematic; it is by no means incompatible with
genuine innovation nor with wider humanistic commitments. In reading Jauss, one is not reading the work of a speculative philosopher, a
literary critic, or a pure theoretician of poetics. One is, first of all,
reading the work of a specialist of French literature who has made
contributions to a remarkably diverse number of topics, from medieval genre theory to Marcel Proust.[1] But, beyond this, one is also
reading the work of a theoretically informed, learned, and enlightened
expert whose work fully warrants extended theoretical discussion
and didactic application.

The methodology of the Konstanz school is mostly referred to as
Rezeptionsästhetik, a word that does not lend itself easily to translation into English. We speak, in this country, of reader-response criticism or, more imaginatively (though also more controversially) of
"affective stylistics."[2] These terms stress reading as a constitutive
element of any text but, except for the implicit connotations of
"stylistic" or "poetics," they put less emphasis on the far-reaching,
traditional word "aesthetics" that remains of central importance to
Jauss and his associates. What has to be called, somewhat awkwardly,
the "aesthetics of reception" has itself been well received in this
country. It has been a two-way process; the University of Konstanz
may be as far removed from a large urban center as is possible in
today's Germany but there is nothing provincial about the Konstanz
school. From the start, in 1963, the colloquia of the group included
participants from the United States and a recent anthology of their
main position papers includes contributions from Michael Riffaterre
and Stanley Fish.[3] Conversely, leading members of the Konstanz
group such as Wolfgang Iser, Jurij Striedter, and Hans Robert Jauss
himself often teach in this country, some on a permanent basis.
Leading American journals publish and review their papers; the
books of Wolfgang Iser, whose field is English literature, have been
translated and are being extensively used and debated by American
specialists of narrative fiction. With the publication of this collection
of essays by Hans Robert Jauss the introduction of the Konstanz
school to American readers is made complete. It makes available
some of the most lucidly argued theoretical documents to have originated in the group. They are indeed so clear and convincing as to require little introduction. Since they are rooted, however, in a meth-

odological and philosophical tradition only remotely comparable to our own, it may be useful to see how Jauss's presuppositions are revealed and put into perspective by approaches that developed in different circumstances.

The aim of the Konstanz theoreticians can be derived from the general title given to their main publication series: Poetics *and* Hermeneutics.[4] The *and* that appears in this combination is not as obvious as it might seem. Hermeneutics is, by definition, a process directed toward the determination of meaning; it postulates a transcendental function of understanding, no matter how complex, deferred, or tenuous it might be, and will, in however mediated a way, have to raise questions about the extralinguistic truth value of literary texts. Poetics, on the other hand, is a metalinguistic, descriptive or prescriptive discipline that lays claim to scientific consistency. It pertains to the formal analysis of linguistic entities as such, independently of signification; as a branch of linguistics, it deals with theoretical models prior to their historical realization. Hermeneutics belongs traditionally to the sphere of theology and its secular prolongation in the various historical disciplines; unlike poetics, which is concerned with the taxonomy and the interaction of poetic structures, hermeneutics is concerned with the meaning of specific texts. In a hermeneutic enterprise, reading necessarily intervenes but, like computation in an algebraic proof, it is a means toward an end, a means that should finally become transparent and superfluous; the ultimate aim of a hermeneutically successful reading is to do away with reading altogether.[5] It is not so easy to say how reading is involved, if at all, in poetics. If—to abuse once more one of the most outworn examples in literature—on noting that Homer refers to Achilles as a lion, I conclude that Achilles is courageous, this is a hermeneutic decision; if, on the other hand, I examine, with Aristotle, whether Homer is using a simile or a metaphor,[6] this is a consideration in the sphere of poetics. The two procedures have very little in common. It is clear, however, from this loaded example (loaded because, by selecting a figure of speech, one has in fact pre-empted the question) that one has to have "read" the text in terms of poetics to arrive at a hermeneutic conclusion. One has to have become aware that it is a figure, otherwise one would simply take it to mean that Achilles has changed species or that Homer has taken leave of his senses. But one also has to read it hermeneutically to "understand" it as poetics: one has to acknowledge Achilles' courage as well as his humanity to notice that something occurs in the language that does not normally occur in the natural or social world, that a lion can be substituted for a man. All that this hasty piece of improvised poetics is meant to suggest is that hermeneutics and poetics, different and distinct as they are, have a way of becoming entangled, as indeed they have since Aristotle and before. One can look upon the history of literary theory as the continued attempt to disentangle this knot and to record the reasons for failing to do so.

The boldness of the Konstanz school in calling their approach a poetics as well as a hermeneutics measures the scope and the burden of its contribution. In practice, the distribution of competences as well as the rather complex methodological genealogy of the group has divided the emphasis among its various members. Some go back to the structural analyses of the Prague linguistic circle and find their ancestry among the more technical aspects of phenomenology, including the work of the Polish philosopher Roman Ingarden. In their case, the primary emphasis falls on poetics (*Werkstruktur*) rather than on hermeneutics (*Interpretationssystem*).[7] Others find their antecedents among philosophers of history and interpretation rather than in the structural analysis of language and of consciousness; their primary emphasis is on hermeneutics. The synthesis, the articulation of poetics with hermeneutics remains the common aim of all aestheticians of reception, but the attempted solutions as well as the techniques of reading that lead to these solutions vary, depending on the starting position. If, mostly for the sake of convenience, one chooses to divide the group into poeticians and hermeneuts, then Hans Robert Jauss undoubtedly belongs among the latter. This may give him the appearance of being more traditional, or at least more concerned with tradition, than some of his associates, yet it makes his approach particularly instructive for American readers whose legitimate impatience with the technicalities of formal analysis sends them in search of models for historical understanding.

Jauss's relationship to the hermeneutic tradition is itself by no means simple or uncritical. He fully shares in the stance that unites all members of the group in their common rejection of "essentialist" conception of literary art. The suspicion of essentialism arises whenever the study of the production or of the structure of literary texts is pursued at the expense of their reception, at the expense of the individual or collective patterns of understanding that issue from their reading and evolve in time. In "Literary History as a Challenge to Literary Theory (Chapter 1 of this volume), the closest Jauss came to writing an actual manifesto, the polemical thrust of the passages in which he sets his methods apart from those of his predecessors allows one to situate this new pragmatism, or this new materialism, within the tradition of German scholarship. Jauss differentiates himself sharply from both the formalistic and the Marxist tendencies that were prevalent at the time. The grounds for his critical attitude toward Marxism (or, to be more precise, toward a certain type of social realism) as well as toward form, turn out to be remarkably similar. Georg Lukács, an avowed Marxist, is criticized for reasons that differ little from those invoked with regard to the anything but Marxist Ernst Robert Curtius. For all their ideological differences, both adhere to the classical creed of the canonical work as the aesthetic incarnation of a universal essence. Curtius's canon, which is that of the masterpieces of the Western neo-Latin tradition, differs entirely from Lukács's, which is that of nineteenth century realism as it culminates in Balzac and dissolves with Flaubert. But the disagreements between various canons are less important to Jauss than the canonical conception itself, in which the work is assumed to transcend history because it encompasses the totality of its tensions within itself. Lukács and Curtius both remain faithful to such a conception. Even Hans-Georg Gadamer, Jauss's teacher at Heidelberg whom he has consistently acknowledged as a determining influence, is being reproached for his commitment to a canonical idea of tradition, which, in Germany, often tends to coincide with the canonization of the Age of Goethe. Jauss's work is part of a reaction against an orthodoxy, an orthodoxy that refuses to admit, as Hegel is supposed to have stated in his *Aesthetics*, that the end of classicism is also the end of art. Hence his continued concern with modernity as the crux of literary history. The question remains to be considered whether Jauss's own historical procedure can indeed claim to free itself from the coercion of a model that is perhaps more powerful, and for less controllable reasons, than its assumed opponents believe.

The strength of Jauss's method stems from a refinement of the established rules for the historical understanding of literature. His interest is no longer directed toward the definition of an actual canon but toward the dynamic and dialectical process of canon formation — a notion that is familiar, in this country, to readers of T. S. Eliot and, more recently and in a very different mode, of Harold Bloom.[8] Such a critique of historical positivism coupled with a critique of essentialism is not in itself new; few historians still believe that a work of the past can be understood by reconstructing, on the basis of recorded evidence, the set of conventions, expectations, and beliefs that existed at the time of its elaboration. What is different and effective in the approach suggested by Jauss are the reasons (implicitly) given for this impossibility: the historical consciousness of a given period can never exist as a set of openly stated or recorded propositions. It exists instead, in Jauss's terminology, as a "horizon of expectation." The term, which derives from Husserl's phenomenology of perception in its application to the experience of consciousness, implies that the condition of existence of a consciousness is not available to this consciousness in a conscious mode, just as, in a perception, conscious attention is possible only upon a background, or horizon, of distraction.[9] Similarly, the "horizon of expectation" brought to a work of art is never available in objective or even objectifiable form, neither to its author nor to its contemporaries or later recipients.

This complicates, but also enriches, the process of historical description to a considerable degree. A dialectic of understanding as a complex interplay between knowing and not-knowing, is built within the very process of literary history. The situation is comparable to the dialogical relationship that develops between the analyst and his interlocutor in psychoanalysis. Neither of the two knows the experience being discussed; they may indeed not even know whether such an experience ever existed. The subject is separated from it by mechanisms of repression, defense, displacement and the like, whereas, to the analyst, it is available only as a dubiously evasive symptom. But this difficulty does not prevent a dialogical discourse of at least some interpretative value from taking place. The two "horizons," that of individual experience and that of methodical understanding, can engage each other and they will undergo modifications in the process, though none of the experiences may ever become fully explicit.

The analogy with psychoanalysis (which Jauss does not use) underscores the epistemological complexity of the historian's task. Both analyst and historian point to a cognition that, for reasons variously identified as psychological, epistemological, or, in the case of Heidegger, ontological, is not available as an actual presence and therefore requires a labor of interpretation or of reading prior even to determining whether it can ever be reached. We have come to expect this degree of hermeneutic intricacy from any philosophical or psychological analysis but, surprisingly enough, a similar subtlety is rarely demanded from historians and, among historians, least of all from literary historians—although, according to the logic of the situation with its implied stress on reading rather than knowing, literary history, rather than psychoanalysis or epistemology, should be the privileged example, the model case. This surprise is in fact not surprising at all, since the reluctance is itself the symptom of an anxiety of not-knowing that may reach further than pragmatic historians may wish to know. Be this as it may, in Jauss's defense of a history

and an aesthetics of reception, the model for the historical understanding of literature finally comes of age, as it were, by ways of the
negative implications contained in the term "horizon of expectation."
His critical descriptions of earlier literary histories draw their energy
from this insight and, with few exceptions, these descriptions will be
found hard to refute. Jauss's critique of the preconscious or unconscious[10] assumptions that underlie canonical literary history constitutes a major contribution, all the more relevant for us since the
same problem exists in this country in a less thematized, more diffused, and therefore all the more coercive way.

The same point of departure, the duplicitous epistemology of the
historical consciousness, allows Jauss to defend a far-reaching synthesis between the private and the public dimensions of the literary
work. This synthesis constitutes the programmatic and forward-look-
ing, as opposed to the critical, aspects of his work. Thus the passage
from the individual to the collective or the social aspects of the work
is implicit in the model of the "horizon": just as the anonymous
background of a perception is general and nondifferentiated with regard to the individual perception that stands foregrounded and silhouetted[11] against it, the particular work, at the moment of its production, stands out in its singularity from the collective grayness of
received ideas and ideologies. Preconscious or subconscious expectations are always collective and therefore, to a degree, "received."
They are the outcome of a reception by means of which the individual work becomes part of a landscape against which new works will,
in turn, be silhouetted. Translated from spatial metaphors into epistemological categories, the process can be stated in terms of question
and answer: the question occurs as an individual disruption of an
answer that has become common knowledge but which, under the effect of this new question, can now be seen to have itself been an individual response to an earlier, collective question. As the answer metamorphoses into a question, it becomes like an individual, tree, or
portrait set within a stylized landscape and it reveals, by the same
token, a live background behind its background, in the form of a
question from which it now can itself *stand out*. The question-and-
answer structure, like the foreground-background or the conscious-
preconscious structures, are abyssal frames that engender each other
without end or *telos*. In the process, however, they create a sequence
of apparent syntheses that convey an impression of methodological
mastery. Jauss can legitimately claim that the "horizon of expectation" mediates between the private inception and the public reception of the work. And he can also claim that it mediates between the

self-enclosed structure and its outside effect or *Wirkung*. To the extent that the background is collective or "common," it is, at first, nondifferentiated and unstructured; under the impact of the individually structured questions, as understood and identified by the historian-interpreter, it becomes aware of itself as background and acquires, in its turn, the coherence necessary for its organization and potential transformation. A clear example of this process occurs on page 27: Emma Bovary, a character in a fictional construct, whose mind is like an amorphous bundle of aberrations against which the beauty of her shape stands silhouetted, engenders, in the mind of her readers, a critical awareness of social conventions strong enough to put these conventions in question. The historical reading as reception mediates between the formal structure and social change.

In the final analysis, the procedure provides a model for the articulation between structure and interpretation. At the moment of its inception, the individual work of art stands out as unintelligible with regard to the prevailing conventions. The only relation it has to them is that of contemporaneity or of synchrony, an entirely contingent and syntagmatic relationship between two elements that happen to coincide in time but are otherwise entirely alien to each other. The differentiation that separates the work from its setting is then inscribed in the historical, diachronic motion of its understanding (*Horizontswandel*), which ends in the discovery of properties held in common between the work and its projected history. Unlike the relationship between the work and its historical present, the relationship between the work and its future is not purely arbitrary. It contains elements of genuine paradigmatic similarity that can circulate freely between the formal singularity of the work and the history of its reception. Put in somewhat more technical terms, one would say that, in Jauss's historical model, a syntagmatic displacement within a synchronic structure becomes, in its reception, a paradigmatic condensation within a diachrony. Attributes of difference and of similarity can be exchanged thanks to the intervention of temporal categories: by allowing the work to exist in time without complete loss of identity, the alienation of its formal structure is suspended by the history of its understanding. Chiasmic patterns of this type never fail to carry the promise of totalization.

One sees that the methodological rewards for the willingness to give up the illusion of unmediated understanding are considerable. Nor are they purely theoretical: Jauss is entirely willing to submit his hermeneutical model to the concrete test of practical interpretation and to refine it in the process. The lack of compatibility between literary theory and practice that plagues the study of literature everywhere, thus also seems to be on the way of being overcome by a judicious aesthetics of reception. The persuasiveness of the argument, the validity of the critique of traditional canonical literary history, the considerable contributions to the interpretation of particular texts combine to bear witness to the merits of a method whose influence on the theory and the pedagogy of literary studies has been entirely beneficial. It is an impressive record. If one wishes, in the true spirit of the method, to question in turn the horizon of expectation of the aesthetics of reception, then one should begin by acknowledging the merits of a theory that enables one to ask such a question within a productive context.

Some writers, not very remote from Jauss in time and place, have denied the efficacy of a theory of interpretation based on the public reception of a work of literature and have discarded it as a mere side-effect devoid of hermeneutic interest. Walter Benjamin's dogmatic pronouncement at the onset of his essay entitled "The Task of the Translator" is a relevant case in point: "Nowhere does a concern for the reception of a work of art or of an artform aver itself fruitful for its understanding. . . . No poem is addressed to a reader, no painting to its beholder, no symphony to its listeners."[12] The passage is quoted by Rainer Warning, together with a passage from Adorno, as a prime example of author or production oriented essentialism.[13] But is this really the case? When Jauss identifies the power of canonical essences in the writings of Curtius, Lukács, and Gadamer, he is on safe ground, but when the same is being said about Benjamin, Adorno, and Heidegger—three names that, for all that separates them, belong together in this context—things are not so simple. Benjamin, for instance, in the very essay from which the just-quoted passage is taken, could not be more explicit in his critique of Platonic essences as a model for history when he rejects the validity of the notion of copy or representation (*Abbild*) as an approach to literary texts. Nor could one be more eloquently explicit than he is, in the same essay, about the historicity of literary understanding—although the notion of history that Benjamin here invokes certainly differs considerably from Jauss's. By invoking the "translation" rather than the reception or even the reading of a work as the proper analogon for its understanding, the negativity inherent in the process is being recognized: we all know that translations can never succeed and that the task (*Aufgabe*) of the translator also means, as in the parlance of competitive sports, his having to give up, his defeat "by default." But "translation" also directs, by implication, the attention to language, rather than perception, as the possible locus for this negative moment. For translation is, by definition, intralinguistic, not a relationship between a subject and an object, or a foreground and a background, but between one linguistic function and another. Throughout the essay, Benjamin's point is that translation, as well as the insuperable difficulty that inhabits its project, exposes certain tensions that pertain specifically to language: a possible incompatibility between proposition (*Satz*) and denomination (*Wort*) or between the literal and what he calls the symbolic meaning of a text or, within the symbolic dimension itself, between what is being symbolized and the symbolizing function. The conflict is stated, in most general terms, as existing between what language means (*das Gemeinte*) and the manner in which it produces meaning (*die Art des Meinens*). It is certainly true that, in Benjamin's essay and elsewhere in his writings, these tensions are, to some degree, suspended in what he refers to as pure language: *die reine Sprache*. But it is equally clear that this apparent transcendence does not occur in the realm of art but in that of the sacred. Between Benjamin's *reine Sprache* and Valéry's *poésie pure* there is very little in common. Far from being nostalgia or a prophecy of the sacred, poetic language, of which the inherent inadequacy is made explicit in its translation, is what has to be forgotten to find access to the sacred: in the poetic translations that Hölderlin made of Sophocles "meaning collapses from abyss to abyss, until it threatens to lose itself in the bottomless depths of language." In such a sentence, "abyss" should perhaps be read as technically and neutrally as in any trivial "mise en abîme." The existential pathos is counterbalanced by the fact that these "bottomless depths" of language are also its most manifest and ordinary grammatical dimensions, the specific linguistic categories that Benjamin can list with some precision. What this does to Benjamin's subsequent claims of transcendence (or to their perhaps falacious understanding *as* transcendence) is not our present concern. It establishes however that, as far as poetry and its history are concerned, there can be no question of essences. The rejection of a conception of poetry as message or reception is not the result of an essentialist conception of literature but of the critique of such a conception. With numerous qualifications, something similar could be said of Heidegger's essay "On the Origin of the Work of Art," which Jauss summarizes (and dismisses) as an assertion of a "timeless present" or a "self sufficient presence" (p. 63) of the work of art, a simplification that does scant justice to Heidegger's dialectical concept of historical preservation (*Bewahrung*) on which Jauss himself, possibly by way of Gadamer, is dependent.

The point is not to oppose to each other philosophical traditions some of which Jauss could easily enlist on his side of the question. Rather, the reference to Benjamin's essay draws attention to the possibility that a concept such as "horizon of expectation" is not necessarily applicable, without further elaboration, to the arts of language. For all the obstacles to understanding mentioned by Benjamin belong specifically to language rather than to the phenomenal world; consequently, the expectation that they could be mastered by analogy with processes that stem from the psychology of perception is by no means certain. Husserl himself, among others, could be invoked to caution against the possibility of such a mistranslation.[14] The hermeneutics of experience and the hermeneutics of reading are not necessarily compatible. This does not imply that the solutions proposed by Jauss are inadequate or that the recourse to perception can or should be avoided altogether; the opposite is the case. It does mean, however, that the horizon of Jauss's methodology, like all methodologies, has limitations that are not accessible to its own analytical tools. The limitation, in this case, has to do with linguistic factors that threaten to interfere with the synthesizing power of the historical model. And it also means that these same factors will then exercise a more or less occult power over Jauss's own discourse, especially over the details of his textual interpretations.

At first sight, this hardly seems to be the case. Jauss is by no means adverse to taking the linguistic aspects of texts into consideration, nor is he in any way on the defensive in dealing with the work of linguists. His preference, however, goes to linguists who attempt to mediate between the communicative and the aesthetic function of language, to what one could call the stylists of communication theory. Jauss has argued from the start that the recognition of the formal and aesthetic aspects of a text are not to be separated from historical investigations having to do with its reception; a good formalist, by the strength of his own performance, has to become a historian. The Czech linguist Felix V. Vodička, whose work is often cited with approval by Jauss and other Konstanz theoreticians, has made this explicit in his conception of reception as the historical "concretization" of a linguistic structure. The element of negativity that, in Jauss's horizon of expectation is located in the nonawareness of the background, resides, in Vodička and in the Prague linguists generally, in the characterization of literary language as a language of *signs*. Just as an element of not-knowing is built within the model of the horizon, the concept of literary sign implies an element of indeterminacy and of arbitrariness. In the words of Jan Mukařovský, a leading figure of the Prague Linguistic Circle, as quoted by Vodička: "Although the work of literature is closely dependent in its effect on communication by signs, it depends on it in such a manner that it is the dialectical negation of an actual communication."[15] The ensuing polysemy is mastered by inscribing it within the historical and social continuum of particular receptions or "concretizations." Structural aesthetics as practiced by the Prague circle are therefore far from being a threat to Jauss. His historical concepts seem to dovetail perfectly with their linguistic terminology. This theoretical alliance achieves a genuine synthesis between hermeneutics and poetics. Is this to say that Benjamin's anxieties about the semantics of poetic language are convincingly laid to rest by the concerted investigations of both linguists and historians?

The answer will depend on a term that until now we were able to keep in abeyance. When Vodička speaks of concretizations, he strongly insists that these are *aesthetic* concretizations, just as Jauss's reception is an *aesthetic* reception, an *aesthetic* process. How "aesthetic" is to be understood here is not self-evident. For Mukařovský, the aesthetic quality of the work of literature, like its historical quality, is a function of its sign-structure. In the analysis of poetic diction "the structure of the linguistic sign holds the center of attention, whereas the (nonpoetic) functions are oriented toward extralinguistic instances and goals exceeding the linguistic sign."[16] The focus, in poetic texts, on the process of signification rather than on significance is what is said to be specifically aesthetic. The arbitrary and conventional aspects of the sign thus acquire value as aesthetic features and it is by this same conventionality that the collective, social, and historical dimensions of the work can be reintegrated. This is the very point at which the procedures of a historian such as Jauss and poeticians such as Vodička or Mukařovský converge. It is Jauss's considerable merit to have perceived and demonstrated the linkage between reception and semiotics. The condensation of literary history and structural analysis occurs by ways of the category of the aesthetic and depends for its possibility on the stability of this category.

This stability, however, remains problematic for many philosophers. A concatenation of the aesthetic with the meaning-producing powers of language is a strong temptation to the mind but, precisely for that reason, it also opens up a Pandora's box. The aesthetic is, by definition, a seductive notion that appeals to the pleasure principle, a eudaemonic judgment that can displace and conceal values of truth and falsehood likely to be more resilient to desire than values of pleasure and pain. Nietzsche, who is acutely aware of aesthetic powers as tools of the will, warns that judgments based on pleasure or on pain "are the silliest *expressions* of judgments imaginable—by which, of course, I (Nietzsche) do not mean to say that the judgments which become audible in this manner have to be silly."[17] Aesthetic reactions can never be considered as central causes (*Ursachen*) but only as trivial side-effects (*Nebensachen*): "they are value judgments *of the second order* which are derived from a centrally dominant value; they consider the useful and the harmful in a purely affective mode and are therefore absolutely volatile and dependent."[18] The considerable interest they hold for the historian or for the critical philosopher is symptomatological rather than systematic: they are philosophically significant to the extent that their power to mislead points to other causes. Hegel's massively misunderstood treatment of the aesthetic as a provisional (*vorläufig*, a word that also occurs in Benjamin[19]) form of cognition is entirely in the spirit of his continuators Kierkegaard and Nietzsche. This means, among other things, that whenever the aesthetic is invoked as an appeal to clarity and control, whenever, in other words, a symptom is made into a remedy for the disorder that it signals, a great deal of caution is in order. Jauss's straightforward equation of the aesthetic with the pleasure principle, as in the essay on Valéry and Goethe, or as is implicit in his subsequent book on *Aesthetic Experience and Literary Hermeneutics*[20], is in itself symptomatic. And when this same principle is then made to link up with the more objective properties of language revealed by linguistic analysis, the suspicion arises that aesthetic judgment has trespassed beyond its legitimate epistemological reach. As is to be expected in such a case, the traces of this transgression become noticeable by the omission, rather than by the misrepresentation, of certain features of language.

Characteristic of such omissions is Jauss's lack of interest, bordering on outright dismissal, in any considerations derived from what has, somewhat misleadingly, come to be known as the "play" of the signifier, semantic effects produced on the level of the letter rather than of the word or the sentence and which therefore escape from the network of hermeneutic questions and answers. Such a concern with "the instances of the letter" is particularly in evidence, as is well known, among certain French writers not generally included within Jauss's own critical canon of relevant *Fachliteratur*. He has always treated such Parisian extravagances with a measure of suspicion and even when, under the pressure of their persistence as well as of genuine affinities between their enterprise and his own, he acknowledged some of their findings, it has always been a guarded and partial re-cognition. There are good pedagogical and ideological reasons, of local rather than general interest, for this reserve. The tactics of ex-clusion, on the other hand, are so familiar as to constitute, within the community of literary scholarship, a mass reaction: in a long tra-dition, more familiar even in the world of *haute couture* than of literary theory, what is made in Paris is often thought of as more fashionable than sound. What is in fashion in Paris is tolerable only as window display, not for everyday wear. Yet, as we know from Baudelaire, fashion, *la mode*, is itself a highly significant and, pre-cisely, aesthetic and historical category that historians should not underestimate. When it becomes fashionable to dismiss fashion, clearly something interesting is going on, and what is being discarded as *mere* fashion must also be more insistent, and more threatening, than its frivolity and transcience would seem to indicate. What is being dismissed, in the context of our question, is the play of the signifier, the very same topic (if it can thus be called) which Friedrich Schlegel singled out when the displeasure of his readers, the accusation of fri-volity, forced him, in 1800, to suspend publication of the *Athenäum*.[21]

In the practice of his own textual interpretation, Jauss pays little attention to the semantic play of the signifier and when, on rare oc-casions, he does so, the effect is quickly reaestheticized before any-thing unpleasant might occur—just as any word-play is so easily dis-armed by assimilating it to the harmlessness of a mere pun or *calem-bour*. Thus, in a recent article that makes use of one of Baudelaire's Spleen poems as a textual example,[22] Jauss comments judiciously on the lines in which the name of the eighteenth-century painter Boucher is made to pseudo-rhyme with the word "débouché" (uncorked)

> . . . un vieux boudoir
> Où les pastels plaintifs et les pâles Boucher,
> Seuls, respirent l'odeur d'un flacon débouché.

In a rare Lacanian moment, Jauss suggests that what he calls a "grotesque" effect of verbal play—the rhyme-pair Boucher/débouché —is also something more uncanny: "The still harmonius representa-tion of the last perfume escaping from the uncorked bottle overturns (*kippt um*) into the dissonant connotation of a 'decapitated' rococo painter Boucher" (p. 157). After having gone this far, it becomes very hard to stop. Should one not also notice that this bloody scene is made gorier still by the presence of a proper name (Boucher) which, as a common name, means butcher, thus making the "pâle Boucher" the agent of his own execution? This pale and white text of recollection (the first line of the poem is "J'ai plus de souvenirs que si j'avais mille ans") turns red with a brutality that takes us out of the inwardness of memory, the ostensible *theme* of the poem, into a very threatening literality to which an innocent art-term such as "dissonance" hardly does justice. Much more apt is Jauss's very concrete and undecorous, almost colloquial, word "umkippen" (to overturn), which "overturns" the beheaded Boucher as if he were himself an uncorked "flacon" spilling his blood. That this would happen to the proper name of a painter, and by means of a merely "grotesque" and frivolous play on words tells us a great deal about the difficult-to-control borderline (or lack of it) between the aesthetics of *homo ludens* and the literal incisiveness of *Wortwitz*. For reasons of decorum, the gap that Jauss has opened, by his own observation, in the aesthetic texture of the language is at once reclosed, as if the commentator felt that he might betray the integrity of the text with which he is dealing.

This hesitation, this restraint before giving in to the coarseness and the potential violence of the signifier is by no means to be condemned as a lack of boldness. After all, Baudelaire himself does not threaten us, or himself, directly, and by keeping the menace wrapped up, as it were, within a play of language, he does not actually draw blood. He seems to stop in time, to fence with a foil[23] —for how could anyone be hurt by a mere rhyme? Yet, the poetic restraint exercised by Baudelaire differs entirely from the aesthetic restraint exercised by Jauss. For the play on words, as we all know from obscene jokes, far from preserving decorum dispenses with it quite easily, as Baudelaire dispensed with it to the point of attracting the attention of the *police des moeurs*. What it does not dispense with, unlike decorum (a classical and aesthetic concept), is the ambiguity of a statement that because it is a verbal thrust and not an actual blow, allows itself to be taken figurally but, in so doing, opens up the way to the performance of what it only seems to feign or prefigure. The false rhyme on Boucher/débouché is a figure, a paranomasis. But only after we have, with the assistance of H. R. Jauss, noticed and recognized it as such does the actual threat inherent in the fiction produced by the actual hands of the painter (who is also a butcher) become manifest. This no longer describes an aesthetic but a poetic structure, a structure that has to do with what Benjamin identified as a nonconvergence of "meaning" with "the devices that produce meaning," or what Nietzsche has in mind when he insists that eudaemonic judgments are inadequate "means of expression" of a cognition. Since this poetic (as distinguished from aesthetic) structure has to do with the necessity of deciding whether a statement in a text is to be taken as a figure or *à la lettre*, it pertains to rhetoric. In this particular instance, Jauss has come upon the rhetorical dimension of language; it is significant that he has to draw back in the face of his own discovery.

But how can it be said that Jauss swerves from the consideration of rhetoric where he has so many perceptive and relevant things to say about it, and does so without any trace of the restraint for which I am both praising and blaming him in his gloss on Baudelaire's poem? An extended study of his writings, going well beyond the decorous limits of an introduction, would show that something similar to what happens in the essay on Spleen occurs whenever rhetorical categories are at stake. One hint may suffice. In a polemical exchange with Gadamer about the rhetoric of classicism (p. 30), classical art is assimilated to a rhetoric of mimesis (the Aristotelian rhetorical category par excellence), and opposed to medieval and modern art, which are said to be nonmimetic and nonrepresentational. A rhetorical trope serves as the ground of a historical system of periodization that allows for the correct understanding of meaning; once again, a poetic and a hermeneutic category have been seamlessly articulated. But if this assertion seems so reasonable, is it not because it corresponds to a received idea of literary history rather than being the result of a rigorous linguistic analysis? The alternative to *mimesis* would be, one assumes, allegory, which all of us associate with medieval and, at least since Benjamin, with modern art. If we then ask whether Jauss's own model for reading, the horizon of expectation, is classical or modern, one would have to say that it is the former. For it is certainly, like all hermeneutic systems, overwhelmingly mimetic: if literary understanding involves a horizon of expectation it resembles a sense of perception, and it will be correct to the precise extent that it "imitates" such a perception. The negativity inherent in the Husserlian model is a negativity within the sensory itself and not its negation, let alone its "other." It is impossible to conceive of a phenomenal experience that would not be mimetic, as it is impossible to conceive of an aesthetic judgment that would not be dependent on imitation as a constitutive category, also and especially when the judgment, as is the case in Kant, is interiorized as the consciousness of a subject. The concept of nonrepresentational art stems from painting and from a pictorial aesthetic that is firmly committed to the phenomenalism of art. The allegory, or allegoresis, which Jauss opposes to mimesis, remains firmly rooted in the classical phenomenalism of an aesthetics of representation.

"Allegory," however, is a loaded term that can have different implications. A reference to Walter Benjamin can again be helpful, all

the more so since Jauss alludes to him in the same essay on Baudelaire from which I have been quoting. In his treatment of allegory
Benjamin plays, by anticipation, the part of Hamann in a debate in
which Jauss would be playing the part of Herder. For him, allegory
is best compared to a commodity; it has, as he puts it in a term taken
from Marx, *Warencharakter*, "matter that is death in a double sense
and that is anorganic." The "anorganic" quality of allegory is, however, not equivalent, as Jauss's commentary seems to suggest (p. 179),
to the negation of the natural world; the opposition between organic
and anorganic, in Benjamin, is not like the opposition between *or-
ganisch* and *aorganisch*, familiar from the terminology of idealist philosophy in Schelling and also in Hölderlin. The commodity is anorganic because it exists as a mere piece of paper, as an inscription or a
notation on a certificate. The opposition is not between nature and
consciousness (or subject) but between what exists as language and
what does not. Allegory is material or materialistic, in Benjamin's
sense, because its dependence on the letter, on the literalism of the
letter, cuts it off sharply from symbolic and aesthetic syntheses.
"The subject of allegory can only be called a grammatical subject";
the quotation is not from Benjamin but from one of the least valued
sections of Hegel's *Lectures on Aesthetics*,[24] the canonical bible, still
for Heidegger, of the phenomenalism of art. Allegory names the rhetorical process by which the literary text moves from a phenomenal,
world-oriented to a grammatical, language-oriented direction. It thus
also names the moment when aesthetic and poetic values part com-
pany. Everyone has always known that allegory, like the commodity
and unlike aesthetic delight, is, as Hegel puts it, "icy and barren."[25]
If this is so, can one then still share Jauss's confidence that "the allegorical intention, pursued to the utmost of *rigor mortis*, can still
reverse (*umschlagen*) this extreme alienation into an appearance of
the beautiful" (205)?[26] If the return to the aesthetic is a turning
away from the language of allegory and of rhetoric, then it is also a
turning away from literature, a breaking of the link between poetics
and history.

The debate between Jauss and Benjamin on allegory is a debate between the classical position, here represented by Jauss, and a tradition[27] that undoes it, and that includes, in the wake of Kant, among
others Hamann, Friedrich Schlegel, Kierkegaard, and Nietzsche. The
debate occurs in the course of interpreting Baudelaire's poem "Spleen
II." The poem deals with history as recollection, *souvenir*, Hegel's
Erinnerung. Jauss's precise and suggestive reading carefully traces
the manner in which an inner state of mind (spleen) is first compared

to an outside object (ll. 2 and 5), then asserted to *be* such an object
(l. 6), then becomes the voice of a speaking subject that declares itself to be an object (l. 8), and finally culminates in the dialogical relationship of an apostrophe by this subject to a material object that
has itself acquired consciousness:

> — Désormais tu n'es plus, ô matière vivante!
> Qu'un granit entouré d'une vague épouvante, . . .
> [ll. 19-20] [28]

At the conclusion of the poem, the enigmatic figure of "Un vieux
sphinx" appears and is said, however restrictively and negatively, to
be singing

> Un vieux sphinx . . .
> Ne chante qu'aux rayons du soleil qui se couche.
> [ll. 22-24]

Jauss convincingly identifies this sphinx as the figure of the poetic
voice and his song as the production of the text of "Spleen II" (pp. 169,
170). We rediscover the not unfamiliar, specular (that is to say solar and
phenomenal) conception of a "poetry of poetry,"[29] the self-referen-
tial text that thematizes its own invention, prefigures its own reception, and achieves, as aesthetic cognition and pleasure, the recovery
from the most extreme of alienations, from the terror of encrypted
death. "The dissonance of the statement is aesthetically harmonized
by the assonance and the balance between the various textual layers"
(p. 182). "In a successfully elaborated form, the literary representation
of terror and anxiety is always already, thanks to aesthetic sublimation,
overcome" (p. 167). The promise of aesthetic sublimation is powerful-
ly argued, in a manner that leaves little room for further questioning.
   The assurance that further questioning nevertheless should take
place has little to do with one's own spleen, with pessimism, nihilism
or the historical necessity to overcome alienation. It depends on
powers of poetic analysis, which it is in no one's power to evade. One
of the thematic textual "layers" of "Spleen II" that remain constant
throughout the text is that of the mind as a hollow container, box,
or grave and the transformation of this container, or of the corpse
contained in it, into a voice:

> mon triste cerveau.
> C'est une pyramide, un immense caveau,
> Qui contient plus de morts que la fosse commune.
> — Je suis un cimetière abhorré de la lune,
>
> . . . .
> — Désormais tu n'es plus, ô matière vivante!

Qu'un granit entouré d'une vague épouvante,
Assoupi dans le fond d'un Saharah brumeux;
Un vieux sphinx ignoré du monde insoucieux,
Oublié sur la carte, et dont l'humeur farouche
Ne chante qu'aux rayons du soleil qui se couche.

The transformation occurs as one moves from mind (as recollection) to pyramid and to sphinx. It occurs, in other words, by an itinerary that travels by way of Egypt. Egypt, in Hegel's *Aesthetics*, is the birthplace of truly symbolic art, which is monumental and architectural, not literary. It is the art of memory that remembers death, the art of history as *Erinnerung*. The emblem for interiorized memory, in Hegel, is that of the buried treasure or mine (*Schacht*), or perhaps, a well.[30] Baudelaire, however, fond though he is of well-metaphors, uses "pyramid," which connotes, of course, Egypt, monument and crypt, but which also connotes, to a reader of Hegel, the emblem of the sign as opposed to the symbol.[31] The sign, which pertains specifically to language and to rhetoric, marks, in Hegel, the passage from sheer inward recollection and imagination to thought (*Denken*), which occurs by way of the deliberate forgetting of substantial, aesthetic, and pictorial symbols.[32] Baudelaire, who in all likelihood never heard of Hegel, happens to hit on the same emblematic sequence[33] to say something very similar. The decapitated painter lies, as a corpse, in the crypt of recollection and is replaced by the sphinx who, since he has a head and a face, can be apostrophized in the poetic speech of rhetorical figuration. But the sphinx is not an emblem of recollection but, like Hegel's sign, an emblem of forgetting. In Baudelaire's poem he is not just "oublié" but "oublié sur la carte," inaccessible to memory because he is imprinted on paper, because he is himself the inscription of a sign. Contrary to Jauss's assertion—"for who could say with more right than the sphinx: j'ai plus de souvenirs que si j'avais mille ans"—the sphinx is the one least able to say anything of the sort. He is the grammatical subject cut off from its consciousness, the poetic analysis cut off from its hermeneutic function, the dismantling of the aesthetic and pictorial world of "le soleil qui se couche" by the advent of poetry as allegory. What he "sings" can never be the poem entitled "Spleen"; his song is not the sublimation but the forgetting, by inscription, of terror, the dismemberment of the aesthetic whole into the unpredictable play of the literary letter. We could not have reached this understanding without the assistance of Jauss's reading. His work confronts us with the enigma of the relationship between the aesthetic and the poetic and, by so doing, it demonstrates the rigor of its theoretical questioning.

Paul de Man

Translator's Preface
Timothy Bahti

I recently came across a scholarly article (in German) on contemporary "aesthetics of reception" that was utterly forgettable except that, within the space of eleven pages, it displayed no fewer than 106 footnotes. This is an example, perhaps, not only of a certain tendency toward overkill in German scholarship, but also of the degree of close attention and learned debate being given to that development in literary studies that is also known as the Konstanz School. As Paul de Man notes in his Introduction, Hans Robert Jauss and his colleagues are engaged in rethinking the methods of literary study, and this is more an enterprise of literary scholarship than it is a project in literary theory or a part of today's myriad debates on the philosophical and ideological assumptions of the human sciences. It is in this spirit of literary scholarship—rather than one of partisan affiliation—that I have translated the essays collected here, and would make several prefatory remarks.

Widely discussed in both West and East Germany since its organization as a loosely collective position in the late Sixties, and increasingly well known to the Germanophonic audience in France and America, the Konstanz School is for the most part unknown to English-speaking audiences and has until now been largely limited to two translated books by Wolfgang Iser. As a scholar of English literature and a theorist working in large part within the Anglo-American philosophic tradition, Iser could appeal to this audience on its native ground. Now, with the appearance of this work by Jauss in English, the more *historical* position of the other leading Constance representative can finally be broadly appreciated. I believe that Jauss's position obviates, or at least reformulates in more interesting and productive ways, many of the difficulties of the various Anglo-American theories of "reader response" (from I. A. Richards to the present) or the neo-Aristotelian ideas about emotions elicited by literary form, at the same time that it circumvents the objections to considerations of the reader as they are presented in W. K. Wimsatt's argument against the "affective fallacy" or other essays of the New Criticism—and Jauss does both precisely through his engagement of the historical dimension of literary understanding. In this, he belongs to a line of twentieth-century German critics that includes Walter Benjamin, Erich Auerbach, Theodor Adorno, and Peter Szondi, and that constitutes the backbone of Germany's contribution to literary studies in this century, distinguishing it from the more ahistorical contributions of French, English, and American theory and criticism. Given this difference in intellectual contexts, then, Jauss's work deserves not a loose translation that might make it all too easily assimilable into our current critical situation, but rather a precise translation that would allow for a close, rigorous, truly critical reception. It is such a translation that I have tried to provide.

Jauss's German is often not easy, and I have not attempted to simplify it when transposing it into English. His terminologies and conceptual frameworks, on the other hand, can perhaps be made more accessible through several brief references. Jauss was trained within the German tradition of Romance philology, a tradition familiar to American readers in the work of Auerbach, E. R. Curtius, and Leo Spitzer, and one to which Jauss has remained ever faithful. His other major training was under the philosopher Hans-Georg Gadamer, who was himself a student of Heidegger. If it took *Being and Time* more than thirty years to find its English translation, Gadamer's *Truth and Method* appeared in English within fifteen years of its German publication, and thus the historical hermeneutics that it represents, and that Jauss develops further—both drawing upon the work of the English philosopher R. G. Collingwood—can be supposed to meet with a ready and potentially informed audience. In the essays collected here, Jauss's other main theoretical resources are Kant's critique of aesthetic judgment, Husserl's phenomenology, and Russian Formalism together with Prague Structuralism. Kant has long been adopted by Anglo-American thought—indeed, he remains almost the last German philosopher taken seriously by analytic philosophy. Husserlian phenomenology has been widely disseminated in some American university circles, especially its extension into social phenomenology (Schütz's concept of the *Lebenswelt* or "life-world") that Jauss finds particularly useful. And Russian Formalism and Prague Structuralism have become parts of mainstream American literary theory and criticism through the efforts of René Wellek, Victor Erlich, and others. Thus Jauss's work ought to find a receptive audience here in America, even if his own combination of various intellectual sources represents a major new position within the competing methodologies that characterize the current pluralism of our discipline. Whenever possible, I have sought to assist this reception through reference in the notes to existing English translations of his sources, although I have in each case translated quoted material from the original versions.

The portions of the first essay, "Literary History as a Challenge to Literary Studies," that originally appeared in translation in *New Literary History* (1970) have been thoroughly retranslated for the sake of accuracy and completeness. On the other hand, I am grateful for permission to have lightly retouched David Wilson's excellent translation of "History of Art and Pragmatic History" (in *New Perspectives in German Literary Criticism*, ed. Richard E. Amacher and Victor Lange [Princeton, N.J., 1979]) in order to ensure terminological and stylistic consistency within the volume. All the other essays collected here have been translated from the German by myself for the first time. I am grateful for the encouragement of Hans Robert Jauss, Paul de Man, and Wlad Godzich in undertaking this translation, as well as for the patient efforts of the editors at the University of Minnesota Press in seeing this volume into print. The shortcomings of the translation, of course, remain my own.

Timothy Bahti
Ithaca, New York

Toward an Aesthetic of Reception

Chapter 1
Literary History as
a Challenge to Literary Theory

I

In our time literary history has increasingly fallen into disrepute, and not at all without reason. The history of this worthy discipline in the last one hundred and fifty years unmistakably describes the path of a steady decline. Its greatest achievements all belong to the nineteenth century. To write the history of a national literature counted, in the times of Gervinus and Scherer, De Sanctis and Lanson, as the crowning life's work of the philologist. The patriarchs of the discipline saw their highest goal therein, to represent in the history of literary works [*Dichtwerke*] the idea of national individuality on its way to itself. This high point is already a distant memory. The received form of literary history scarcely scratches out a living for itself in the intellectual life of our time. It has maintained itself in requirements for examinations by the state system of examinations that are themselves ready for dismantling. As a compulsory subject in the high school curriculum, it has almost disappeared in Germany. Beyond that, literary histories are still to be found only, if at all, on the bookshelves of the educated bourgeoisie who for the most part opens them, lacking a more appropriate literary dictionary, to answer literary quiz questions.[1]

In university course catalogs literary history is clearly disappearing. It has long been no secret that the philologists of my generation even rather pride themselves in having replaced the traditional presentation of their national literature by periods and as a whole with lectures on the history of a problem or with other systematic approaches. Scholarly production offers a corresponding picture:

3

collective projects in the form of handbooks, encyclopedias, and (as the latest offshoot of the so-called "publisher's synthesis") series of collected interpretations have driven out literary histories as unserious and presumptuous. Significantly, such pseudohistorical collections seldom derive from the initiative of scholars, rather most often from the whim of some restless publisher. Serious scholarship on the other hand precipitates into monographs in scholarly journals and presupposes the stricter standard of the literary critical methods of stylistics, rhetoric, textual philology, semantics, poetics, morphology, historical philology, and the history of motifs and genres. Philological scholarly journals today are admittedly in good part still filled with articles that content themselves with a literary historical approach. But their authors find themselves facing a twofold critique. Their formulations of the question are, from the perspective of neighboring disciplines, qualified publicly or privately as pseudoproblems, and their results put aside as mere antiquarian knowledge. The critique of literary theory scarcely sees the problem any more clearly. It finds fault with classical literary history in that the latter pretends to be only one form of history writing, but in truth operates outside the historical dimension and thereby lacks the foundation of aesthetic judgment demanded by its object—literature as one of the arts.[2]

This critique should first be made clear. Literary history of the most convenient forms tries to escape from the dilemma of a mere annal-like lining-up of the facts by arranging its material according to general tendencies, genres, and what-have-you, in order then to treat within these rubrics the individual works in chronological series. In the form of an excursis, the authors' biography and the evaluation of their oeuvre pop up in some accidental spot here, in the manner of an occasional aside. Or this literary history arranges its material unilinearly, according to the chronology of great authors, and evaluates them in accordance with the schema of "life and works"; the lesser authors are here overlooked (they are settled in the interstices), and the development of genres must thereby also unavoidably be dismembered. The second form is more appropriate to the canon of authors of the classics; the first is found more often in the modern literatures that have to struggle with the difficulty—growing up to and in the present—of making a selection from a scarcely surveyable list of authors and works.

But a description of literature that follows an already sanctioned canon and simply sets the life and work of the writers one after another in a chronological series is, as Gervinus already remarked, "no history; it is scarcely the skeleton of a history."[3] By the same token, no historian would consider historical a presentation of literature by genres that, registering changes from work to work, followed the unique laws of the forms of development of the lyric, drama, and novel and merely framed the unclarified character of the literary development with a general observation (for the most part borrowed from historical studies) concerning the *Zeitgeist* and the political tendencies of the age. On the other hand it is not only rare but almost forbidden that a literary historian should hold judgments of quality concerning the works of past ages. Rather, he prefers to appeal to the ideal of objectivity of historiography, which only has to describe "how it really was." His aesthetic abstinence has good grounds. For the quality and rank of a literary work result neither from the biographical or historical conditions of its origin [*Entsteh- ung*], nor from its place in the sequence of the development of a genre alone, but rather from the criteria of influence, reception, and posthumous fame, criteria that are more difficult to grasp. And if a literary historian, bound by the ideal of objectivity, limits himself to the presentation of a closed past, leaving the judgment of the literature of his own, still-unfinished age to the responsible critics and limiting himself to the secure canon of "masterpieces," he remains in his historical distance most often one to two generations behind the latest development in literature. At best he partakes of the contemporary engagement with literary phenomena of the present as a passive reader, and thereby becomes in the formation of his judgment a parasite of a criticism that he silently despises as "unscholarly." What then should a historical study of literature still be today, a study that—taking up a classical definition of the interest in history, that of Friedrich Schiller—can promise so little instruction to the "thoughtful observer," no imitative model at all to the "active man of the world," no important information to the "philosopher," and everything else but a "source of the noblest pleasure" to the reader?[4]

II

Citations customarily call upon an authority to sanction a step in the process of scholarly reflection. But they can also remind us of a former way of posing a question, to prove that an answer that has become classic is no longer satisfactory, that it has itself become historical again and demands of us a renewal of the process of question and answer. Schiller's answer to the question of his inaugural lecture at Jena on 26 May 1789, "What Is and Toward What End Does One

Study Universal History," is not only representative of the historical understanding of German idealism; it is also illuminating for a critical survey of the history of our discipline. For it indicates the expectations under which the literary history of the nineteenth century sought to fulfill the legacy of the idealist philosophy of history in competition with general historiography. At the same time it lets one recognize why the epistemological ideal of the historicist school had to lead to a crisis, and also why it had to draw the decline of literary history along with it.

Gervinus can serve as our chief witness. He authored not only the first scholarly presentation of a *History of the Poetic National Literature of the Germans* [*Geschichte der poetischen Nationalliteratur der Deutschen*](1835-42), but also the first (and only) theory of historiography [*Historik*] written by a philologist.[5] His *Fundamentals of the Theory of Historiography* develop the main thoughts of Wilhelm von Humboldt's text, *On the Task of the Historian* [*Über die Aufgabe des Geschichtsschreibers*] (1821) into a theory with which Gervinus elsewhere also established the great task of a history of "high" literature. The literary historian will only then become a writer of history when, researching his object of study, he has found "the one basic idea that permeates precisely that series of events that he took upon himself as his object, that appears in them, [and] brings them into connection with world events."[6] This guiding idea — for Schiller still the general teleological principal that allows us to conceive of the world-historical progress of humanity — already appears in Humboldt in the separate manifestations of the "idea of national individuality."[7] And when Gervinus then makes this "ideal mode of explanation" of history his own, he implicitly places Humboldt's "historical idea"[8] in the service of nationalist ideology: a history of German national literature ought to show how "the wise direction in which the Greeks had led humanity, and toward which the Germans (in accordance with their particular characteristics) had always been disposed, was taken up again by these [Germans] with free consciousness."[9] The universal idea of enlightened philosophy of history disintegrated into the multiplicity of the history of national individualities and finally narrowed itself to the literary myth that precisely the Germans were called to be the true successors of the Greeks — for the sake of that idea, "that the Germans alone in their purity were created to realize."[10]

The process made evident by the example of Gervinus is not only a procedure typical of the *Geistesgeschichte* of the nineteenth century. It also contained a methodological implication for literary history as for all historiography when the historicist school brought the teleological model of idealist philosophy of history into disrepute. When one rejected the solution of the philosophy of history—to comprehend the course of events from an "end, an ideal high point" of world history—as unhistorical,[11] how then was the coherence of history, never given as a whole, to be understood and represented? The ideal of universal history thereby became, as Hans-Georg Gadamer showed, a dilemma for historical research.[12] In Gervinus's formulation, the historian "can only wish to represent complete series of events, for he cannot judge where he does not have the final scenes before him."[13] National histories could serve as closed series so long as one saw them peak politically in the fulfilled moment of national unification, or literarily in the high point of a national classic. Yet their progression toward the "final scene" must inevitably bring back the old dilemma. Thus in the last analysis Gervinus only made a virtue of necessity when—in notable agreement with Hegel's famous diagnosis of "the end of the artistic period"—he dispensed with the literature of his own post-classical age as merely a symptom of decline, and gave to the "talents that now lack a goal" the advice that they would better occupy themselves with the real world and the state.[14]

But the historicist historian seemed to be freed from the dilemma of the closure and continuation of history wherever he limited himself to periods that he could place before him up through the "final scene," and describe in their own completeness without regard for that which followed from them. History as the representation of periods thus also promised to fulfill the methodological ideal of the historicist school to the fullest extent. Thereafter, when the unfolding of national individuality was no longer satisfactory as a guiding thread, literary history chiefly strung closed periods one after another. The "fundamental law of writing history, according to which the historian should disappear before his object, which should itself step forward in full objectivity,"[15] could be observed most immediately with the period, an individual meaningful whole [Sinnganzen] set off by itself. If "full objectivity" demands that the historian ignore the standpoint of his present time, the value and significance of a past age must also be recognizable independent of the later course of history. Ranke's famous utterance of 1854 gives a theological foundation to this postulate: "But I maintain that each period is immediate vis-à-vis God, and that its value depends not at all on what followed from it, but rather on its own existence, on its own self."[16] This new answer to the question as to how the concept of "progress" in history is to be conceived, assigns the task of a new theodicy to the historian: when the historian considers and represents "each period as something valid for itself," he justifies God before the philosophy of history as progress, a philosophy that values periods only as steps for the following generation and thereby presupposes a preference for later periods—in other words, an "injustice of the godhead."[17] Ranke's solution to the problem left behind by the philosophy of history was nonetheless purchased at the expense of cutting the thread between history's past and present—between the period "as it really was" and that "which followed from it." In its turning away from the Enlightenment philosophy of history, historicism sacrificed not only the teleological construction of universal history, but also the methodological principle that, according to Schiller, first and foremost distinguishes the universal historian and his method: namely, "to join the past with the present"[18]—an inalienable understanding, only ostensibly speculative, that the historicist school could not brush aside without paying for it,[19] as the further development in the field of literary history also indicates.

The achievement of nineteenth-century literary history stood and fell with the conviction that the idea of national individuality was the "invisible part of every fact,"[20] and that this idea made the "form of history"[21] representable even in a series of literary works. To the extent that this conviction disappeared, the thread connecting events had to disappear as well, past and present literature fall apart into separate spheres of judgment,[22] and the selection, determination, and evaluation of literary facts become problematic. The turn toward positivism is primarily conditioned by this crisis. Positivist literary history believed it could make a virtue of its necessity if it borrowed the methods of the exact natural sciences. The result is only too well known: the application of the principle of pure causal explanation to the history of literature brought only externally determining factors to light, allowed source study to grow to a hypertrophied degree, and dissolved the specific character of the literary work into a collection of "influences" that could be increased at will. The protest was not long in coming. Geistesgeschichte armed itself with literature, set an aesthetics of irrational creation in opposition to the causal explanation of history, and sought the coherence of literature [*Dichtung*] in the recurrence of atemporal ideas and motifs.[23] In Germany Geistesgeschichte allowed itself to be drawn into the preparation and foundation of the "people's" [*völkischen*] literary studies of National Socialism. After the war, new methods relieved it and completed the process of de-ideologization, but did not thereby take upon themselves the classical task of literary history. The representation of literature in its immanent history and in its relation to pragmatic history lay outside the interests of the history of ideas and concepts, as well as outside the interests of research into tradition that flourished in the wake of the Warburg School. The history of ideas strove secretly for a renewal of the history of philosophy in the mirror of literature;[24] the research into tradition neutralized the lived praxis of history when it sought the focal point of knowledge in the origin or in the atemporal continuity of tradition, and not in the presence and uniqueness of a literary phenomenon.[25] The recognition of the enduring within perpetual change released one from the labor of historical understanding. The continuity of the classical heritage, raised to the highest idea, appeared in Ernst Robert Curtius's monumental work (which set a legion of epigonal *topoi*-researchers to work) in the tension between creation and imitation, between "great literature" [Dichtung] and "mere literature" that is immanent in the literary tradition and not historically mediated: a timeless classicism of masterpieces raised itself above that which Curtius called the "unbreakable chain, the tradition of mediocrity,"[26] and left history behind as a *terra incognita*.

The gap between the historical and the aesthetic consideration of literature is no more spanned here than it already was in Benedetto Croce's literary theory, with its division of poetry and nonpoetry held *ad absurdum*. The antagonism between pure literature [Dichtung] and time-bound literature was only to be overcome when its founding aesthetics was put into question and it was recognized that the opposition between creation and imitation characterizes only the literature of the humanist period of art, but can no longer grasp modern literature or even, already, medieval literature. Literary sociology and the work-immanent method[27] disassociated themselves from the approaches of the positivist and idealist schools. They widened even further the gap between history and literature [Dichtung]. This is most clearly seen in the opposed literary theories of the Marxist and Formalist schools that must stand at the center of this critical survey of the prehistory of contemporary literary studies.

III

Both schools have in common the turning away from positivism's blind empiricism as well as from the aesthetic metaphysics of Geistesgeschichte. They sought, in opposite ways, to solve the problem of how the isolated literary fact or the seemingly autonomous literary work could be brought back into the historical coherence of literature and once again be productively conceived as evidence of the social process, or as a moment of literary evolution. But there is as yet still no great literary history that could be identified as a product of these two attempts, that would have retold the old histories of national literatures from the new Marxist or Formalist premises, reformed their sanctioned canon, and represented world literature as a process, with a view toward its emancipatory social or perceptually formative [wahrnehmungsbildende] function. Through their one-sidedness, the Marxist and the Formalist literary theories finally arrived at an aporia, the solution to which demanded that historical and aesthetic considerations be brought into a new relationship.

The original provocation of Marxist literary theory that is also always renewed is that it denies their own histories to art and to the corresponding forms of consciousness of ethics, religion, or metaphysics. The history of literature, like that of art, can no longer maintain the "appearance of its independence" when one has realized that its production presupposes the material production and social praxis of human beings, that even artistic production is a part of the "real life-process" of the appropriation of nature that determines the history of human labor or development. Only when this "active life-process" is represented "does history stop being a collection of dead facts."[28] Thus literature and art can be viewed as a process "only in relation to the praxis of historical human beings," in their "social function" (Werner Krauss),[29] conceived as one of the coeval "kinds of human appropriation of the world" and represented as part of the general process of history in which man overcomes the natural condition in order to work his way up to being human (Karl Kosík).[30]

This program, recognizable in *The German Ideology* (1845/46) and other early writings of Karl Marx only in its initial tendencies, still awaits its realization, at least for the history of art and literature. Already shortly after its birth, with the *Sickingen* debate of 1859,[31] Marxist aesthetics was drawn under the spell of an approach conditioned by the concepts of periods and genres, an approach that still dominates the arguments between Lukács, Brecht, and others in the Expressionism debate of 1934-38:[32] literary realism's problem of imitation or reflection [Wiederspiegelung]. Nineteenth-century realist art theory—provocatively directed against the romantics who kept their distance from reality, by literary figures forgotten today (Champfleury, Duranty); ascribed *post festum* by literary history to the great novelists Stendhal, Balzac, and Flaubert; and raised to the dogma of socialist realism in the twentieth century during the Stalinist era—arose and remained in a noteworthy dependence on the classical aesthetics of *imitatio naturae*. At the same time as the modern concept of art as the "signature of creative man," as the realization of the unrealized, as a potential constructive or formative of reality was being advanced against the "metaphysical tradition of the identity of being and nature, and the determination of the work of man as the 'imitation of nature,' "[33] Marxist aesthetics still, or again, believed it must legitimate itself with a theory of copying. To be sure, in its concept of art it puts "reality" in the place of "nature," but it then once again endows the reality placed before art with characteristic features of that nature that was apparently overcome, with exemplary obligation and essential completeness.[34] Measured against the original antinaturalist position of Marxist theory,[35] its contraction upon the mimetic ideal of bourgeois realism can only be adjudged as a throwback to a substantialist materialism. For beginning with Marx's concept of labor, and with a history of art understood within the dialectic of nature and labor, the material horizon of conditions and objective praxis, Marxist aesthetics did not have to shut itself off from the modern development of art and literature, which its doctrinaire criticism has up to the most recent past put down as decadent because "true reality" is missing. The argument of the last years, in which this verdict has been canceled step by step, is to be interpreted at once as a process in which Marxist aesthetics sets to work with secular tardiness against the reduction of the work of art to a merely *copying* function, in order finally to do justice to the long-supressed insight into art's character as *formative* of reality.

The orthodox theory of reflection stands in the way of this genuine task of a dialectical-materialist literary history and in the way of the solution of the correlative problem of how one is to determine the achievement and influence of literary forms as an independent kind of objective human praxis. The problem of the historical and processlike connection of literature and society was put aside in an often reproving manner by the games of Plechanov's[36] method: the reduction of cultural phenomena to economic, social, or class equivalents that, as the given reality, are to determine the origin of art and literature, and explain them as a merely reproduced reality. "Whoever begins with the economy as something given and not further deducible, as the deepest fundamental cause of all and the unique reality that suffers no further inquiry—he transforms the economy into its result, into a thing, an autonomous factor of history, and thereby promotes a fetishization of economy."[37] The "ideology of the economic factor" that Karl Kosík thus takes to court forced the history of literature into a parallelism that the historical phenomenon of literary production, in its diachrony as well as its synchrony, continually refutes.

Literature, in the fullness of its forms, allows itself to be referred back only in part and not in any exact manner to concrete conditions of the economic process. Changes in the economic structure and rearrangements in the social hierarchy happened before the present age mostly in long, drawn-out processes, with scarcely visible caesurae and few spectacular revolutions. Since the number of ascertainable determinants in the "infrastructure" remained incomparably smaller than the more rapidly changing literary production of the "superstructure," the concrete multiplicity of works and genres had to be traced back to always the same factors or conceptual hypostases, such as feudalism, the rise of the bourgeois society, the cutting-back of the nobility's function, and early, high, or late capitalist modes of production. Also, literary works are variously permeable of events in historical reality, according to their genre or to the form pertaining to their period, which led to the conspicuous neglecting of nonmimetic genres, as opposed to the epic. In searching for social equivalents, sociologism not accidentally held to the traditional series of masterpieces and great authors, since their originality seemed to be interpretable as immediate insight into the social process or—in the case of insufficient insight—as involuntary expression of changes occurring in the "basis."[38] The dimensions specific to the historicity of literature are thereby obviously diminished. For an important work, one that indicates a new direction in the literary process, is surrounded by an unsurveyable production of works that correspond to the traditional expectations or images concerning reality, and that thus in their social index are to be no less valued than the solitary novelty of the great work that is often comprehended only later. This dialectical relationship between the production of the new and the reproduction of the old can be grasped by the theory of reflection only when it no longer insists on the homogeneity of the contemporary in the temporal misrepresentation of a harmonizing arrangement of social conditions and the literary phenomena reflecting them, side by side. With this step, however, Marxist aesthetics arrives at a difficulty that Marx already foresaw: "the unequal relationship of the development of the material production . . . to the artistic."[39] This difficulty, behind which the specific historicity of literature hides itself, can be solved by the theory of reflection only at the cost of its self-cancellation [*Selbstaufhebung*].

The claim to formulate dialectically the theory of reflection thus entangled its leading representative Georg Lukács in striking contradictions.[40] They come into view with his explanation of the normative value of classical art as well as with his canonization of Balzac for modern literature, but also with his concept of totality and its correlate, the "immediacy of reception." When Lukács relies on Marx's famous fragment on classical art, and claims that even Homer's influence today is "inseparably bound to the age and the means of production in which or, respectively, under which Homer's work arose,"[41] he once again implicitly presupposes as answered that which, according to Marx, was still to be explained: why a work "can still provide [us] aesthetic pleasure"[42] when as the mere reflex of a long-overcome form of social development it would still be serving only the historian's interest. How can the art of a distant past survive the annihilation of its socioeconomic basis, if one denies with Lukács any independence to the artistic form and thus also cannot explain the ongoing influence of the work of art as a process formative of history? Lukács helps himself along in this dilemma with the time-honored concept of the "classical" that is nonetheless transcendent of history, that can bridge the gap between past art and present influence, even in the case of its content, only with determinations of a timeless ideality[43]—and thus precisely not in a dialectical-materialist mediation. For modern literature, as is well known, Lukács raised Balzac and Tolstoy to the classical norm of realism. From this viewpoint, the history of modern literature takes on the form of an already honorable humanist schema of the writing of art history: given its classical high point in the nineteenth-century bourgeois novel, the view describes the trajectory of a decline, loses itself in the artistic modes of decadence that are alien to reality, and is to regain its ideality to the extent that it reproduces the modern social reality in forms such as typification, individualization, or "organic narration"—forms that have already become historical, and been canonized by Lukács.[44]

The historicity of literature that is concealed by the classicism of orthodox Marxist aesthetics is also missed by Lukács where he seemingly gives a dialectical interpretation to the concept of reflection, as, for example, in his commentary on Stalin's theses "On Marxism in Linguistics"[45]: "Each superstructure not only reflects reality, but actively takes a position for or against the old or the new basis."[46] How are literature and art, as superstructure, supposed to be able "actively" to take a position vis-à-vis their social basis when on the other hand, according to Engels, in this "reciprocal influence" economic necessity will "in the last instance" nonetheless prevail and determine the "kind of change and further development" of social reality,[47] and when therefore the step toward the new is always one-sidedly preordained for literary and artistic production by an inevitably altered economic basis? This undialectical one-sidedness is also not eliminated when, with Lucien Goldmann, one reforms the connection between literature and social reality along the "homology" of structures instead of contents.

Goldmann's attempts toward a literary history of French classicism and a sociology of the novel postulate a series of "world views" that are class-specific, then degraded by late capitalism since the nineteenth century, and finally reified; these must—here the not-yet-overcome classicism betrays itself—satisfy the ideal of "coherent expression" that he allows only for great writers.[48] So here too, as already with Lukács, literary production remains confined to a secondary function, always only reproducing in harmonious parallel with the economic process. This harmonization of "objective signification" and "coherent expression," of given social structure and imitative artistic phenomenon, implicitly presupposes the classic-idealist unity of content and form, essence and appearance[49]—only now, in place of the idea, the material side, that is, the economic factor, is explained as substance. This has as its consequence that the social dimension of literature and art with respect to their reception is likewise limited to the secondary function of only allowing an already previously known (or ostensibly known) reality to be *once again recognized*.[50] Whoever confines art to reflection also restricts its influence—here the disowned heritage of Platonic mimesis takes its revenge—to the recognition of the already known. But it is precisely at this point that the possibility of grasping the revolutionary character of art is foreclosed to Marxist aesthetics: the characteristic that it can lead men beyond the stabilized images and prejudices of their historical situation toward a new perception of the world or an anticipated reality.

Marxist aesthetics can only escape from the aporias of the theory of reflection, and once again become aware of the specific historicity of literature, when it acknowledges with Karl Kosík that: "Each work of art has a doubled character within an indivisible unity: it is the expression of reality, but it also forms the reality that exists not next to the work, nor before the work, but precisely only in the work."[51] First attempts to win back the dialectical character of historical praxis for art and literature stand out in the literary theories of Werner Krauss, Roger Garaudy, and Karl Kosík. Krauss, who in his studies of Enlightenment literary history rehabilitated the consideration of literary forms since, in them, "a great measure of social influence [has] stored itself," defines the socially *formative* function of literature as follows: "Literature [Dichtung] moves in the direction of an awareness [*Vernehmen*]. Therefore the society that is addressed produces itself within the literature: style is its law—through the cognizance of the style the literature's address can also be deciphered."[52] Garaudy turns against that "realism closed within itself" to redefine the character of the work of art, as "realism without bounds," from the perspective of the human present open toward the future as work and myth: "For reality, when it includes human beings, is no longer just that which it is, but also everything that is missing in it, everything that it must still become."[53] Kosík solves the dilemma of Marx's fragment on classical art—how and why a work of art can survive the conditions under which it originated—with a definition of the character of art that historically mediates the essence and influence of a work of art and brings them into a dialectical unity: "The work lives to the extent that it has influence. Included within the influence of a work is that which is accomplished in the consumption of the work as well as in the work itself. That which happens with the work is an expression of what the work is. . . . The work is a work and lives as a work for the reason that it *demands* an interpretation and '*works*' [influences, *wirkt*] in many meanings."[54]

The insight that the historical essence of the work of art lies not only in its representational or expressive function but also in its influence must have two consequences for a new founding of literary history. If the life of the work results "not from its autonomous existence but rather from the reciprocal interaction of work and mankind,"[55] this perpetual labor of understanding and of the active reproduction of the past cannot remain limited to the single work. On the contrary, the relationship of work to work must now be brought into this interaction between work and mankind, and the historical coherence of works among themselves must be seen in the interrelations of production and reception. Put another way: literature and art only obtain a history that has the character of a process when the succession of works is mediated not only through the producing subject but also through the consuming subject—through the interaction of author and public. And if on the other hand "human reality is not only a production of the new, but also a (critical and dialectical) reproduction of the past,"[56] the function of art in the process of this perpetual totalizing can only come into view in its independence when the specific achievement of artistic form as well is no longer just mimetically defined, but rather is viewed dialectically as a medium capable of forming and altering perception, in which the "formation of the senses" chiefly takes place.[57]

Thus formulated, the problem of the historicity of artistic forms is a belated discovery of Marxist literary studies. For it had already posed itself forty [fifty] years ago to the Formalist school that they were fighting, at that moment when it was condemned to silence by the prevailing holders of power, and driven into the diaspora.

IV

The beginnings of the Formalists, who as members of the "Society for the Study of Poetic Language" (*Opoyaz*) came forth with programmatic publications from 1916 on, stood under the aegis of a rigorous foregrounding of the artistic character of literature. The theory of the formal method[58] raised literature once again to an independent object of study when it detached the literary work from all historical conditions and like the new structural linguistics defined its specific result purely functionally, as "the sum-total of all the stylistic devices employed in it."[59] The traditional distinction between "poetry" [Dichtung] and literature thus becomes dispensable. The artistic character of literature is to be ascertained solely from the opposition between poetic and practical language. Language in its practical function now represents as "a nonliterary series" all remaining historical and social conditioning of the literary work; this work is described and defined as a work of art precisely in its specific differentiation (*écart poétique*), and thus not in its functional relationship to the nonliterary series. The distinction between poetic and practical language led to the concept of "artistic perception," which completely severed the link between literature and lived praxis. Art now becomes the means of disrupting the automatization of everyday perception through "estrangement" or "defamiliarization" (*ostraneniye*). It follows that the reception of art also can no longer exist in the naive enjoyment of the beautiful, but rather demands the differentiation of form, and the recognition of the operation. Thus the process of perception in art appears as an end in itself, the "tangibility of form" as its specific characteristic and the "discovery of the operation" as the principle of a theory. This theory made art criticism into a rational method in conscious renunciation of historical knowledge, and thereby brought forth critical achievements of lasting value.

Another achievement of the Formalist school meanwhile cannot be overlooked. The historicity of literature that was at first negated returned with the extension of the Formalist method, and placed it before a problem that forced it to rethink the principles of diachrony. The literariness of literature is conditioned not only synchronically by the opposition between poetic and practical language, but also diachronically by the opposition to the givens of the genre and the preceding form of the literary series. When the work of art is "perceived against the background of other works of art and in association with them," as Viktor Shklovsky formulates it,[60] the interpretation of the work of art must also take into consideration its relation to other forms that existed before it did. With this the Formalist school began to seek its own way back into history. Its new project distinguished itself from the old literary history in that it gave up the former's fundamental image of a gradual and continuous process and opposed a dynamic principle of *literary evolution* to the classical concept of *tradition*. The notion of an organic continuity lost its former precedence in art history and the history of style. The analysis of literary evolution discovers in the history of literature the "dialectical self-production of new forms,"[61] describing the supposedly peaceful and gradual course of tradition [*Überlieferung*] as a procession with fracturing changes, the revolts of new schools, and the conflicts of competing genres. The "objective spirit" of unified periods was thrown out as metaphysical speculation. According to Viktor Shklovsky and Jurij Tynjanov, there exists in each period a number of literary schools at the same time, "wherein one of them represents the canonized height of literature"; the canonization of a literary form leads to its automatization, and demands the formation of new forms in the lower stratum that "conquer the place of the older ones," grow to be a mass phenomenon, and finally are themselves in turn pushed to the periphery.[62]

With this project, that paradoxically turned the principle of literary *evolution* against the organic-teleological sense of the classical concept of evolution, the Formalist school already came very close to a new historical understanding of literature in the realm of the origin, canonization, and decay of genres. It taught one to see the work of art in its history in a new way, that is, in the changes of the systems of literary genres and forms. It thus cut a path toward an understanding that linguistics had also appropriated for itself: the understanding that pure synchrony is illusory, since, in the formulation of Roman Jakobson and Jurij Tynjanov, "each system necessarily comes forth as evolution and on the other hand evolution inevitably carries with it the character of a system."[63] To see the work in *its* history, that is, comprehended within literary history defined as "the succession of systems,"[64] is however not yet the same as to see the work of art in *history*, that is, in the historical horizon of its origination, social function, and historical influence. The historicity of literature does not end with the succession of aesthetic-formal systems; the evolution of literature, like that of language, is to be determined not only immanently through its own unique relationship of diachrony and synchrony, but also through its relationship to the general process of history.[65]

From this perspective on the reciprocal dilemma of Formalist and Marxist literary theory, a consequence can be seen that was not drawn by either of them. If on the one hand literary evolution can be comprehended within the historical change of systems, and on the other hand pragmatic history can be comprehended within the processlike linkage of social conditions, must it not then also be possible to place the "literary series" and the "nonliterary series" into a relation that comprehends the relationship between literature and history without forcing literature, at the expense of its character as art, into a function of mere copying or commentary?

V

In the question thus posed, I see the challenge to literary studies of taking up once again the problem of literary history, which was left unresolved in the dispute between Marxist and Formalist methods. My attempt to bridge the gap between literature and history, between historical and aesthetic approaches, begins at the point at which both schools stop. Their methods conceive the *literary fact* within the closed circle of an aesthetics of production and of representation. In doing so, they deprive literature of a dimension that inalienably belongs to its aesthetic character as well as to its social function: the dimension of its reception and influence. Reader, listener, and spectator — in short, the factor of the audience — play an extremely limited role in both literary theories. Orthodox Marxist aesthetics treats the reader — if at all — no differently from the author: it inquires about his social position or seeks to recognize him in the structure of a represented society. The Formalist school needs the reader only as a perceiving subject who follows the directions in the text in order to distinguish the [literary] form or discover the [literary] procedure. It assumes that the reader has the theoretical understanding of the philologist who can reflect on the artistic devices, already knowing them; conversely, the Marxist school candidly equates the spontaneous experience of the reader with the scholarly interest of historical materialism, which would discover relationships between superstructure and basis in the literary work. However, as Walther Bulst has stated, "no text was ever written to be read and interpreted philologically by philologists,"[66] nor, may I add, historically by historians. Both methods lack the reader in his genuine role, a role as unalterable for aesthetic as for historical knowledge: as the addressee for whom the literary work is primarily destined.

For even the critic who judges a new work, the writer who conceives of his work in light of positive or negative norms of an earlier work, and the literary historian who classifies a work in its tradition and explains it historically are first simply readers before their reflexive relationship to literature can become productive again. In the triangle of author, work, and public the last is no passive part, no chain of mere reactions, but rather itself an energy formative of history. The historical life of a literary work is unthinkable without the active participation of its addressees. For it is only through the process of its mediation that the work enters into the changing horizon-of-experience of a continuity in which the perpetual inversion occurs from simple reception to critical understanding, from passive to active reception, from recognized aesthetic norms to a new production that surpasses them. The historicity of literature as well as its communicative character presupposes a dialogical and at once processlike relationship between work, audience, and new work that can be conceived in the relations between message and receiver as well as between question and answer, problem and solution. The closed circle of production and of representation within which the methodology of literary studies has mainly moved in the past must therefore be opened to an aesthetics of reception and influence if the problem of comprehending the historical sequence of literary works as the coherence of literary history is to find a new solution.

The perspective of the aesthetics of reception mediates between passive reception and active understanding, experience formative of norms, and new production. If the history of literature is viewed in this way within the horizon of a dialogue between work and audience that forms a continuity, the opposition between its aesthetic and its historical aspects is also continually mediated. Thus the thread from the past appearance to the present experience of literature, which historicism had cut, is tied back together.

The relationship of literature and reader has aesthetic as well as historical implications. The aesthetic implication lies in the fact that the first reception of a work by the reader includes a test of its aesthetic value in comparison with works already read.[67] The obvious historical implication of this is that the understanding of the first reader will be sustained and enriched in a chain of receptions from generation to generation; in this way the historical significance of a work will be decided and its aesthetic value made evident. In this process of the history of reception, which the literary historian can only escape at the price of leaving unquestioned the presuppositions that guide his understanding and judgment, the reappropriation of past works occurs simultaneously with the perpetual mediation of past and present art and of traditional evaluation and current literary attempts. The merit of a literary history based on an aesthetics of reception will depend upon the extent to which it can take an active part in the ongoing totalization of the past through aesthetic experience. This demands on the one hand—in opposition to the objectivism of positivist literary history—a conscious attempt at the formation of a canon, which, on the other hand—in opposition to the classicism of the study of traditions—presupposes a critical revision if not destruction of the received literary canon. The criterion for the formation of such a canon and the ever necessary retelling of literary history is clearly set out by the aesthetics of reception. The step from the history of the reception of the individual work to the history of literature has to lead to seeing and representing the historical sequence of works as they determine and clarify the coherence of literature, to the extent that it is meaningful for us, as the prehistory of its present experience.[68]

From this premise, the question as to how literary history can today be methodologically grounded and written anew will be addressed in the following seven theses.

VI

Thesis 1. A renewal of literary history demands the removal of the prejudices of historical objectivism and the grounding of the traditional aesthetics of production and representation in an aesthetics of reception and influence. The historicity of literature rests not on an organization of "literary facts" that is established *post festum*, but rather on the preceding experience of the literary work by its readers.

R. G. Collingwood's postulate, posed in his critique of the prevailing ideology of objectivity in history — "History is nothing but the re-enactment of past thought in the historian's mind"[69] — is even more valid for literary history. For the positivistic view of history as the "objective" description of a series of events in an isolated past neglects the artistic character as well as the specific historicity of literature. A literary work is not an object that stands by itself and that offers the same view to each reader in each period.[70] It is not a monument that monologically reveals its timeless essence. It is much more like an orchestration that strikes ever new resonances among its readers and that frees the text from the material of the words and brings it to a contemporary existence: "words that must, at the same time that they speak to him, create an interlocutor capable of understanding them."[71] This dialogical character of the literary work also establishes why philological understanding can exist only in a perpetual confrontation with the text, and cannot be allowed to be reduced to a knowledge of facts.[72] Philological understanding always remains related to interpretation that must set as its goal, along with learning about the object, the reflection on and description of the completion of this knowledge as a moment of new understanding.

History of literature is a process of aesthetic reception and production that takes place in the realization of literary texts on the part of the receptive reader, the reflective critic, and the author in his continuing productivity. The endlessly growing sum of literary "facts" that winds up in the conventional literary histories is merely left over from this process; it is only the collected and classified past and therefore not history at all, but pseudo-history. Anyone who considers a series of such literary facts as a piece of the history of literature confuses the eventful character of a work of art with that of historical matter-of-factness. The *Perceval* of Chrétien de Troyes, as a literary event, is not "historical" in the same sense as, for example, the Third Crusade, which was occurring at about the same time.[73] It is not a "fact" that could be explained as caused by a series of situational preconditions and motives, by the intent of a historical action as it can be reconstructed, and by the necessary and secondary consequences of this deed. The historical context in which a literary work appears is not a factical, independent series of events that exists apart from an observer. *Perceval* becomes a literary event only for its reader, who reads this last work of Chrétien with a memory of his earlier works and who recognizes its individuality in comparison with these and other works that he already knows, so that he gains a new criterion for evaluating future works. In contrast to a political event, a literary event has no unavoidable consequences subsisting on their own that no succeeding generation can ever escape. A literary event can continue to have an effect only if those who come after it still or once again respond to it—if there are readers who again appropriate the past work or authors who want to imitate, outdo, or refute it. The coherence of literature as an event is primarily mediated in the horizon of expectations of the literary experience of contemporary and later readers, critics, and authors. Whether it is possible to comprehend and represent the history of literature in its unique historicity depends on whether this horizon of expectations can be objectified.

VII

Thesis 2. The analysis of the literary experience of the reader avoids the threatening pitfalls of psychology if it describes the reception and the influence of a work within the objectifiable system of expectations that arises for each work in the historical moment of its appearance, from a pre-understanding of the genre, from the form and themes of already familiar works, and from the opposition between poetic and practical language.

My thesis opposes a widespread skepticism that doubts whether an analysis of aesthetic influence can approach the meaning of a work of art at all or can produce, at best, more than a simple sociology of taste. René Wellek in particular directs such doubts against the literary theory of I. A. Richards. Wellek argues that neither the individual state of consciousness, since it is momentary and only personal, nor a collective state of consciousness, as Jan Mukařovský assumes the effect a work of art to be, can be determined by empirical means.[74] Roman Jakobson wanted to replace the "collective state of consciousness" by a "collective ideology" in the form of a system of norms that exists for each literary work as *langue* and that is actualized as *parole* by the receiver—although incompletely and never as a whole.[75] This theory, it is true, limits the subjectivity of the influence, but it still leaves open the question of which data can be used to comprehend the influence of a particular work on a certain public and to incorporate it into a system of norms. In the meantime there are empirical means that had never been thought of before—literary data that allow one to ascertain a specific disposition of the audience for each work (a disposition that precedes the psychological reaction as well as the subjective understanding of the individual reader). As in the case of every actual experience, the first literary experience of a previously unknown work also demands a "foreknowledge which is an element of the experience itself, and on the basis of which anything new that we come across is available to experience at all, i.e., as it were readable in a context of experience."[76]

A literary work, even when it appears to be new, does not present itself as something absolutely new in an informational vacuum, but predisposes its audience to a very specific kind of reception by announcements, overt and covert signals, familiar characteristics, or implicit allusions. It awakens memories of that which was already read, brings the reader to a specific emotional attitude, and with its beginning arouses expectations for the "middle and end," which can then be maintained intact or altered, reoriented, or even fulfilled ironically in the course of the reading according to specific rules of the genre or type of text. The psychic process in the reception of a text is, in the primary horizon of aesthetic experience, by no means only an arbitrary series of merely subjective impressions, but rather the carrying out of specific instructions in a process of directed perception, which can be comprehended according to its constitutive motivations and triggering signals, and which also can be described by a textual linguistics. If, along with W. D. Stempel, one defines the initial horizon of expectations of a text as paradigmatic isotopy, which is transposed into an immanent syntagmatic horizon of expectations to the extent that the utterance grows, then the process of reception becomes describable in the expansion of a semiotic system that accomplishes itself between the development and the correction of a system.[77] A corresponding process of the continuous establishing and altering of horizons also determines the relationship of the individual text to the succession of texts that forms the genre. The new text evokes for the reader (listener) the horizon of expectations and rules familiar from earlier texts, which are then varied, corrected, altered, or even just reproduced. Variation and correction determine the scope, whereas alteration and reproduction determine the borders of a genre-structure.[78] The interpretative reception of a text always presupposes the context of experience of aesthetic perception: the question of the subjectivity of the interpretation and of the taste of different readers or levels of readers can be asked meaningfully only when one has first clarified which transsubjective horizon of understanding conditions the influence of the text.

The ideal cases of the objective capability of such literary-historical frames of reference are works that evoke the reader's horizon of expectations, formed by a convention of genre, style, or form, only in order to destroy it step by step—which by no means serves a critical purpose only, but can itself once again produce poetic effects. Thus Cervantes allows the horizon of expectations of the favorite old tales of knighthood to arise out of the reading of *Don Quixote*, which the adventure of his last knight then seriously parodies.[79] Thus Diderot, at the beginning of *Jacques le Fataliste*, evokes the horizon of expectations of the popular novelistic schema of the "journey" (with the fictive questions of the reader to the narrator) along with the (Aristotelian) convention of the romanesque fable and the providence unique to it, so that he can then provocatively oppose to the promised journey- and love-novel a completely unromanesque "vérité de l'histoire": the bizarre reality and moral casuistry of the enclosed stories in which the truth of life continually denies the mendacious character of poetic fiction.[80] Thus Nerval in the *Chimères* cites, combines, and mixes a quintessence of well-known romantic and occult motifs to produce the horizon of expectations of a mythical metamorphosis of the world only in order to signify his renunciation of romantic poetry. The identifications and relationships of the mythic state that are familiar or disclosable to the reader dissolve into an unknown to the same degree as the attempted private myth of the lyrical "I" fails, the law of sufficient information is broken, and the obscurity that has become expressive itself gains a poetic function.[81]

There is also the possibility of objectifying the horizon of expectations in works that are historically less sharply delineated. For the specific disposition toward a particular work that the author anticipates from the audience can also be arrived at, even if explicit signals are lacking, through three generally presupposed factors: first, through familiar norms or the immanent poetics of the genre; second, through the implicit relationships to familiar works of the literary-historical surroundings; and third, through the opposition between fiction and reality, between the poetic and the practical function of language, which is always available to the reflective reader during the reading as a possibility of comparison. The third factor includes the possibility that the reader of a new work can perceive it within the narrower horizon of literary expectations, as well as within the wider horizon of experience of life. I shall return to this horizonal structure, and its ability to be objectified by means of the hermeneutics of question and answer, in the discussion of the relationship between literature and lived praxis (see XII).

VIII

Thesis 3. Reconstructed in this way, the horizon of expectations of a work allows one to determine its artistic character by the kind and the degree of its influence on a presupposed audience. If one characterizes as aesthetic distance the disparity between the given horizon of expectations and the appearance of a new work, whose reception can result in a "change of horizons" through negation of familiar experiences or through raising newly articulated experiences to the level of consciousness, then this aesthetic distance can be objectified historically along the spectrum of the audience's reactions and criticism's judgment (spontaneous success, rejection or shock, scattered approval, gradual or belated understanding).

The way in which a literary work, at the historical moment of its appearance, satisfies, surpasses, disappoints, or refutes the expectations of its first audience obviously provides a criterion for the determination of its aesthetic value. The distance between the horizon of expectations and the work, between the familiarity of previous aesthetic experience and the "horizonal change"[82] demanded by the reception of the new work, determines the artistic character of a literary work, according to an aesthetics of reception: to the degree that this distance decreases, and no turn toward the horizon of yet-unknown experience is demanded of the receiving consciousness, the closer the work comes to the sphere of "culinary" or entertainment art [*Unterhaltungskunst*]. This latter work can be characterized by an aesthetics of reception as not demanding any horizonal change, but rather as precisely fulfilling the expectations prescribed by a ruling standard of taste, in that it satisfies the desire for the reproduction of the familiarly beautiful; confirms familiar sentiments; sanctions wishful notions; makes unusual experiences enjoyable as "sensations"; or even raises moral problems, but only to "solve" them in an edifying manner as predecided questions.[83] If, conversely, the artistic character of a work is to be measured by the aesthetic distance with which it opposes the expectations of its first audience, then it follows that this distance, at first experienced as a pleasing or alienating new perspective, can disappear for later readers, to the extent that the original negativity of the work has become self-evident and has itself entered into the horizon of future aesthetic experience, as a henceforth familiar expectation. The classical character of the so-called masterworks especially belongs to this second horizonal change;[84] their beautiful form that has become self-evident, and their seemingly unquestionable "eternal meaning" bring them, according to an aesthetics of reception, dangerously close to the irresistibly convincing and enjoyable "culinary" art, so that it requires a special effort to read them "against the grain" of the accustomed experience to catch sight of their artistic character once again (see section X).

The relationship between literature and audience includes more than the facts that every work has its own specific, historically and sociologically determinable audience, that every writer is dependent on the milieu, views, and ideology of his audience, and that literary success presupposes a book "which expresses what the group expects, a book which presents the group with its own image."[85] This objectivist determination of literary success according to the congruence of the work's intention with the expectations of a social group always leads literary sociology into a dilemma whenever later or ongoing influence is to be explained. Thus R. Escarpit wants to presuppose a "collective basis in space or time" for the "illusion of the lasting quality" of a writer, which in the case of Molière leads to an astonishing prognosis: "Molière is still young for the Frenchman of the twentieth century because his world still lives, and a sphere of culture, views, and language still binds us to him. . . . But the sphere becomes ever smaller, and Molière will age and die when the things which our culture still has in common with the France of Molière die" (p. 117). As if Molière had only mirrored the "mores of his time" and had only remained successful through this supposed intention! Where the congruence between work and social group does not exist, or no longer exists, as for example with the reception of a work in a foreign language, Escarpit is able to help himself by inserting a "myth" in between: "myths that are invented by a later world for which the reality that they substitute for has become alien" (p. 111). As if all reception beyond the first, socially determined audience for a work were only a "distorted echo," only a result of "subjective myths," and did not itself have its objective a priori once again in the received work as the limit and possibility of later understanding! The sociology of literature does not view its object dialectically enough when it determines the circle of author, work, and audience so one-sidedly.[86] The determination is reversible: there are works that at the moment of their appearance are not yet directed at any specific audience, but that break through the familiar horizon of literary expectations so completely that an audience can only gradually develop for them.[87] When, then, the new horizon of expectations has achieved more general currency, the power of the altered aesthetic norm can be demonstrated in that the audience experiences formerly successful works as outmoded, and withdraws its appreciation. Only in view of such horizonal change does the analysis of literary influence achieve the dimension of a literary history of readers,[88] and do the statistical curves of the bestsellers provide historical knowledge.

A literary sensation from the year 1857 may serve as an example. Alongside Flaubert's *Madame Bovary*, which has since become world-famous, appeared his friend Feydeau's *Fanny*, today forgotten. Although Flaubert's novel brought with it a trial for offending public morals, *Madame Bovary* was at first overshadowed by Feydeau's novel: *Fanny* went through thirteen editions in one year, achieving a success the likes of which Paris had not experienced since Chateaubriand's *Atala*. Thematically considered, both novels met the expectations of a new audience that—in Baudelaire's analysis—had foresworn all romanticism, and despised great as well as naive passions equally:[89] they treated a trivial subject, infidelity in a bourgeois and provincial milieu. Both authors understood how to give to the conventional, ossified triangular relationship a sensational twist that went beyond the expected details of the erotic scenes. They put the worn-out theme of jealousy in a new light by reversing the expected relationship between the three classic roles: Feydeau has the youthful lover of the *femme de trente ans* beome jealous of his lover's husband despite his having already fulfilled his desires, and perishing over this agonizing situation; Flaubert gives the adulteries of the doctor's wife in the provinces—interpreted by Baudelaire as a sublime form of *dandysme*—the surprise ending that precisely the laughable figure of the cuckolded Charles Bovary takes on dignified traits at the end. In the official criticism of the time, one finds voices that reject *Fanny* as well as *Madame Bovary* as a product of the new school of *réalisme*, which they reproach for denying everything ideal and attacking the ideas on which the social order of the Second Empire was founded.[90] The audience's horizon of expectations in 1857, here only vaguely sketched in, which did not expect anything great from the novel after Balzac's death,[91] explains the different success of the two novels only when the question of the effect of their narrative form is posed. Flaubert's formal innovation, his principle of "impersonal narration" (*impassibilité*)—attacked by Barbey d'Aurevilly with the comparison that if a story-telling machine could be cast of English steel it would function no differently than Monsieur Flaubert[92]—must have shocked the same audience that was offered the provocative contents of *Fanny* in the inviting tone of a confessional novel. It could also find incorporated in

Feydeau's descriptions the modish ideals and surpressed desires of a stylish level of society,[93] and could delight without restraint in the lascivious central scene in which Fanny (without suspecting that her lover is watching from the balcony) seduces her husband—for the moral indignation was already diminished for them through the reaction of the unhappy witness. As *Madame Bovary*, however, became a worldwide success, when at first it was understood and appreciated as a turning-point in the history of the novel by only a small circle of connoisseurs, the audience of novel-readers that was formed by it came to sanction the new canon of expectations; this canon made Feydeau's weaknesses—his flowery style, his modish effects, his lyrical-confessional cliches—unbearable, and allowed *Fanny* to fade into yesterday's bestseller.

IX

Thesis 4. The reconstruction of the horizon of expectations, in the face of which a work was created and received in the past, enables one on the other hand to pose questions that the text gave an answer to, and thereby to discover how the contemporary reader could have viewed and understood the work. This approach corrects the mostly unrecognized norms of a classicist or modernizing understanding of art, and avoids the circular recourse to a general "spirit of the age." It brings to view the hermeneutic difference between the former and the current understanding of a work; it raises to consciousness the history of its reception, which mediates both positions; and it thereby calls into question as a platonizing dogma of philological metaphysics the apparently self-evident claims that in the literary text, literature [Dichtung] is eternally present, and that its objective meaning, determined once and for all, is at all times immediately accessible to the interpreter.

The method of historical reception[94] is indispensable for the understanding of literature from the distant past. When the author of a work is unknown, his intent undeclared, and his relationship to sources and models only indirectly accessible, the philological question of how the text is "properly"—that is, "from its intention and time"—to be understood can best be answered if one foregrounds it against those works that the author explicitly or implicitly presupposed his contemporary audience to know. The creator of the oldest branches of the *Roman de Renart*, for example, assumes—as his prologue testifies—that his listeners know romances like the story of

Troy and *Tristan*, heroic epics (*chansons de geste*), and verse fables (*fabliaux*), and that they are therefore curious about the "unprecedented war between the two barons, Renart and Ysengrin," which is to overshadow everything already known. The works and genres that are evoked are then all ironically touched on in the course of the narrative. From this horizonal change one can probably also explain the public success, reaching far beyond France, of this rapidly famous work that for the first time took a position opposed to all the long-reigning heroic and courtly poetry.[95]

Philological research long misunderstood the originally satiric intention of the medieval *Reineke Fuchs* and, along with it, the ironic-didactic meaning of the analogy between animal and human natures, because ever since Jacob Grimm it had remained trapped within the romantic notion of pure nature poetry and naive animal tales. Thus, to give yet a second example of modernizing norms, one could also rightly reproach French research into the epic since Bédier for living—unconsciously—by the criteria of Boileau's poetics, and judging a nonclassical literature by the norms of simplicity, harmony of part and whole, probability, and still others.[96] The philological-critical method is obviously not protected by its historical objectivism from the interpreter who, supposedly bracketing himself, nonetheless raises his own aesthetic preconceptions to an unacknowledged norm and unreflectively modernizes the meaning of the past text. Whoever believes that the "timelessly true" meaning of a literary work must immediately, and simply through one's mere absorption in the text, disclose itself to the interpreter as if he had a standpoint outside of history and beyond all "errors" of his predecessors and of the historical reception—whoever believes this "conceals the involvement of the historical consciousness itself in the history of influence." He denies "those presuppositions—certainly not arbitrary but rather fundamental—that govern his own understanding," and can only feign an objectivity "that in truth depends upon the legitimacy of the questions asked."[97]

In *Truth and Method* Hans-Georg Gadamer, whose critique of historical objectivism I am assuming here, described the principle of the history of influence, which seeks to present the reality of history in understanding itself,[98] as an application of the logic of question and answer to the historical tradition. In a continuation of Collingwood's thesis that "one can understand a text only when one has understood the question to which it is an answer,"[99] Gadamer demonstrates that the reconstructed question can no longer stand within its original horizon because this historical horizon is always already enveloped within the horizon of the present: "Understanding is always the process of the fusion of these horizons that we suppose to exist by themselves."[100] The historical question cannot exist for itself; it must merge with the question "that the tradition is for us."[101] One thereby solves the question with which René Wellek described the aporia of literary judgment: should the philologist evaluate a literary work according to the perspective of the past, the standpoint of the present, or the "verdict of the ages"?[102] The actual standards of a past could be so narrow that their use would only make poorer a work that in the history of its influence had unfolded a rich semantic potential. The aesthetic judgment of the present would favor a canon of works that correspond to modern taste, but would unjustly evaluate all other works only because their function in their time is no longer evident. And the history of influence itself, as instructive as it might be, is as "authority open to the same objections as the authority of the author's contemporaries."[103] Wellek's conclusion—that there is no possibility of avoiding our own judgment; one must only make this judgment as objective as possible in that one does what every scholar does, namely, "isolate the object"[104]—is no solution to the aporia, but rather a relapse into objectivism. The "verdict of the ages" on a literary work is more than merely "the accumulated judgment of other readers, critics, viewers, and even professors";[105] it is the successive unfolding of the potential for meaning that is embedded in a work and actualized in the stages of its historical reception as it discloses itself to understanding judgment, so long as this faculty achieves in a controlled fashion the "fusion of horizons" in the encounter with the tradition.

The agreement between my attempt to establish a possible literary history on the basis of an aesthetics of reception and H.-G. Gadamer's principle of the history of influence nonetheless reaches its limit where Gadamer would like to elevate the concept of the classical to the status of prototype for all historical mediation of past with present. His definition, that "what we call 'classical' does not first require the overcoming of historical distance—for in its own constant mediation it achieves this overcoming,"[106] falls out of the relationship of question and answer that is constitutive of all historical tradition. If classical is "what says something to the present as if it were actually said to it,"[107] then for the classical text one would not first seek the question to which it gives an answer. Doesn't the classical, which "signifies itself and interprets itself,"[108] merely describe the result of what I called the "second horizonal change": the unquestioned, self-evident character of the so-called "masterwork," which conceals its original negativity within the retrospective horizon of an exemplary tradition, and which necessitates our regaining the "right horizon of questioning" once again in the face of the confirmed classicism? Even with the classical work, the receiving consciousness is not relieved of the task of recognizing the "tensional relationship between the text and the present."[109] The concept of the classical that interprets itself, taken over from Hegel, must lead to a reversal of the historical relationship of question and answer,[110] and contradicts the principle of the history of influence that understanding is "not merely a reproductive, but always a productive attitude as well."[111]

This contradiction is evidently conditioned by Gadamer's holding fast to a concept of classical art that is not capable of serving as a general foundation for an aesthetics of reception beyond the period of its origination, namely, that of humanism. It is the concept of *mimesis*, understood as "recognition," as Gadamer demonstrates in his ontological explanation of the experience of art: "What one actually experiences in a work of art and what one is directed toward is rather how true it is, that is, to what extent one knows and recognizes something and oneself."[112] This concept of art can be validated for the humanist period of art, but not for its preceding medieval period and not at all for its succeeding period of our modernity, in which the aesthetics of mimesis has lost its obligatory character, along with the substantialist metaphysics ("knowledge of essence") that founded it. The epistemological significance of art does not, however, come to an end with this period-change, whence it becomes evident that art was in no way bound to the classical function of recognition.[113] The work of art can also mediate knowledge that does not fit into the Platonic schema if it anticipates paths of future experience, imagines as-yet-untested models of perception and behavior, or contains an answer to newly posed questions.[114] It is precisely concerning this virtual significance and productive function in the process of experience that the history of the influence of literature is abbreviated when one gathers the mediation of past art and the present under the concept of the *classical*. If, according to Gadamer, the classical *itself* is supposed to achieve the overcoming of historical distance through its constant mediation, it must, as a perspective of the hypostatized tradition, displace the insight that classical art at the time of its production did not yet appear "classical": rather, it could open up new ways of seeing things and preform new experiences that only in historical distance—in the recognition of what is now familiar—give rise to the appearance that a timeless truth expresses itself in the work of art.

The influence of even the great literary works of the past can be compared neither with a self-mediating event nor with an emanation: the tradition of art also presupposes a dialogical relationship of the present to the past, according to which the past work can answer and "say something" to us only when the present observer has posed the question that draws it back out of its seclusion. When, in *Truth and Method*, understanding is conceived—analogous to Heidegger's "event of being" [*Seinsgeschehen*] —as "the placing of oneself within a process of tradition in which past and present are constantly mediated,"[115] the "productive moment which lies in understanding"[116] must be shortchanged. This productive function of progressive understanding, which necessarily also includes criticizing the tradition and forgetting it, shall in the following sections establish the basis for the project of a literary history according to an aesthetics of reception. This project must consider the historicity of literature in a threefold manner: diachronically in the interrelationships of the reception of literary works (see X), synchronically in the frame of reference of literature of the same moment, as well as in the sequence of such frames (see XI), and finally in the relationship of the immanent literary development to the general process of history (see XII).

X

Thesis 5. The theory of the aesthetics of reception not only allows one to conceive the meaning and form of a literary work in the historical unfolding of its understanding. It also demands that one insert the individual work into its "literary series" to recognize its historical position and significance in the context of the experience of literature. In the step from a history of the reception of works to an eventful history of literature, the latter manifests itself as a process in which the passive reception is on the part of authors. Put another way, the next work can solve formal and moral problems left behind by the last work, and present new problems in turn.

How can the individual work, which positivistic literary history determined in a chronological series and thereby reduced to the status of a "fact," be brought back into its historical-sequential realtionship and thereby once again be understood as an "event"? The theory of the Formalist school, as already mentioned, would solve this problem with its principle of "literary evolution," according to which the new work arises against the background of preceding or competing works, reaches the "high point" of a literary period as a successful form, is quickly reproduced and thereby increasingly automatized, until finally, when the next form has broken through, the former vegetates on as a used-up genre in the quotidian sphere of literature. If one were to analyze and describe a literary period according to this program—which to date has hardly been put into use[117]—one could expect a representation that would in various respects be superior to that of the conventional literary history. Instead of the works standing in closed series, themselves standing one after another and unconnected, at best framed by a sketch of general history—for example, the series of the works of an author, a particular school, or one kind of style, as well as the series of various genres—the Formalist method would relate the series to one another and *discover the evolutionary alternating relationship of functions and forms*.[118] The works that thereby stand out from, correspond to, or replace one another would appear as moments of a process that no longer needs to be construed as tending toward some end point, since as the *dialectical self-production of new forms* it requires no teleology. Seen in this way, the autonomous dynamics of literary evolution would furthermore eliminate the dilemma of the criteria of selection: the criterion here is the work as a new form in the literary series, and not the self-reproduction of worn-out forms, artistic devices, and genres, which pass into the background until at a new moment in the evolution they are made "perceptible" once again. Finally, in the Formalist project of a literary history that understands itself as "evolution" and—contrary to the usual sense of this term—excludes any directional course, the historical character of a work becomes synonymous with literature's historical character: the "evolutionary" significance and characteristics of a literary phenomenon presuppose innovation as the decisive feature, just as a work of art is perceived against the background of other works of art.[119]

The Formalist theory of "literary evolution" is certainly one of the most significant attempts at a renovation of literary history. The recognition that historical changes also occur within a system in the field of literature, the attempted functionalization of literary development, and, not least of all, the theory of automatization—these are achievements that are to be held onto, even if the one-sided canonization of change requires a correction. Criticism has already displayed the weaknesses of the Formalist theory of evolution: mere opposition or aesthetic variation does not suffice to explain the growth of literature; the question of the direction of change of literary forms remains unanswerable; innovation for itself does not alone make up artistic character; and the connection between literary evolution and social change does not vanish from the face of the earth through its mere negation.[120] My thesis XII responds to the last question; the problematic of the remaining questions demands that the descriptive literary theory of the Formalists be opened up, through an aesthetics of reception, to the dimension of historical experience that must also include the historical standpoint of the present observer, that is, the literary historian.

The description of literary evolution as a ceaseless struggle between the new and the old, or as the alternation of the canonization and automatization of forms reduces the historical character of literature to the one-dimensional actuality of its changes and limits historical understanding to their perception. The alterations in the literary series nonetheless only become a historical sequence when the opposition of the old and new form also allows one to recognize their specific mediation. This mediation, which includes the step from the old to the new form in the interaction of work and recipient (audience, critic, new producer) as well as that of past event and successive reception, can be methodologically grasped in the formal and substantial problem "that each work of art, as the horizon of the 'solutions' which are possible after it, poses and leaves behind."[121] The mere description of the altered structure and the new artistic devices of a work does not necessarily lead to this problem, nor, therefore, back to its function in the historical series. To determine this, that is, to recognize the problem left behind to which the new work in the historical series is the answer, the interpreter must bring his own experience into play, since the past horizon of old and new forms, problems and solutions, is only recognizable in its further mediation, within the present horizon of the received work. Literary history as "literary evolution" presupposes the historical process of aesthetic reception and production up to the observer's present as the condition for the mediation of all formal oppositions or "differential qualities" ["*Differenzqualitäten*"] .[122]

Founding "literary evolution" on an aesthetics of reception thus not only returns its lost direction insofar as the standpoint of the literary historian becomes the vanishing point—but not the goal!—of the process. It also opens to view the temporal depths of literary experience, in that it allows one to recognize the variable distance between the actual and the virtual significance of a literary work. This means that the artistic character of a work, whose semantic potential Formalism reduces to innovation as the single criterion of value, must in no way always be immediately perceptible within the horizon of its first appearance, let alone that it could then also already be exhausted in the pure opposition between the old and the new form. The distance between the actual first perception of a work and its virtual significance, or, put another way, the resistance that the new work poses to the expectations of its first audience, can be so great that it requires a long process of reception to gather in that which was unexpected and unusable within the first horizon. It can thereby happen that a virtual significance of the work remains long unrecognized until the "literary evolution," through the actualization of a newer form, reaches the horizon that now for the first time allows one to find access to the understanding of the misunderstood older form. Thus the obscure lyrics of Mallarmé and his school prepared the ground for the return to baroque poetry, long since unappreciated and therefore forgotten, and in particular for the philological reinterpretation and "rebirth" of Góngora. One can line up the examples of how a new literary form can reopen access to forgotten literature. These include the so-called "renaissances"— so-called, because the word's meaning gives rise to the appearance of an automatic return, and often prevents one from recognizing that literary tradition can not transmit itself alone. That is, a literary past can return only when a new reception draws it back into the present, whether an altered aesthetic attitude willfully reaches back to reappropriate the past, or an unexpected light falls back on forgotten literature from the new moment of literary evolution, allowing something to be found that one previously could not have sought in it.[123]

The new is thus not only an *aesthetic* category. It is not absorbed into the factors of innovation, surprise, surpassing, rearrangement, or alienation, to which the Formalist theory assigned exclusive importance. The new also becomes a *historical* category when the diachronic analysis of literature is pushed further to ask which historical moments are really the ones that first make new that which is new in a literary phenomenon; to what degree this new element is already perceptible in the historical instant of its emergence; which distance, path, or detour of understanding were required for its realization in content; and whether the moment of its full actualization was so influential that it could alter the perspective on the old, and thereby the canonization of the literary past.[124] How the relationship of poetic theory to aesthetically productive praxis is represented in this light has already been discussed in another context.[125] The possibilities of the interaction between production and reception in the historical change of aesthetic attitudes are admittedly far from exhausted by these remarks. Here they should above all illustrate the dimension into which a diachronic view of literature leads when it would no longer be satisfied to consider a chronological series of literary facts as already the historical appearance of literature.

XI

Thesis 6. The achievements made in linguistics through the distinction and methodological interrelation of diachronic and synchronic analysis are the occasion for overcoming the diachronic perspective—previously the only one practiced—in literary history as well. If the perspective of the history of reception always bumps up against the functional connections between the understanding of new works and the significance of older ones when changes in aesthetic attitudes are considered, it must also be possible to take a synchronic cross-section of a moment in the development, to arrange the heterogeneous multiplicity of contemporaneous works in equivalent, opposing, and hierarchical structures, and thereby to discover an overarching system of relationships in the literature of a historical moment. From this the principle of representation of a new literary history could be developed, if further cross-sections diachronically before and after were so arranged as to articulate historically the change in literary structures in its epoch-making moments.

Siegfried Kracauer has most decisively questioned the primacy of the diachronic perspective in historiography. His study "Time and History"[126] disputes the claim of "General History" to render comprehensible events from all spheres of life within a homogeneous medium of chronological time as a unified process, consistent in each historical moment. This understanding of history, still standing under the influence of Hegel's concept of the "objective spirit," presupposes that everything that happens contemporaneously is equally informed by the significance of this moment, and it thereby conceals the actual noncontemporaneity of the contemporaneous.[127] For the multiplicity of events of one historical moment, which the universal historian believes can be understood as exponents of a unified content, are de facto moments of entirely different time-curves, conditioned by the laws of their "special history,"[128] as becomes immediately evident in the discrepancies of the various "histories" of the arts, law, economics, politics, and so forth: "The shaped times of the diverse areas overshadow the uniform flow of time. Any historical period must therefore be imagined as a mixture of events which emerge at different moments of their own time."[129]

It is not in question here whether this state of affairs presupposes a primary inconsistency to history, so that the consistency of general history always only arises retrospectively from the unifying viewpoint and representation of the historian; or whether the radical doubt concerning "historical reason," which Kracauer extends from the pluralism of chronological and morphological courses of time to the fundamental antinomy of the general and the particular in history, in fact proves that universal history is philosophically illegitimate today. For the sphere of literature in any case, one can say that Kracauer's insights into the "coexistence of the contemporaneous and non-contemporaneous,"[130] far from leading historical knowledge into an aporia, rather make apparent the necessity and possibility of discovering the historical dimension of literary phenomena in synchronic cross-sections. For it follows from these insights that the chronological fiction of the moment that informs all contemporaneous phenomena corresponds as little to the historicity of literature as does the morphological fiction of a homogeneous literary series, in which all phenomena in their sequential order only follow immanent laws. The purely diachronic perspective, however conclusively it might explain changes in, for example, the histories of genres according to the immanent logic of innovation and automatization, problem and solution, nonetheless only arrives at the properly historical dimension when it breaks through the morphological canon, to confront the work that is important in historical influence with the historically worn-out, conventional works of the genre, and at the same time does not ignore its relationship to the literary milieu in which it had to make its way alongside works of other genres.

The historicity of literature comes to light at the intersections of diachrony and synchrony. Thus it must also be possible to make the literary horizon of a specific historical moment comprehensible as that synchronic system in relation to which literature that appears contemporaneously could be received diachronically in relations of noncontemporaneity, and the work could be received as current or not, as modish, outdated, or perennial, as premature or belated.[131] For if, from the point of view of an aesthetics of production, literature that appears contemporaneously breaks down into a heterogeneous multiplicity of the noncontemporaneous, that is, of works informed by the various moments of the "shaped time" of their genre (as the seemingly present heavenly constellations move apart astronomically into points of the most different temporal distance), this multiplicity of literary phenomena nonetheless, when seen from the point of view of an aesthetics of reception, coalesces again for the audience that perceives them and relates them to one another as works of *its* present, in the unity of a common horizon of literary expectations, memories, and anticipations that establishes their significance.

Since each synchronic system must contain its past and its future as inseparable structural elements,[132] the synchronic cross-section of the literary production of a historical point in time necessarily implies further cross-sections that are diachronically before and after. Analogous to the history of language, constant and variable factors are thereby brought to light that can be localized as functions of a system. For literature as well is a kind of grammar or syntax, with relatively fixed relations of its own: the arrangement of the traditional and the uncanonized genres; modes of expression, kinds of style, and rhetorical figures; contrasted with this arrangement is the much more variable realm of a semantics: the literary subjects, archetypes, symbols, and metaphors. One can therefore seek to erect for literary history an analogy to that which Hans Blumenberg has postulated for the history of philosophy, elucidating it through examples of the change in periods and, in particular, the successional relationship of Christian theology and philosophy, and grounding it in his historical logic of question and answer: a "formal system of the explanation of the world . . . , within which structure the reshufflings can be localized which make up the process-like character of history up to the radicality of period-changes."[133] Once the substantialist notion of a self-reproducing literary tradition has been overcome through a functional explanation of the processlike relationships of production and reception, it must also be possible to recognize behind the *transformation* of literary forms and contents those *reshufflings* in a literary system of world-understanding that make the horizonal change in the process of aesthetic experience comprehensible.

From these premises one could develop the principle of representation of a literary history that would neither have to follow the all too familiar high road of the traditional great books, nor have to lose itself in the lowlands of the sum-total of all texts that can no longer be historically articulated. The problem of selecting that which is important for a new history of literature can be solved with the help of the synchronic perspective in a manner that has not yet been attempted: a horizonal change in the historical process of "literary evolution" need not be pursued only throughout the web of all the diachronic facts and filiations, but can also be established in the altered remains of the synchronic literary system and read out of further cross-sectional analyses. In principle, a representation of literature in the historical succession of such systems would be possible through a series of arbitrary points of intersection between diachrony and synchrony. The historical dimension of literature, its eventful continuity that is lost in traditionalism as in positivism, can meanwhile be recovered only if the literary historian finds points of intersection and brings works to light that articulate the processlike character of "literary evolution" in its moments formative of history as well as its caesurae between periods. But neither statistics nor the subjective willfulness of the literary historian decides on this histori-cal articulation, but rather the history of influence: that "which re-sults from the event" and which from the perspective of the present constitutes the coherence of literature as the prehistory of its present manifestation.

XII

Thesis 7. The task of literary history is thus only completed when literary production is not only represented synchronically and dia-chronically in the succession of its systems, but also seen as "special history" in its own unique relationship to "general history." This relationship does not end with the fact that a typified, idealized, satiric, or utopian image of social existence can be found in the literature of all times. The social function of literature manifests itself in its genuine possibility only where the literary experience of the reader enters into the horizon of expectations of his lived praxis, preforms his understanding of the world, and thereby also has an effect on his social behavior.

The functional connection between literature and society is for the most part demonstrated in traditional literary sociology within the narrow boundaries of a method that has only superficially re-placed the classical principle of *imitatio naturae* with the determina-tion that literature is the representation of a pregiven reality, which therefore must elevate a concept of style conditioned by a particular period—the "realism" of the nineteenth century—to the status of the literary category par excellence. But even the literary "structuralism" now fashionable,[134] which appeals, often with dubious justification, to the archetypal criticism of Northrop Frye or to the structural anthropology of Claude Lévi-Strauss, still remains quite dependent on this basically classicist aesthetics of representation with its schematizations of "reflection" [Wiederspiegelung] and "typification." By interpreting the findings of linguistic and literary structuralism as archaic anthropological constants disguised in literary myths—which it not infrequently manages only with the help of an obvious allegorization of the text[135]—it reduces on the one hand historical existence to the structures of an original social nature, on the other hand literature to this nature's mythic or symbolic expression. But with this viewpoint, it is precisely the eminently social, i.e., socially *formative* function of literature that is missed. Literary structuralism —as little as the Marxist and Formalist literary studies that came before it—does not inquire as to how literature "itself turns around to help inform . . . the idea of society which it presupposes" and has helped to inform the processlike character of history. With these words, Gerhard Hess formulated in his lecture on "The Image of Society in French Literature" (1954) the unsolved problem of a union of literary history and sociology, and then explained to what extent French literature, in the course of its modern development, could claim for itself to have first discovered certain law-governed characteristics of social existence.[136] To answer the question of the socially formative function of literature according to an aesthetics of reception exceeds the competence of the traditional aesthetics of representation. The attempt to close the gap between literary-historical and sociological research through the methods of an aesthetics of reception is made easier because the concept of the *horizon of expectations* that I introduced into literary-historical interpretation[137] also has played a role in the axiomatics of the social sciences since Karl Mannheim.[138] It likewise stands in the center of a methodological essay on "Natural Laws and Theoretical Systems" by Karl R. Popper, who would anchor the scientific formation of theory in the prescientific experience of lived praxis. Popper here develops the problem of observation from out of the presupposition of a "horizon of expectations," thereby offering a basis of comparison for my attempt to determine the specific achievement of literature in the general process of the formation of experience, and to delimit it vis-à-vis other forms of social behavior.[139]

According to Popper, progress in science has in common with prescientific experience the fact that each hypothesis, like each observation, always presupposes expectations, "namely those that constitute the horizon of expectations which first makes those observations significant and thereby grants them the status of observations."[140] For progress in science as for that in the experience of life, the most important moment is the "disappointment of expectations": "It resembles the experience of a blind person, who runs into an obstacle and thereby experiences its existence. Through the falsification of our assumptions we actually make contact with 'reality.' The refutation of our errors is the positive experience that we gain from reality."[141] This model certainly does not sufficiently explain the process of the scientific formation of theory,[142] and yet it can well illustrate the "productive meaning of negative experience" in lived praxis,[143] as well as shed a clearer light upon the specific function of literature in social existence. For the reader is privileged above the (hypothetical) nonreader because the reader—to stay with Popper's image—does not first have to bump into a new obstacle to gain a new experience of reality. The experience of reading can liberate one from adaptations, prejudices, and predicaments of a lived praxis in that it compels one to a new perception of things. The horizon of expectations of literature distinguishes itself before the horizon of expectations of historical lived praxis in that it not only preserves actual experiences, but also anticipates unrealized possibility, broadens the limited space of social behavior for new desires, claims, and goals, and thereby opens paths of future experience.

The pre-orientation of our experience through the creative capability of literature rests not only on its artistic character, which by virtue of a new form helps one to break through the automatism of everyday perception. The new form of art is not only "perceived against the background of other art works and through association with them." In this famous sentence, which belongs to the core of the Formalist credo,[144] Viktor Shklovsky remains correct only insofar as he turns against the prejudice of classicist aesthetics that defines the beautiful as *harmony of form and content* and accordingly reduces the new form to the secondary function of giving shape to a pregiven content. The new form, however, does not appear just "in order to relieve the old form that already is no longer artistic." It also can make possible a new perception of things by preforming the content of a new experience first brought to light in the form of literature. The relationship between literature and reader can actualize itself in the sensorial realm as an incitement to aesthetic perception as well as in the ethical realm as a summons to moral reflection.[145] The new literary work is received and judged against the background of other works of art as well as against the background of the everyday experience of life. Its social function in the ethical realm is to be grasped according to an aesthetics of reception in the same modalities of question and answer, problem and solution, under which it enters into the horizon of its historical influence.

How a new aesthetic form can have moral consequences at the same time, or, put another way, how it can have the greatest conceivable impact on a moral question, is demonstrated in an impressive manner by the case of *Madame Bovary*, as reflected in the trial that was instituted against the author Flaubert after the prepublication of the work in the *Révue de Paris* in 1857. The new literary form that compelled Flaubert's audience to an unfamiliar perception of the "well-thumbed fable" was the principle of impersonal (or uninvolved) narration, in conjunction with the artistic device of the so-called *style indirect libre*, handled by Flaubert like a virtuoso and in a perspectively consequential manner. What is meant by this can be made clear with a quotation from the book, a description that the prosecuting attorney Pinard accused in his indictment as being immoral in the highest degree. In the novel it follows upon Emma's first "false step" and relates how she catches sight of herself in the mirror after her adultery:

Seeing herself in the mirror she wondered at her face. Never had her eyes been so large, so black, or so deep. Something subtle spread about her being transfigured her.

She repeated: "I have a lover! a lover!", delighting at the idea as at that of a second puberty that had come to her. So at last she was going to possess those joys of love, that fever of happiness of which she had despaired. She was entering upon something marvelous where all would be passion, ecstasy, delirium.

The prosecuting attorney took the last sentences for an objective depiction that included the judgment of the narrator and was upset over the "glorification of adultery" which he held to be even much more dangerous and immoral than the false step itself.[146] Yet Flaubert's accuser thereby succumbed to an error, as the defense immediately demonstrated. For the incriminating sentences are not any objective statement of the narrator's to which the reader can attribute belief, but rather a subjective opinion of the character, who is thereby to be characterized in her feelings that are formed according to novels. The artistic device consists in bringing forth a mostly inward discourse of the represented character without the signals of direct discourse ("So I am at last going to possess") or indirect discourse ("She said to herself that she was therefore at last going to possess"), with the effect that the reader himself has to decide whether he should take the sentence for a true declaration or understand it as an opinion characteristic of this character Indeed, Emma Bovary is "judged, simply through a plain description of her existence, out of her own feelings."[147] This result of a modern stylistic analysis agrees exactly with the counterargument of the defense attorney Sénard, who emphasized that the disillusion began for Emma already from the second day onward: "The dénouement for morality is found in each line of the book"[148] (only that Sénard himself could not yet name the artistic device that was not yet recorded at this time!). The consternating effect of the formal innovations of Flaubert's narrative style became evident in the trial: the impersonal form of narration not only compelled his readers to perceive things differently—"photographically exact," according to the judgment of the time—but at the same time thrust them into an alienating uncertainty of judgment. Since the new artistic device broke through an old novelistic convention—the moral judgment of the represented characters that is always unequivocal and confirmed in the description—the novel was able to radicalize or to raise new questions of lived praxis, which during the proceedings caused the original occasion for the accusation—alleged lasciviousness—to recede wholly into the background. The question with which the defense went on its counterattack turned the reproach, that the novel provides nothing other than the "story of a provincial woman's adulteries," against the society: whether, then, the subtitle to *Madame Bovary* must not more properly read, "story of the education too often provided in the provinces."[149] But the question with which the prosecuting attorney's *réquisitoire* reaches its peak is nonetheless not yet thereby answered: "Who can condemn that woman in the book? No one. Such is the conclusion. In the book there is not a character who can condemn her. If you find a wise character there, if you find a single principle there by virtue of which the adultery might be stigmatized, I am in error."[150]

If in the novel none of the represented characters could break the staff across Emma Bovary, and if no moral principle can be found valid in whose name she would be condemnable, then is not the ruling "public opinion" and its basis in "religious feeling" at once called into question along with the "principle of marital fidelity"? Before what court could the case of *Madame Bovary* be brought if the formerly valid social norms—public opinion, religious sentiment, public morals, good manners—are no longer sufficient to reach a verdict in this case?[151] These open and implicit questions by no means indicate an aesthetic lack of understanding and moral philistinism on the part of the prosecuting attorney. Rather, it is much more that in them the unsuspected influence of a new art form comes to be expressed, which through a new *manière de voir les choses* was able to jolt the reader of *Madame Bovary* out of the self-evident character of his moral judgment, and turned a predecided question of public morals back into an open problem. In the face of the vexation that Flaubert, thanks to the artistry of his impersonal style, did not offer any handhold with which to ban his novel on grounds of the author's immorality, the court to that extent acted consistently when it acquitted Flaubert as writer, but condemned the literary school that he was supposed to represent, but that in truth was the as yet unrecognized artistic device:

Whereas it is not permitted, under the pretext of portraying character and local color, to reproduce in their errors the facts, utterances and gestures of the characters whom the author's mission it is to portray; that a like system, applied to works of the spirit as well as to productions of the fine arts, leads to a realism which would be the negation of the beautiful and the good, and which, giving birth to works equally offensive to the eye and to the spirit, would commit continual offences against public morals and good manners. [152]

Thus a literary work with an unfamiliar aesthetic form can break through the expectations of its readers and at the same time confront them with a question, the solution to which remains lacking for them in the religiously or officially sanctioned morals. Instead of further examples, let one only recall here that it was not first Bertolt Brecht, but rather already the Enlightenment that proclaimed the competitive relationship between literature and canonized morals, as Friedrich Schiller not least of all bears witness to when he expressly claims for the bourgeois drama: "The laws of the stage begin where the sphere of worldly laws end." [153] But the literary work can also—and in the history of literature this possibility characterizes the latest period of our modernity—reverse the relationship of question and answer and in the medium of art confront the reader with a new, "opaque" reality that no longer allows itself to be understood from a pregiven horizon of expectations. Thus, for example, the latest genre of novels, the much-discussed *nouveau roman*, presents itself as a form of modern art that according to Edgar Wind's formulation, represents the paradoxical case "that the solution is given, but the problem is given up, so that the solution might be understood as a problem." [154] Here the reader is excluded from the situation of the immediate audience and put in the position of an uninitiated third party who in the face of a reality still without significance must himself find the questions that will decode for him the perception of the world and the interpersonal problem toward which the answer of the literature is directed.

It follows from all of this that the specific achievement of literature in social existence is to be sought exactly where literature is not absorbed into the function of a *representational* art. If one looks at the moments in history when literary works toppled the taboos of the ruling morals or offered the reader new solutions for the moral casuistry of his lived praxis, which thereafter could be sanctioned by the consensus of all readers in the society, then a still-little-studied area of research opens itself up to the literary historian. The gap between literature and history, between aesthetic and historical knowledge, can be bridged if literary history does not simply describe the process of general history in the reflection of its works one more time, but rather when it discovers in the course of "literary evolution" that properly *socially formative* function that belongs to literature as it competes with other arts and social forces in the emancipation of mankind from its natural, religious, and social bonds.

If it is worthwhile for the literary scholar to jump over his ahistorical shadow for the sake of this task, then it might well also provide an answer to the question: toward what end and with what right can one today still—or again—study literary history?

Chapter 2
History of Art
and Pragmatic History

I

At first sight, history in the realm of the arts presents two contradictory views. With the first, it would appear that the history of architecture, music, or poetry is more consistent and more coherent than that of society. The chronological sequence of works of art is more closely connected than a chain of political events, and the more gradual transformations of style are easier to follow than the transformations of social history. Valéry once said that the difference between art history and social history was that in the former the products were "filles visibles les unes des autres," whereas in the latter "chaque enfant semble avoir mille pères et réciproquement."[1] One might conclude from this that the claim "man makes his history himself" is most strongly borne out in the realm of the arts.

With the second view, the paradigms of art historiography, in their prescientific and then in their positivistic phase,[2] show that this greater consistency of detail is purchased at the price of an overall inconsistency as regards the links between art genres as well as their relation to the general historical and social process. Before it turned to tracing the history of style, art history had always taken the form of artists' biographies, which were linked only through chronological order. The literary historiography of the humanists also began with "stories," i.e., biographies of writers, in the order of their dates of death, sometimes divided up into categories of authors.[3] The model was Plutarch's *Lives*, which also established the pattern of "parallels." This form of integration, which until the end of the eighteenth century underlay the response to classical art and the dispute over its

46

exemplary character, belonged specifically to the first stage of the "histories of art appreciation."[4] For the literary form of "parallels" presupposes the idea of perfection as a criterion that transcends time, even when authors or works extend it to "genres" of art or to national "golden ages." The historical appearance of art splits up into a variety of different elemental courses, each of which is directed towards its own "point of perfection" and, through aesthetic norms, can be compared with earlier histories or "forerunners." The appearance of all histories in the arts can then be joined together again in the composite historical picture of a periodic recurrence of the golden age—a picture that is typical of humanistic historiography, and also of Voltaire's social history.[5]

A second stage of the "histories" came about through historicism (overestimation of historical singularity) in its positivistic phase. The principle of explaining a work of art by the sum of its historical conditions meant that, with every work, study had to start right from scratch, so that the "beginnings" could be ascertained from its sources, and the determinant factors of time and environment could be extracted from the author's life. The question of sources, which inevitably leads to the question of sources of sources, loses its way in "histories" just as completely as that of the link between life and work. Thus the sequential link between one work and the next is lost in a historical vacuum, which would be obvious simply from the chronological order if it were not concealed by the vague generalization of "currents" or "schools," or bridged by an external nexus, borrowed from pragmatic history—first and foremost, that of nationhood. As against this, the question may justifiably be asked whether art history can in fact do anything else but borrow its overall coherance from pragmatic history.

Between the first and second stages of the "histories" lies the historicism of the Enlightenment, in which art history played a not insignificant role. The epochal turning point at which singular history, together with the newly founded *philosophie de l'histoire*, won the battle against plural histories,[6] began at the start of the eighteenth century through insights arrived at in the study of art. The dispute that flared up again at the height of French classicism concerning the exemplary character of classical art, brought both sides—the *Anciens* and the *Modernes*—ultimately to the same conclusion, which was that ancient and modern art in the long run could not be measured against the same standard of perfection (*Beau absolu*), because each epoch had its own customs, its own tastes, and therefore its own ideas of beauty (*Beau relatif*). The discovery of the historical element of beauty, and the historical perception of art that it initiated, led up to the historicism of the Enlightenment.[7] In the eighteenth century, this process resulted in an increasing emphasis on the temporal element of both art history and philosophical history, which since Fénelon's *Projet d'un traité sur l'histoire* (1714) had deliberately employed the unifying means and classical norms of the epic to legitimize its superiority over the merely factual ruler-and-state type of history.[8]

Winckelmann's *Geschichte der Kunst des Altertums* (1764) is the first landmark of the new historiography of art, which was made possible through the historicizing of antiquity, and was set on its way by the abandoning of comparative description in the form of "parallels." In turning away from the traditional "history of artists," Winckelmann sets the new "history of art" the task of "teaching the origin, the growth, the change and the decline of the same, together with the different styles of nations, times, and artists."[9] Art history, as Winckelmann inaugurated it, does not need to borrow its overall coherence from pragmatic history, since it can claim a greater consistency of its own: "The arts . . . , like all inventions, began with necessity; afterwards one sought beauty, and finally there followed the superfluous: these are the three outstanding stages of art."[10] As opposed to the course of events in pragmatic history, the sequence of works in the art of antiquity is distinguished by a complete and therefore normative course: in the realm of the arts, the historical element can complete itself naturally. Friedrich Schlegel, who carried this principle over to poetry, looked for and found in Greek poetry "a complete natural history of art and of taste," in the course of which "even the incompleteness of the earlier stages and the degeneration of the later" could take on exemplary significance.[11] Herder's critique of Winckelmann can, in this context, be interpreted as an attempt logically to extend the temporal element of art history to "the whole sequence of times,"[12] and to assert the historical universality of beauty, as opposed to the singularized art of the Greeks which had nevertheless been raised to the level of a norm.[13] Poetry "as a tool or as an artistic product and flower of civilization and humanity" reveals through its history something that "could only be brought about progressively in the great course of times and nations."[14] And here the point is reached at which art history and social history enter into a relationship that raises a new question: whether the history of art, which is usually regarded as a dependent "poor relative" of general history, might not once have been the head of the family, and might not once again become a paradigm of historical knowledge.

II

The decay of the traditional form of literary history, shaped in the nineteenth century and now drained of all exemplary scholarly character, makes it almost impossible for us to realize the great status that was enjoyed by art history at its birth, with the formation of historical perception in the thought of the Enlightenment, in the philosophy of history of the German idealists, and at the beginning of historicism. With the turning away from traditional histories, chronicles, and accounts of rulers, states, and wars, the history of the arts seemed like a paradigm of the new form of history, which—above all—could claim a philosophical interest: "Tous les peuples ont produit des héros et des politiques: tous les peuples ont éprové des révolutions: toutes les histoires sont presque égales pour qui ne veut mettre que des faits dans sa mémoire. Mais quiconque pense, et, ce qui est encore plus rare, quiconque a du goût, ne compte que quatre siècles dans l'histoire de monde."[15] Pragmatic histories are of monotonous uniformity; only through the perfection of the arts can the human spirit rise to its own particular greatness and leave behind works that engage not only the memory, but also thought and taste. Thus Voltaire justifies the new undertaking of his *Siècle de Louis XIV* (1751). Voltaire's changeover to the "philosophy of history" was followed by Winckelmann and Herder's founding of the history of art and literature. They made the same claims, and made their criticisms of traditional political and war history no less clearly.

Before his famous works, Winckelmann wrote down *Gedanken vom mündlichen Vortrag der neuern allgemeinen Geschichte* (1754), to distinguish "what is truly useful in history" from the "nice and beautiful." He sets himself apart from "our pragmatic scribes" and from the "diverse general histories," demands "great examples" and "decisive studies," sets up a canon: "Of scholars and artists, general history immortalizes only inventors, not copyists; only originals, not collectors: a Galileo, Huygens, and Newton, not a Viviani, not a Hopital . . . ," and thus follows the basic principle: "Everything subordinate belongs to specialist history."[16] The new demands of Winckelmann's *Geschichte der Kunst des Altertums* (1764) denigrate not only the previous "history of artists," but also the chronological presentation of previous history. The history of art is to be "no mere narration of chronology and changes within it," but history and system all in one; it is to bring out the complete "essence of art" and the idea of beauty throughout its historical development.[17]

For Herder, too, the advantages of a history of the poetry of times and nations were clear. This can be seen from the panoramic presentation of current poetry with which, in his "Humanitäts-Briefen" of 1796, he refers to the historical-philosophical problem of the *Querelle*: "In this gallery of different ways of thinking, aspirations and desires, we certainly come to know periods and nations more deeply than along the deceptive, dreary route of their political and war history. In the latter we seldom see more of a people than how it let itself be governed and killed; in the former we learn how it thought, what it hoped and wished for, how it enjoyed itself, and how it was led by its teachers or its inclinations."[18] The history of the arts becomes a medium through which the historical individuation of the human spirit is presented throughout the course of times and nations. Thus the ideality of the Greeks, which Winckelmann had still maintained, is pushed back into its historical setting, the normative element of perfection carried over to the diversity of individual beauty, and the world-historical study of poetry related to a conception of history that has no further need of any immanent teleology[19] and yet again promises the aesthete a coherent whole. Those aspects of a natural history of art that are still to be found in Herder—the imagery of growth and old age, the cyclic completion of every culture, and the "classical" as the "highest of its (respective) kind"— bring into view the coherence of art history in the traditional way as conditioned by the outcome of the *Querelle*. The trailblazing approach with which Herder outstripped this immanent teleology as well as the progressive theory of the arts, arose out of his return to the tradition of biblical hermeneutics. Herder—as Weber showed— developed a theory of beauty that once more asserted its historical universality against the relativism of national and epochal individualities: the beautiful, which is no longer something metaphysically definable or essentially imitable, can be reconstructed through the hermeneutic critical process as the "supra-historical" quintessence of historical manifestations, taking on an eidetic form for the expert or the critic.[20] Thus history exposes itself to "aesthetic study as a spiritual continuity in a sense different from that of the literalness of facts."[21]

We shall look later at the question of whether the historian of fully developed historicism owes something to Herder's *Ästhetiker* and whether in fact the hermeneutic science of history of the nineteenth century had a latent paradigm in the *poetic heuristics*[22] of art history. The course that literary and art history followed in the nineteenth century can be characterized through the progressive reduction of all claims to advance a unique insight of their own. Under historicism, which entailed the historical study of ancient and modern art as a new paradigm of historical experience, art history handed over lock, stock, and barrel its legitimacy as a medium for aesthetic, philosophical, or hermeneutic reflection. The new history of national literatures, however, became an ideal counterpart to political history, and claimed to develop, through the context of all literary phenomena, the idea of how national individuality could attain its identity, from quasi-mythical beginnings to the fulfillment of national classicism.

Positivism gradually reduced this ideological orientation through a greater emphasis on science, but this merely left research into literary history without *any* particular framework. What Herder said of the old annalistic literary history can again be applied to the positivistic, which is a mere imitation of the external linking of events in pragmatic history: it "steps through nations and times with the quiet tread of a miller's mule."[23] The modern theory of literary studies, dating from the First World War, lays emphasis on stylistic, formalist, and structural methods, and in turning away from positivism has also turned away from literary history. Now the literary historian tends to keep quiet when the discussion is of problems of the discipline of history and historical hermeneutics. But even today the history of literature can still awaken that same interest it took on in the ideas of the Enlightenment and the period of Idealism, if only the appearance and function of literature in history are liberated from the rigid conventions and false causalities of literary history, and the historicity of literary works is put in its rightful perspective, opposed to the positivistic idea of knowledge and the traditionalist idea of art.

III

The form of literary history sanctioned by the historian is conceivably the worst medium through which to display the historicity of literature. It covers up the paradox of all art history, which Droysen touched on when he explained why the past reality of historical facts and their posterior interpretation are different, as for instance with pictures in an art-gallery: "Art history establishes a connection between them which, in themselves, they do not have, for which they are not painted, and from which there arises a sequence, a continuity, under the influence of which the painters of these pictures stood without being aware of it."[24]

Representing the "objective facts" of literary history are data of works, authors, trends, and periods. But even when their chronology can be fully confirmed, their interconnection, as seen in retrospect by the literary historian, is quite different from that "which once in its present [time] had a thousand other connections than those which concern us historically."[25] The retrospectively established, "actual" connection of literary "facts" captures neither the continuity in which a past work arose, nor that in which the contemporary reader or historian recognizes its meaning and importance. What has been the "event" of a literary work cannot be directly gauged from the facts listed by literary history. The question, left open by Droysen, as to how one is to extract from the sequence of works that continuity in which works are first created and received, can be answered only when one realizes that the analogy between "literary facts" and "historical facts" is an epiphenomenon.[26] This analogy, positivistic in origin, debases the historicity of the work of art and at the same time the interconnection of literary works. As a literary fact, or intersecting point of definable factors, the literary work forfeits its historically concrete appearance. This latter has its basis in the form and meaning created by the author, realized by his readers, and to be realized by them over and over again. When literary history adopted the paradigm of positivistic history, reducing the experience of literature to causal links between work and work and author and author, the historical communication between author, work, and reader disappeared behind an hypostatized succession of monographs that retained history only in name.[27]

Behind the appearances of literary history, however, there is basically no objective link between work and work that is not brought about by the creating and receiving subjects of literature.[28] It is this intersubjective communication that separates the historicity of literature from the factual objectivity of pragmatic history. But this difference narrows if one follows Droysen's critique of the dogma of "objective facts," and accepts that diffuse events are only "understood and combined through the interpretation [of them] as a coherent process, as a complex of cause and effect, of aim and fulfillment, in short as a fact," and that these same events can also be interpreted differently from "the point of view of the new fact" or from the later standpoint of the observer.[29] In this way Droysen gave back to the historical fact its basic character as an event, which like the work of art is an open field as far as interpretation is concerned. For it is not only the "right of historical study" but also an equally primary right of aesthetic interpretation, to view works or "facts in the light of the significance they have gained through their effects."[30] And so the analogy that constitutes the link between art history and pragmatic history lies in the character both of the work of art and of the historical fact as an event—a character which in both cases was leveled out by positivism's objectivist idea of knowledge.

The problem of the connections and structural interactions of art history and pragmatic history is one that needs to be looked at again. On the one hand, one must infer, from Droysen's critique of the objectivism of the historical school, that there may have been unacknowledged fictional narrative forms and aesthetic categories of the history of style that made possible this classical form of historiography. And, on the other hand, one must ask whether Droysen's idea of "the event," which includes the consequences of things as well as the standpoint of the retrospective observer, does not itself presuppose the paradigm of the past work of art and its undefined meaning.

IV

"The study of history is not an encyclopaedia of historical sciences, or a philosophy (or theology) of history, or a physics of the historical world, or—least of all—a poetics for historiography. It must set itself the task of being an organon of historical thought and research."[31] Droysen's science of history is, in its approach, hermeneutic. This makes it hard for it to give the lie to the expectation that it will merely be a "poetics for historiography," like Gervinus' *Grundzüge der Historik* (1837). The fact that it also implies a philosophy (the continuity of progressive historical *work*) and a theology of history (the highest aim of a *theodicy*) is less harmful to its claims to independence than the suspicion that history is an art, and therefore cannot be raised to the status of a science. For the method of investigating sources—the "physics of the historical world"—could not suffice to assure history of this status. Despite its triumphs—as Droysen ironically points out—people hailed "as the greatest historian of our time the man who, in his presentation [of history], was closest to the novels of Walter Scott" (p. 322). Droysen's polemic against Ranke and the objectivist ideal of historicism is aimed principally at exposing the illusions that accompany the apparently objective narration of traditional facts.

The first is the illusion of the completed process. Although every historian knows that our knowledge of history must always remain incomplete, the prevailing form of the narrative creates "the illusion, and wants to create it, that we are faced with a complete process of historical things, a finished chain of events, motives and purposes"

(p. 144). The historical narrative uses the law of fiction, that even disparate elements of a story come closer and closer together for the reader, and ultimately combine in a picture of the whole; if this aesthetic effect is to be avoided and the imagination prevented from closing the gaps, then special preventive measures are required that, paradoxically, are more common to modern artistic prose than to historiography.

The second is the illusion of the first beginning and the definitive end. Here, with a sagacity rare for his time, Droysen uncovered and denounced the "false doctrine of the so-called organic development in history" (p. 152): "It is completely beyond the scope of historical research to get to a point that would be . . . the beginning, the sudden origin" (p. 150). It is untrue of history "that all conditions for the later are present in the earlier" (p. 141), and it is equally untrue that things in history have as definite a conclusion as Ranke makes out in his history of the period of the Reformation—for "what has become bears in itself all elements of new unrest" (p. 298). When the historical narrative proceeds genetically and tries to explain things from the standpoint of their origin, it once more falls back upon a law of fiction—namely, the Aristotelian definition of the poetic fiction, which must have a beginning, a middle, and an end: a beginning that does not originate out of something else, and an end that can be followed by nothing.

The third illusion is that of an objective picture of the past. Whoever believes with Ranke that the historian need only disregard his own partiality and cause his present to be forgotten (p. 306), in order to capture an undistorted past, is as little able to guarantee the truth of the resulting "pictures from the past or illustrations of what is long since lost" as are "poets and novelists" (p. 27). Even if a past could be "established in the full breadth of its former present" (p. 27), in the past things themselves there would still not be that "criterion for the important and the characteristic" that can be gained only by reflecting on the standpoint from which the whole variety of phenomena can be viewed as a (relative) whole. "Only the thoughtless can be objective,"[32] for: "Here the 'facts' only seem to be speaking, alone, exclusive, 'objective.' They would be dumb without the narrator, who makes them speak" (§91).

The epic fictions of the completed process, of the first beginning and the definitive end, and of the self-presenting past, are the consequences of what Droysen showed to be the illusion of romantic historicism according to which the historian need only repeat the pure facts as extracted from his sources, "and the resulting illusion of facts handed down then being passed off as history" (§360). The flourishing historiography of the nineteenth century, which sought to disavow the artistic character of history writing in order to gain recognition as a science, devolved on a fictionalization of its subject matter to the extent that it followed the principle that the historian must efface himself in order for history to be able to tell its own story. The poetics of this method is no different from that of the contemporary peak of literature—the historical novel. However, it is not enough to characterize this new poetics of historical narrative by the material revelation and poetic, anecdotal animation of the past with which Sir Walter Scott's novels satisfied the historically curious. Scott's ability to bully scientific historiography into an individualized presentation of the past, such as history had never been capable of before, also was due to a principle of form.

What so impressed A. Thierry, Barante, and other historians of the Twenties, in Scott's novels, was not only the suggestive power of historical color and detail, the individual physiognomy of a past epoch, and the perspective enabling historical events to be pursued through persons instead of through the usual impersonal actions. It was also, above all, the new form of the "drama"—one of Scott's major claims to fame—by which his contemporaries meant not so much the dramatic plot-weaving as the still unfamiliar dramatic form of the narrative: as the narrator of the historical novel remains completely in the background, the story can unfold itself like a play, giving the reader the illusion that he himself is present at the drama of the persons involved. This also means that the reader is put in the position of being able to make his own judgments and draw his own moral conclusions—which had previously always been denied him by argumentative historians like Hume or Robertson.[33] These analogies between the poetics of the historical novel and the ideal of objectivity sought by contemporary historiography speak for themselves.[34] In both cases we have a narrator who is explicitly withdrawn, but implicitly present, all the while communicating and passing judgment —this situation arising out of the illusion of an unmediated presentation of the past. Even more than the novelist Scott, who could delegate his narrative functions to his characters—or hide them through perspectives—the historian Ranke continually reveals himself through *a posteriori* viewpoints and aesthetic classifications that could have played no part in the lives of those who actually experienced the historical event. That he defiantly cuts the thread joining the period "as it actually was" with that "which resulted from it" becomes painfully obvious whenever a judgment, selection, motivation, or linking of events presupposes the hindsight of the historian, and whenever the impression has to be conveyed that a view made possible only by this hindsight and by the aftereffects of the event in question was a pattern inherent in that original event. In Ranke's historiography, these inconsistencies are concealed by the illusion of a completed process—and this in a manner no longer reminiscent of Scott's handling of historical plots, but of the stylistic approach to the sequential continuity of events evinced by the form of art history.

V

We can now illustrate the thesis that Ranke's historiography is determined by aesthetic categories that fall in with the latent paradigm of the history of style, by analyzing the period of the English War as presented in Ranke's *Französische Geschichte* (Chap. I, 3; 1852-1861).[35] History of style, in the form created by Winckelmann, has the following characteristics: a turning point through the introduction of something new (change of style);[36] division into phases (e.g., the four phases of Greek art: older style, high, beautiful, and the style of imitators); the completeness of periods (styles have clear beginnings and a definite end, sealed off by the success of the new).

In Ranke's presentation, the period of the English War starts off in several respects with a radical change to something new. Louis IX, the "original of all religious kings," is succeeded by a king from the same Capetian stock, but "a character of a different kind"—Philip the Fair, a believer in the specifically modern doctrine of power politics (p. 78). He was the first that "with ruthless ambition" dared to "violate" the boundaries to the German Empire maintained by his predecessors—a fact concerning which Ranke has this comment to make: "he knew, or felt, that he was in league with the nature of things" (pp. 78-79). This sentence is a perfect example of a narrative statement (henceforth to be abbreviated n.s.), possible only in retrospect, which the narrator Ranke obviously passes off ("or felt") as coming from the person of Philip. The change to the new is then thematized in the dispute with Pope Boniface VIII, the breaking off of Crusade politics, and the destruction of the Order of the Temple. In the last-named case, Ranke does not even attempt to test the truth of the accusations against the Templars, his reason being that "it is enough for us to take note of the change in ideas" (p. 79). And so the border between the old and the new can be defined in its full, epoch-making significance: "The age that had been enlivened by the ideas of general Christendom, was over (n.s.); the goods from which the profits were to be used in the reconquering of Jerusalem, were collected up and used in the service of the kingdom. . . . Through his [Philip's] whole being there blew already the sharp breeze of modern history" (n.s., p. 80). Historical processes of such a general kind as Ranke had in mind do not, in reality, take over one from the other at a single frontier between old ("was over") and new ("blew already"), but they merge into one another at a variety of levels and crossing-points, sometimes delayed, sometimes premature. Ranke's presentation, which is highly effective from the points of view of narrative and perspective, brushes aside the heterogeneity and gives this new impulse a function that one can only call aesthetic, for here the "change in ideas," like the creation of a new style, proceeds as a sort of event from a definite beginning, and at a stroke changes the whole outlook of the world.

Ranke has stylized the political starting point of this epoch in a manner that betrays him: "But scarcely had this standpoint been adopted of a ruthless, isolated policy oriented toward a furtherance of the state of France, when there occurred an event through which the country was plunged into a general confusion and thrown back completely upon itself" (n.s., pp. 80, 81). With this temporal vagueness ("but scarcely had . . . when there occurred") Ranke surreptitiously introduces a teleology that continues to show itself in the linking and phasing of events right up to the formulation of an end result: "The world was astonished to see not only French flags flying in Normandy, but also the English retreating from the hundred-year possession of Aquitania. They kept nothing except Calais. Perhaps as great a piece of good fortune for the conquered as for the conquerers, for the nations had to separate, if each of them [was to] develop in accordance with its own instincts" (n.s., p. 95). Just like the unfolding of a new style, then, the history of the new epoch also has its purpose, in the light of which all individual contingencies become meaningful and their connection clear—"clear" as the sequence of works representing a particular style, sharing in every change in that style, and revealing only the sort of changes that can be included in a description of that style.

With Ranke's narrative style, the heterogeneous is often absorbed into the general course of things by means of temporal phasing and harmonizing. Heterogeneous elements of an event are brought in as it were in stages ("for centuries" . . . "long since" . . . "finally" . . . [p. 79]), then to be plunged into their main development with the "now" of a vital moment ("And this great faction now made contact with the struggle over the succession" [p. 83]). Or the main action might bring to the fore a long hidden, heterogeneous event through a highly significant "completely," so that it may thereby be incorporated into the general process. Thus, for instance, the new power of the cities is first "prepared in secret," then "supported by all those elements working in the depths," and finally released "completely" by the English War (p. 82). The temporal sequence implied in "completely," in the typical "now" (which not infrequently has the meaning of "at this very moment"), or in the combination "already . . . but" (p. 86), leaves matters of chronology very vague where often it would be difficult to be precise or where precision would destroy the harmonious flow, and it creates out of the contingency of events a continuity of significant moments.

This idealized time sequence, like the history of a style, describes a steady upward and downward movement, except that here the curve runs in the opposite direction, as Ranke follows the line of the decline and subsequent rise of royal power. Corresponding to the culminating-point of a history of style is the moment at which all the heterogeneous trends are homogenized: "Meanwhile, however, the English War had broken out again, and there came a moment at which all these questions, however little they originally had in common, merged into one another" (p. 88). The ideality of this moment is again betrayed by the fact that is obviously not identical with any of the events of this phase (Agincourt, Treaty of Troyes, Henry V's entry into Paris), but rather symbolized the lowest ebb of the French crown. The upward movement begins with a reference to a higher need: "But his [the Dauphin's] sword . . . alone would scarcely have saved him; first he had to separate himself from the . . . union of the Armagnacs . . . if he really wanted to be King of France" (p. 89). Once again the "great and saving moment," which the narrator Ranke dwells on for some time (p. 90), does not coincide with any concrete event. The description of the upward movement homogenizes the events and changes that strengthen the monarchy, and leaves the defeated opposition nothing but its dying moments of decline. And so the idea concealed in the event, but brought out by the narrator as the decisive impulse behind the transition, can be fulfilled by the historical outcome already described — the idea of a new monarchical order, together with which is inaugurated a new idea of the nation "developed in accordance with its own instincts" (p. 95). But the historian, who describes the cut-and-dried historical individuality of this epoch with such apparent objectivity, still owes us the reasons for his interpretation and narrative perspective, which betray themselves in his *parti pris* for the consolidation of the "fixed order" of the monarchy (p. 94) and against the repressed ideas of the towns and estates movement.

VI

While the principle behind Ranke's presentation of history refers back to the latent paradigm of the history of style, Droysen's critique of the narrative presentation and the resultant artistic nature of "objective" historiography presupposes a hermeneutics that arose from the historical approach to art. Droysen tries to shatter the "conventional view . . . that the only type of historical presentation is the narrative" (p. 254) through the distinction of nonnarrative forms of presentation (the "examining," the "didactic," the "discursive") and also through the attempt to draw a borderline between "artistic" and "historical" narrative. His statement that the artistic creation is "a totality, something complete in itself" (p. 285) is aimed at the historical novel ("a picture, a photograph of that which once was," p. 285), and applies equally to the history of the past and to the historical representation of respective epochs by historicism. Underlying this is Droysen's main argument: "That which was, does not interest us because it was, but because in a certain sense it still is, in that it is still effective because it stands in the total context of things which we call the historical, i.e., moral world, the moral cosmos" (p. 275). The narrative form of historical presentation, according to Droysen, can escape the suspicion of being artistic fiction only if, as a mimesis of development, it includes and reflects "our interpretation of important events from this standpoint" (p. 285). But this presentation of history—according to Droysen the only "historically" legitimate one—has its precedent in the hermeneutic process of experiencing and readapting the art of the past. The meaning of a work of art as well is extracted only during the progressive process of its reception; it is not a mystic whole that can reveal itself totally on its first showing.[37] The art of the past, just like history, does not interest merely because it was, but because "in a certain sense it still is" and invites one to new adaptations.

Droysen's argument against the narrative technique leaves unanswered the question of how the classical narrative form of history can be eliminated and how the contrasting didactic form of presentation can be introduced—"in order to use the whole wealth of the past for the enlightenment of our present and for our deeper understanding of it" (p. 275). Droysen seems to have overlooked the fact that the new task "of showing the development of this present and of its thought content" (p. 275), like any "mimesis of development," cannot be performed linguistically without a narrative link—in other words, without the form of "story." This also applies to the individual event if, as Droysen maintains, a historical fact as an event—just like a work of art—is constituted by the range of its possible meanings and can therefore be made concrete only through the interpretation of later observers or performers. Droysen's new definition of the historical fact—"What happens is understood and put together only by interpretation as a coherent event . . . in short, as a fact" (pp. 133-34)—necessarily implies narration if the diffuse event of the past is to be grasped as a totality in the light of its present meaning. In this context, narrative is to be understood primarily as a basic category of historical perception, and only secondarily as a form of historical presentation. The different modes of narrative presentation have, throughout history, been subject to a process consisting of various phases and degrees of literariness and "anti-literariness." Droysen's polemic against the "artistically" closed narrative form of historicism again implies an "anti-literary" form of presentation—with a limited perspective, aware of its own location, and a horizon that is left open; and, paradoxically, the poetics of modern literature offers paradigms for such a presentation.

This interweaving of poetics and history reappears in A. C. Danto's analytical philosophy of history. Danto's premise is: "our knowledge of the past is significantly limited by our ignorance of the future" (p. 16); he bases narrative logic on the posteriority of its statements: "[they] give descriptions of events under which those events could not have been witnessed" (p. 61); historical explanation presupposes "conceptual evidence" (p. 119)[38] and narrative ("A narrative describes and explains at once" [p. 141]); it should not try to reproduce the past, but with the aid of the past "organize present experience" (p. 79). All this is directly in line with Droysen's approach to history, though Danto makes no reference to it. Poetics comes onto the scene when Danto deals with the role of narrative in historical explanation and seeks an equivalent to the unprovable "historical laws" (Chaps. x-xi). He claims to find it in "temporal wholes," which first of all he explains by referring to the historical variability of literary forms (p. 226), and then traces back to definitions (pp. 223 ff.) that are basically just a rehash of the classical, Aristotelian norms of epic fiction. But if the narrative as a form of historical explanation is to keep open the possibility of further narrative statements about the same event (p. 167), the closed horizon of the classical narrative form must be surmounted and the contingency of history made to prevail against the epic tendency of the "story."

"A story is an account, I shall say an explanation, of how the change from beginning to end took place" (p. 234): this corresponds to the Aristotelian definition of the story (*Poetics*, 1450 b)—all the more so as Danto had already substituted "change," in the sense of the tragic dénouement (1450 a; 1452 a) for the mere event as the actual subject of historical explanation (p. 233). In this way Danto falls into the illusion, already uncovered by Droysen, of the first beginning and the definitive end; it immediately gets him into trouble when he observes—but swiftly dismisses as a mere problem of causality—that the "change of things" might be the middle of a history that stretches as far back as it does forwards (p. 240). His thesis "that we are in fact referring to a change when we demand an explanation of some event" (p. 246) also narrows the idea of an event to a homogeneous change, and ignores the fact that in an event not only the change from before to after, but also the aftereffects and the retrospective importance for the observer or for the acting person need to be explained. Danto believes he can achieve homogeneity through what seems to him to be the obvious condition that the historical narrative requires a never-changing subject, and should include only details or episodes that will serve the cause of explanation (p. 250). But this is precisely how Aristotle defined the epic unity of the story (1451 a), at the same time drawing attention to the superiority of fiction—which is concerned with the possible or the general—over history, which can deal only with the factual and the particular (1451 b). If narrative logic, which here is still completely confined to the closed circle of classical poetics, is to fit in with the contingency of history, it could follow the paradigm of the modern novel: since Flaubert, this has systematically dismantled the teleology of the epic story, and developed new narrative techniques in order to incorporate the open horizon of the future into the story of the past, to replace the omniscient narrator by localized perspectives, and to destroy the illusion of completeness through unexpected and unexplained details.

Narrative as a basic form of historical perception and explanation can be viewed throughout in accordance with Danto's analogy to the basic form of literary genres and their historical appearance. Only one must then refute the substantialist misconception that in a history of genres the multiplicity of historical variants is countered by an invariable form which, as "historic law," subsumes every possible historical form of a genre.[39] The history of artistic genres in fact

reveals the existence of forms that possess no greater generality than
that which shows itself in the change of their historical appearance.[40]
What Droysen said of the individuality of nations also applies to the
literary form or artistic genre as historical unit: "They change to the
extent that they have history, and they have history to the extent
that they change" (p. 198). This sentence refers to the basic view
of history in Droysen's *Historik*, the "continuity of progressive historical work" (p. 29), or—in Droysen's interpretation—the ἐπιϑοσις
εις αὐτό, through which according to Aristotle (*De an.*, ii, 4.2) the
species of man differs from that of animals, which can only reproduce *as* species. It is obvious that the history of art, as regards the
historical appearance of its forms, fulfills in a very distinct manner
Droysen's idea of a continuity "in which everything earlier extends
and supplements itself through the later" (p. 12). If it is inherent in
the idea of "historical work" that "with every new and individual
appearance it creates a newness and an addition" (p. 9), then artistic productions correspond to this idea more than other manifestations of historical life, which, in the framework of continuing institutions, change more slowly and not always in such a way that
every change "creates a newness and an addition" as the work of
art in fact can with every new and individual appearance. The analogy between the historical event and the past work of art, which
Droysen's *Historik* presupposes, therefore extends even further. The
history of art, through its manner of progression in time, and the
study of art, through its continuous mediation of past and present
art, can become a paradigm for a history that is to show the "development of this present" (p. 275). But art history can take on
this function only if it itself overcomes the organon-type principle
of the history of style, and thus liberates itself from traditionalism
and its metaphysics of supratemporal beauty. Droysen was already
pointing the way when he tried to bring the histories of individual
arts back into the "progression" of historical work, and when he
spurred on the art history of his day, which was "still only in its
beginning," with the words: "The idea of beauty will progress in
the same measure as the acknowledged beauty of ideas" (p. 230).

VII

The conception of a history of art that is to be based on the historical functions of production, communication, and reception, and
is to take part in the process of continuous mediation of past and
present art, requires the critical abandonment of two contrasting

positions. First, it defies historical objectivism, which remains a convenient paradigm ensuring the normal progress of philological research, but which in the realm of literature can achieve only a semblance of precision, which in the exemplary disciplines of natural and social science scarcely earns it any respect. It also challenges the philological metaphysics of tradition and thereby the classicism of a view of fiction that disregards the historicity of art, in order to confer on "great fiction" its own relation to truth—"timeless present" or "self-sufficient presence"[41]—and a more substantial, organic history—"tradition" or "the authority of the traditional."[42]

Traditionalism, which holds fast to the "eternal store" and guaranteed classical character of "masterpieces" and so creates for itself the spectacle of a *Sonntagsstrasse der Literaturgeschichte* (Sunday street of literary history),[43] can appeal to a secular experience of the fine arts. For, as Droysen remarks in his *Historik* (1857): "No one before Aristotle thought that dramatic poetry might have a history; until about the middle of our century it did not occur to anybody to talk of a history of music."[44] The timelessly beautiful is also subject to historical experience because of historical influences, elements of which will remain in the work of art, and because of the open horizon of its meaning, which becomes apparent in the never-ending process of interpretation; and the fine arts also have a history, to the extent that they do change in this way—these facts are a comparatively recent discovery, which the triumph of historicism could not make self-evident. What Droysen's contemporary Baudelaire provocatively formulated in 1859 as a "théorie rationnelle et historique du beau," illustrated with the outrageous example of clothing fashions, and contrasted with the low-brow bourgeois taste for the "immortal,"[45] has continually been regarded ever since the *Querelle des Anciens et des Modernes* as a new challenge to the classical interpretation of art by the enlightened or historical consciousness.

The conception of tradition that this idea of art goes back to is —according to Theodor W. Adorno—carried over from natural, spontaneous situations (the link between generations, traditions of crafts and trades) to the realm of the mind.[46] This carrying over endows what is past with an authoritative orientation, and sets the creations of the mind into a substantial continuity that supports and harmonizes history, at the cost of suppressing the contrary, the revolutionary, the unsuccessful.[47] In accordance with the image of transmission (*tradere*), the process of historical action here turns into a self-activating movement of imperishable substances or into the sequential effect of original norms. To put it as briefly as possible: "In truth history does not belong to us, but we belong to it."[48]

In the sphere of art, the alteration of the historical praxis of human creativity into a self-sufficient recurrence of formative historical entities reveals itself in the hypostatized metaphor of the *after-life of antiquity*. This stands for a historiographic model that, in the humanist's credo, has its counterpart in the "imitation of the ancient" and, in the course of history, witnesses nothing but the continual alteration of decline and return to classical models and lasting values. But tradition cannot transmit itself by itself. It presupposes a response whenever an "effect" of something past is recognizable in the present. Even classical models are present only where they are responded to: if tradition is to be understood as the historical process of artistic praxis, this latter must be understood as a movement that begins with the recipient, takes up and brings along what is past, and translates or "transmits" it into the present, thus setting it in the new light of present meaning.

Along with the illusion of a self-activating tradition, aesthetic dogmatism also falls into discredit — the belief in an "objective" meaning, which is revealed once and for all in the original work, and which an interpreter can restore at any time, provided he sets aside his own historical position and places himself, without any prejudices, into the original intention of the work. But the form and meaning of a work formative of tradition are not the unchangeable dimensions or appearances of an aesthetic object, independent of perception in time and history: its potential of meaning only becomes progressively visible and definable in the subsequent changes of aesthetic experience, and dialogically so in the interaction between the literary work and the literary public. The tradition-forming potential of a classic work can be seen by its contemporaries only within the horizon of its first "materialization."[49] Only as the horizon changes and expands with each subsequent historical materialization, do responses to the work legitimize particular possibilities of understanding, imitation, transformation, and continuation — in short, structures of exemplary character that condition the process of the formation of literary tradition.

If one wishes to give the name "tradition" to this discontinuous process of an active, normative, and changing reproduction of what is past in the realm of art, then one must do away with the Platonic idea of art and with the substantialist conception of history as an "event of tradition." The receiving consciousness certainly stands among traditions that precondition its way of understanding, but, just as certainly, the traditional cannot be fitted out with predicates and a life of its own, for without the active participation of the receiving mind, these are simply not conceivable. It is therefore a substantialist relapse in his historical hermeneutics when H.-G. Gadamer —obviously indulging a predilection for the classics—expects of the traditional text per se (regardless of whether it is a work of art or a historical document) "that it asks a question of the interpreter. Interpretation . . . always contains a basic reference to the question that has been asked on one. To understand a text means to understand a question."[50] But a past text cannot, of its own accord, across the ages, ask us or later generations a question that the interpreter would not first have to uncover or reformulate for us, proceeding from the answer that the text hands down or appears to contain. Literary tradition is a dialectic of question and answer that is always kept going—though this is often not admitted—from the present interest. A past text does not survive in historical tradition, thanks to old questions that would have been preserved by tradition and could be asked in an identical way for all times including our own. For the question whether an old or allegedly timeless question still—or once again—concerns us, while innumerable other questions leave us indifferent, is decided first and foremost by an interest that arises out of the present situation, critically opposes it, or maintains it.

Walter Benjamin, in his critique of historicism, reaches an analogous conception of historical tradition: "To put into operation experience with history—which for every present is an original experience—is the task of historical materialism. It turns to a consciousness of the present, which shatters the continuum of history."[51] Why this task should fall to the historical materialist alone is not made clear by this essay. For, after all, a historical materialist must presumably believe in a "real historical continuity" if, with Benjamin, he declares his allegiance to the ideas expressed in Engels' letter to Mehring (14 July 1893). Anyone who, with Engels, wishes to proclaim the apparent triumph of thought as "intellectual reflections of changed economic fact," cannot also impute to the conscious mind the achievement of "shattering the continuum of history." According to materialist dogma, he cannot apply any consciousness to the present that is not previously conditioned by changed economic facts in the midst of the real, historical continuity, which, paradoxically, that consciousness is meant to shatter. The famous "tiger leap into the past" (*Geschichtsphilosophische Thesen, xiv*) completely brushes aside historical materialism: Benjamin's anti-traditionalist theory of reception superseded it in the Fuchs essay before he himself realized it.

VII

The classical idea of art as the history of creative spirits and timeless masterpieces, together with its positivistic distortion in the form of innumerable histories of "Man and Work," has since the Fifties been the subject of critical examination conducted in the name of the "structural method." In Anglo-American criticism this proceeded from Northrop Frye's theory of archetypal literature, and in French from Claude Lévi-Strauss; it aimed at a predominantly elitist idea of culture and art, contrasted this with a new interest in primitive art, folklore, and subliterature, and demanded a methodical approach starting with the individual work and finishing with literature as a system.[52] For Frye, literature is an "order of words," not a "piled aggregate of works": "Total literary history gives us a glimpse of the possibility of seeing literature as a complication of a relatively restricted and simple group of formulas that can be studied in primitive culture."[53] Archetypes or "communicable symbols" mediate between the structure of primitive myths and the forms or figures of later art and literature. The historical dimension of literature withdraws behind the omnipresence or transferability of these symbols, which obviously change gradually, with literary means of expression from myth to mimesis; it reemerges only when, at the last moment, Frye attributes to the myth an emancipatory function regarding ritual, so that—like Matthew Arnold—he can set art the task of removing class barriers, enabling it to participate "in the vision of the goal of social effort, the idea of complete and classless society."[54]

The gulf between structure and event, between synchronous system and history, becomes absolute in Lévi-Strauss, who searches behind the myths for nothing but the structure in depth of the closed synchronous system of a functional logic. The latent Rousseauism of this theory is apparent in the chapter "Du mythe au roman" from *L'Origine des manières de table.*[55] When the structural analysis of the Indian myths, which in a single breath are awarded and refused "liberté d'invention"("nous pouvons au moins démontrer la nécessité de cette liberté,"[104]), poses a historical process such as the development from myth to novel, this process appears as an incontrovertible degradation in the general *"débâcle"* of history (pp. 105-106). In this downward movement of the real through the symbolic to the imaginary, the structures of contrast decline into those of repetition. Lévi-Strauss is reminded here of the "serial," which also draws its life from the denatured repetition of original works and, like the "mythe à tiroir," is the subject to a short periodicity and the same "contraintes formelles." But this new version of the old theory of the "decayed matter of culture" (or here, "matter of nature") is contradicted by the fact that in the nineteenth century the serial novel was not the "état dernier de la dégradation du genre romanesque" but, on the contrary, the starting point for the great, "original" novel of the Balzac and Dostoyevsky type—not to mention the fact that the *Mystéres de Paris* kind of novel developed a new mythology of city life that cannot be fitted in with the idea of a decline in the "exténuation du mythe." Ultimately Lévi-Strauss's theory of a decline itself surreptitiously takes on the nature of a new myth, when in the moral outcome of the serial novel he claims to find an equivalent to the closed structure of the myth, "par lequel une société qui se livre à l'histoire croit pouvoir remplacer l'ordre logico-naturel qu'elle a abandonné, à moins qu'elle-même n'ait été abandonée par lui" (p. 106). History as the deviation of society from nature, personified in the "ordre logico-naturel," if one were not to assume that nature herself (comparable to Heidegger's "Kehre") has turned away from man: with this, Heidegger's myth of "Seinsvergessenheit" (forgetfulness of being) is given a worthy, panstructuralistic companionpiece.

For Lévi-Strauss every work of art is completely explicable through its function within the secondary system of reference of society; every act of speech is reduced to a combinatory element in a primary system of signs; all meaning and individuation merges into an anonymous, subjectless system, establishing the priority of a spontaneous natural order over any historical process. And so we may assume, with Paul Ricoeur, that the paradigm of anthropological structuralism will be productive for the methodology of the study of art and literature only if, along with the results of structural analysis, the latter takes up and regains what the former seeks dogmatically to exclude: "une production dialectique, qui fasse advenir le système comme acte et la structure comme événement."[56]

An approach to bridging the gap between structure and event is already to be distinguished in the literary theory of Roland Barthes, who in France paved the way for criticism of the "Lansonist system" of university literary history, and was the first to show what structural analysis of a literary work could really achieve. His Racine interpretation penetrates the historical explanation and naive psychology of literary creation, and establishes a kind of structural anthropology of classical tragedy. The archaic system of characters is transplanted into a surprisingly rich context of functions, a context that extends from the three dimensions of topography right up to metaphysics and the inverted theology of redemption of the Racinian hero, and that stimulates and expands one's historical understanding.[57] The question left open in *L'homme racinien* as to what literature meant to Racine and his contemporaries is, for Barthes, one of those problems that literary history can solve only through a radical conversion "analogous to that which made possible the transition from the chronicles of kings to genuine history." For literary history can only "deal on the level of literary functions (production, communication, consumption), and not on that of the individuals who have exercised these functions."[58] From a scientific point of view, literary history would accordingly be sociologically possible only as a history of the literary institution, while the other side of literature —the individual connection between author and work, between work and meaning—would be left to the subjectivity of criticism, of which Barthes can, quite rightly, make the demand that it confess to its preconceptions if it wants to prove its historical legitimacy.[59] But this raises the question whether the thus legitimized subjectivity or series of interpretations of a work is not itself again "institutionalized" through history, forming a system in his historical sequence. The question also arises as to how one is to conceive the structure of a work in opposition to the structuralist axiom of completeness, remains open to an interpretation that in principle is incapable of completeness and, indeed takes on its specific character as art through this very openness and dependence on individual response.

Barthes has not asked the first of these questions, but his answer to the second is equally exasperating for the dogmatists of positivism and of structuralism.[60] "Ecrire, c'est ébranler le sens du monde, y disposer une interrogation indirecte, à laquelle l'écrivain, par un dernier suspens, s'abstient de répondre. La réponse, c'est chacun de nous qui la donne, y apportant son histoire, son langage, sa liberté; mais comme histoire, langage et liberté changent infiniment, la réponse du monde à l'écrivain est infinie: on ne cesse jamais de répondre à ce qui a été écrit hors de tout réponse: affirmés, puis mis en rivalité, puis remplacés, les sens passent, la question demeure."[61] Here the open structure of the literary work is observed in the open relation between meaning, question, and answer, but the cost of this is a yawning gap of subjective arbitrariness between the past work and its progressive interpretation—a gap that can be bridged only by the historical mediation of question and answer. For the implicit question, which in fact is what first awakens our present interest in the past work, can be obtained only through the answer that the aesthetic object, in its present materialization, holds or seems to hold ready for us. Literary works differ from purely historical documents precisely because they do more than simply document a particular time, and remain "speaking" to the extent that they attempt to solve problems of form or content, and so extend far beyond the silent relics of the past.[62]

If the literary text is taken primarily as an answer, or if the later reader is primarily seeking an answer in it, this by no means implies that the author himself has formulated an explicit answer in his work. The answering character of the text, which provides the historical link between the past work and its later interpretation, is a modality of its structure—seen already from the viewpoint of its reception; it is not an invariable value within the work itself. The answer or meaning expected by the later reader can have been ambivalent or have remained altogether indeterminate in the original work. The degree of indeterminacy can—as Wolfgang Iser has shown—actually determine the degree of aesthetic effectiveness and hence the artistic character of a work.[63] But even the extreme case of an open-structured fictional text, with its quantity of indeterminacy calculated to stimulate the imagination of the active reader, reveals how every fresh response links up with an expected or supposed meaning, the fulfillment or nonfulfillment of which calls forth the implicit question and so sets in motion the new process of understanding. This process emerges most clearly in the history of the interpretation of great works, when the new interpreter is no longer satisfied with the conventionally accepted answer or interpretation, and looks for a new answer to the implied or "posthumous" question. The open, indeterminate structure makes a new interpretation possible, whereas on the other hand the historical communication of question and answer limits the mere arbitrariness of interpretation.

It makes no difference whether the conventionally accepted answer of a text has been given explicitly, ambivalently, or indeterminately by the author himself; or whether it is an interpretation of the work that first arose at its reception. The question implied in the answer presented by the work of art—a question which, according to Barthes, each present must answer in its own way—is now set within a changed horizon of aesthetic experience, and so is no longer asked as it was originally by the past text, but is the result of an interaction between present and past.[64] The question, which enables the past work of art to affect us still or anew, has to be implicit because it presupposes the active mind's testing the conventional answer, finding it convincing or otherwise, discarding it or putting it in a new light so that the question now implied for us may be revealed. In the historical tradition of art, a past work survives not through eternal questions, nor through permanent answers, but through the more or less dynamic interrelationship between question and answer, between problem and solution, which can stimulate a new understanding and can allow the resumption of the dialogue between present and past.

Analysis of the dialectic of question and answer formative of tradition in the history of literature and art is a task that literary criticism has scarcely even begun. It goes beyond the semiotic conception of a new science of literature, which Barthes sees in an all too narrow framework: "It cannot be a science of contents (which can only be suckled by historical science proper), but a science of the conditions of contents, i.e., of forms: what will concern it is the variations of meaning applied and to a certain extent applicable to the works."[65] However, the constantly renewed interpretation is more than an answer left to the discretion of the interpreter, for literary tradition is more than just a variable series of subjective projections or "fulfilled meanings" over a mere matrix or "empty meaning" of works, "which bears all of those."[66] It is not only the formal constitution and variability of the meanings applicable to works that can be described in accordance with the linguistic rules of the sign. The content, the sequence of interpretations as they have appeared historically—this, too, has a logic: that of question and answer, through which the accepted interpretations can be described as a coherence formative of tradition; it also has a counterpart to the language or "literature competence"[67] that is a prerequisite for all transformations: the initial meaning or problem structure of the work, which is its "a priori" content, conditioning all subsequent interpretations, and providing the first instance against which all these must prove themselves. And so there is no reason why the science of literature should not also be a science of contents. And indeed it will have to be, because the science of history cannot relieve it of the task of closing the gap that Barthes, through his formal rigorism, has widened between author and reader, reader and critic, critic and historian, and furthermore between the functions of literature (production, communication, reception).[68] A new science of literature will cease to be a mere auxiliary to history at the moment when it uses the privilege of its still "speaking" sources, and their communication of response and tradition, to attempt to move away from the old "history of development" and towards a new "history of structure"—a move that the science of history is also concerned with making.

IX

How can the history of art and literature contribute towards closing the gap between structural method and historical hermeneutics? This problem is common nowadays to various approaches to a theory of literature that—like my own attempt[69] —regard as necessary the destruction of literary history in its old monographic or "epic" tradition, in order to arouse a new interest in the history and historicity of literature. This is especially true of the French *Nouvelle Critique* and Prague structuralism,[70] whose standpoint we must examine here, at least as it is represented in a few pioneer works.

One representative advocate of the *Nouvelle Critique* is Gérard Genette. In his programmatic essay *Structuralisme et critique littéraire* (1966),[71] he shows different ways in which literary criticism could use structural description, and the theory of style could integrate already current analyses of immanent structures in a structural synthesis. The contrast between intersubjective or hermeneutic analysis and structural analysis would not require literature to be divided into two separate spheres of mythographic or subliterature, on the one hand, and artistic literature, in the exegetic tradition, on the other—as Ricoeur has suggested, in his critique of Lévi-Strauss.[72] For the two methods could expose complementary meanings of the same text: "à propos d'une même oeuvre, la critique herméneutique parlerait le langage de la reprise du sens et de la récréation intérieure, et la critique structurale celui de la parole distante et de la reconstruction intelligible."[73] Thematic criticism, which until now has been concerned almost exclusively with the individual works of authors, would have to relate these to a collective topic of literature, dependent on the attitude, taste, and wishes—in short, the "expectation of the public."[74] Literary production and consumption would act in the same way as *parole* and *langue*; and so it must also be possible to formulate the literary history of a system in a series of synchronous sections, and to translate the mere sequence of autonomous, mutually "influencing" works into a structural history of literature and its functions.[75]

Jean Starobinski, on the other hand, with his new definition of literary criticism (*La relation critique*, 1968), proceeds from the belief that structuralism in its strict form is applicable only to literatures that represent a "regulated play in a regulated society."[76] The moment literature questions the given order of institutions and traditions, oversteps the closed limits of the surrounding society with its sanctioned literature, and thus opens up the dimension of history in a culture, the result is that the synchronous structure of a society and the appearance of its literature as an event no longer belong to the homogeneous texture of the same logos: "la plupart des grandes oeuvres modernes ne déclarent leur relation au monde que sur le mode de refus, de l'opposition, de la contestation."[77] The task of a new criticism will be to bring this "relation différentielle" back into the structural context of literature. This not only requires that thematic criticism open the closed hermeneutic circle between work and interpreter (trajet textuel) onto the work's path to the world of its readers (trajet intentionnel); it also requires that critical understanding should not frustrate the differential or "transgressive" function of the work: if history continually cancels out the protest element and the exceptionality of literature, absorbing it as a paradigm of the next order, the critic must fight against this leveling out of works in the line of tradition, and must hold fast to the differences,[78] thus emphasizing the discontinuity of literature in the history of society.

Furthest from the dogma of the irreconcilability of structural and historical analysis is probably Prague structuralism. Here approaches of Formalist literary theory have been developed into a structural aesthetics, which seeks to comprehend the literary work with categories of aesthetic perception and then to describe the perceived gestalt of the aesthetic object diachronically, in its "concretizations" conditioned by response. The pioneer work of Jan Mukařovský has been continued, particularly by F. Vodička, to form a theory of literary history that is based on the aesthetics of response.[79] In his book *Struktura vývoje* (1969) he sees the main task of literary history in the context of the polarity between the literary work and reality, which is to be materialized and historically described according to the manner of its perception, i.e., the dynamic connections between the work and the literary public.[80] This requires, on the one hand, the reconstruction of the "literary norm," i.e., the "totality of literary postulates" and the hierarchy of literary values of a given period, and, on the other, the ascertainment of the literary structure through the "concretization" of literary works, i.e., through the concrete gestalt that they have assumed in the perception of the public of the time. Prague structuralism therefore sees the structure of a work as a component part of the broader structure of literary history, and sees the latter as a process arising out of the dynamic tension between work and norm, between the historic sequence of literary works and the sequence of changing norms or attitudes of the public: "Between them there is always a certain parallelism, for both creations — the creations of norms and the creation of a new literary reality — proceed from a common base: from the literary tradition that they overcome."[81] This presupposes that aesthetic values, like the "essence" of works of art, only reveal their different forms through a process and are not permanent factors in themselves. The literary work—according to Mukařovský's bold new version of the social character of art—is offered not as a structure that is independent of its reception, but simply as an "aesthetic object," which can therefore be described only in accordance with the succession of its concretizations.

By *concretization*, Vodička means the picture of the work in the consciousness of those "for whom the work is an esthetic object."[82] With this idea, Prague structuralism has taken up and historicized an approach of Roman Ingarden's phenomenological aesthetics. According to the latter, the work, in the polyphonic harmony of its qualities, still had the character of a structure independent of temporal changes in the literary norm; but Vodička disputes the idea that the aesthetic values of a work could be given complete expression through an optimal concretization: "As soon as the work is divided up on its absorption into new contexts (changed state of the language, different literary postulates, changed social structure, new system of spiritual and practical values etc.), one can feel the esthetic effect of precisely those qualities of a work which earlier . . . were not felt as esthetically effective."[83] Only the reception, i.e., the historical life of the work in literature, reveals its structure, in an open series of aspects, through the active interrelationship between the literary work and the literary public. With this theory, Prague structuralism has gained a position for the aesthetics of reception that relieves it of the twin problems of aesthetic dogmatism and extreme subjectivism: "Dogmatism found eternal, unchangeable values in the work, or interpreted the history of responses as a way to the ultimate, correct perception. Extreme subjectivism, on the other hand, saw in all responses proof of individual perception and ideas, and sought only in exceptional cases to overcome this subjectivism through a temporal determination."[84] Vodička's theory of reception links up with the methodological principle that the materialization legitimated by a literary public—which itself can become a norm for other works—is to be distinguished from merely subjective forms of materialization, which do not enter any current tradition as a value judgment: "The object of cognition cannot be all materializations possible with regard to the individual attitude of the reader, but only those which show a confrontation between the structure of the work and the structure of the norms currently valid."[85] Thus the critic who records and publishes a new materialization joins the author and the reader as someone with his own particular function within the "literary community," whose constitution as "literary public" is only one of several perspectives that can offer this theory of a structural literary history as a shot in the arm to the methodologically stagnant sociology of literature.

X

A theory that sets out to destroy the substantialist idea of tradition, and to replace it with a functional idea of history, is bound to be open to the charge of one-sidedness precisely in this sphere of art and literature. Whoever abandons the latent Platonism of the philological method, dismisses as illusory the eternal essence of the work of art and the timeless standpoint of its observer, and begins to regard the history of art as a process of production and reception, in which not identical functions but dialogical structures of question and answer mediate between past and present—such a person must run the risk of missing a specific experience of art that is obviously in opposition to its historicity. Art historiography that follows the principle of the open structure and the perceptually incomplete interpretation of works, in accordance with the process of productive understanding and critical reinterpretation, is concerned primarily with the intellectual and emancipatory function of art.[86] It is not, then, bound to ignore the social and, in the narrower sense, aesthetic character of art—its critical, communicative, and socially influential function and those achievements that the active and the suffering man experiences as impulses of ecstasy, pleasure, and play, and withal as impulses that remove him from his historical existence and his social situation?

It cannot be disputed that the emancipatory and socially formative function of art represents only one side of its historical role in the process of human history. The other side is revealed in the fact that works of art are "directed against the course of time, against disappearance and transience," because they seek to immortalize, i.e., "to confer on the objects of life the dignity of immortalization."[87] And so, according to Kurt Badt, art history also has the task of showing "what art has been able to present of human perfection, for instance even in suffering (Grünewald's *Christus*)."[88] However, recognizing the supratemporal character of this glorifying and immortalizing function does not mean contrasting the historicity of art with the timeless essence of an absolute beauty that has manifested itself only in the immortality of the work. The glorified immortality of the work of art is something that has been created *against* transcience and within history itself.[89] The history of art incorporates the historical appearance of works and their immortality as the result of aesthetic activities of mankind. If, with Karel Kosík, we understand the dialectics of history as a process in which history "contains both the historicity that is transient, sinks into the past and *does not* return, and historical character, the formation of the immortal—i.e. the self-forming and self-creating"[90]—then the history of art is distinguished from other spheres of historical reality by the fact that in it the formation of the immortal is not only visibly carried out through the production of works, but also through reception, by its constant reenactment of the enduring features of works that long since have been committed to the past.

The history of art maintains this special status even if one concurs with the Marxist literary theory that art and literature cannot claim any history of their own, but only become historical insofar as they participate in the general process of historical praxis. The history of art keeps its special position within pragmatic history to the extent that, through the medium of perception and by means of interpretation, it can consciously bring forth the historical capacity of "totalization, in which human praxis incorporates impulses from the past and animates them through this very integration."[91] Totalization, in the sense of "a process of production and reproduction, animation and rejuvenation,"[92] is presented in exemplary form by the history of art. For here—as T. S. Eliot pointed out—it is not only the authentically new work that revises our view of all past works. Here the past work, too, which has the appearance of immortal beauty and—according to Malraux—embodies art as a counter to fate, needs the productive work of understanding in order to be taken out of the imaginary museum and appropriated by the interpretive eye of the present. And here, too, ultimately, art historiography can win back its disputed legitimacy insofar as it seeks out and describes the canons and contexts of works, rejuvenating the great wealth of human experience preserved in past art, and making it accessible to the perception of the present age.

Chapter 3
Theory of Genres
and Medieval Literature

I

The development of a theory not infrequently has an unrecognized or essentially unreflected dependency on the kind and the limitations of the object through which the theory is to be exemplified or to which it is to be applied. This is especially the case with the theory of literary genres. On the one hand, traditional philologists developed it with preference for examples from the classical literary periods—that offered the advantage that the form of a genre could be determined according to canonized rules, and its history followed from work to work according to the intentions and accomplishments of their authors. Structuralist studies opposed this individualizing consideration with a theory that was primarily developed from primitive genres such as, for example, the narrative of myths or the "conte populaire"; from such examples without an individualized artistic character, the theory could demonstrate those simplest structures, functions, and sequences that constitute and differentiate various genres on the basis of a narrative logic.

In contrast to this polarization, it seemed worthwhile to develop a theory of literary genres within a field of inquiry that lies between the opposites of singularity and collectivity, of the artistic character of literature and its merely purposive or social character. Medieval vernacular literatures are especially appropriate for such an attempt. For in this area philological studies have barely gotten beyond individual monographs, themselves often only overviews. These genres are a long way from being sufficiently delimited, let alone historically represented in their historical contemporaneity and sequence.

The generic divisions of the handbooks rest on a convention of the discipline that is scarcely called into question any longer, according to which one promiscuously uses original characterizations, classical genre concepts, and later classifications. In international discussion, Romance literary studies have for a long time failed to advance any contribution to a historical systematics or to the general development of a theory of literary genres.[1] This failure has its material reasons, but also its scholarly-historical ones.

A history and theory of vernacular genres in the Middle Ages bumps up against the particular problem that the structural characteristics of the literary forms—from which the history and theory would begin—themselves first have to be worked out from texts that are, chronologically, highly diffuse. Here we have newly developing literatures that are not immediately dependent on the preceding Latin literature, as concerns either a humanist principle of strict imitation or the canon of a binding poetics. In the Romance vernacular, there was at first scarcely any poetological reflection on genres. "The Vulgate languages and their long-developed typologies only come into the view of the theorists after 1300 with Dante, Antonio da Tempo, and Eustache Deschamps."[2] But medieval theorists judged poetry primarily according to styles, and not according to generic norms.

On the other hand, the modern system of the three basic kinds or "natural forms of literature [Dichtung]" would want to do more than exclude the majority of medieval genres as impure or pseudo-poetic forms.[3] For even the vernacular epic or lyric is difficult to describe within the distinction provided by the modern triad of epic, lyric, and dramatic—and the passion play simply cannot be so described. Basic distinctions such as purposive or purposeless, didactic or fictional, imitative or creative, traditional or individual—which have governed literary understanding since the emancipation of the "fine arts"—were not yet perceived and reflected on; thus it makes no sense to work with a triadic division of literature owed to this emancipatory process, and to heap together with the didactic the remainder of a problematic fourth "literary kind" [Dichtart] —in the Middle Ages, surely the larger part—that doesn't fit into the triadic schema.

In view of such difficulties, a heightened significance was given to the critique that began shortly after 1900 against the pseudo-normative concept of genre in positivistic literary history (understood as "evolutionary" by Brunetière). Croce's aesthetics, which in view of the expressive uniqueness of each work of art still recognized only art itself (or intuition) as a "genre," seemed to free the philologies from the genre problem altogether—a problem that Croce dissolved into the simple question of the utility of various classifications for books. But of course the cutting of a Gordian knot does not lead to any enduring solution to a scholarly problem. Croce's "solution" would certainly not have been accorded any such tenacious success with enthusiasts and opponents if the reaction against the normative genre concept had not been led by the rise of modern stylistics,[4] which similarly declared the "verbal work of art" to be autonomous, and developed methods of ahistorical interpretation for which an initial observation of historical genre-forms appeared superfluous.

With the turn away from the aestheticism of the "work-immanent" method, which produced a record harvest of scholarly monographs but left unanswered the question of the diachronic and synchronic coherence of literary works, began the process of a new, historico-hermeneutic and structuralist development of theory—within which we still stand today. The theory of literary genres is at the point of seeking a path between the Scylla of nominalist skepticism that allows for only aposteriori classifications, and the Charybdis of regression into timeless typologies, a path along which the historicization of genre poetics and of the concept of form are upheld.[5] To initiate a justification of this path with a critique of Croce recommends itself not merely on the grounds of an intradisciplinary discussion. For Croce pushed to an extreme the critique of the universal validity of the canon of genres, a critique that had been growing since the eighteenth century, so that the necessity of founding a historical systematics of literary genres once again becomes apparent.

II

"Every true work of art has violated an established genre, and in this way confounded the ideas of critics who thus found themselves compelled to broaden the genre."[6] What Croce provides here as an annihilating attack upon the normative genre concept once again presupposes (however unconsciously) that precise state of affairs in which the historical reality, the function (understood within the aesthetics of production), and the hermeneutic achievement of the genre concept would be demonstrable. For how else can one answer in a controllable manner the single question considered legitimate by Croce—whether a work of art is a perfectly achieved expression, or only half so, or even not at all[7]—if not through an aesthetic judgment that knows to distinguish within the work of art the unique expression from the expected and generic?

Even a perfect work of art (as the unity of intuition and expression, to use Croce's terms) could be absolute (isolated from everything *expected*) only at the expense of its comprehensibility. Croce considered art a matter of pure individual expression, thereby employing a form of the aesthetics of experience and of genius[8] that is linked to a specific period but was illegitimately generalized by him. But even considered as such, the literary work is conditioned by "alterity," that is, in relation to another, an understanding consciousness. Even where a verbal creation negates or surpasses all expectations, it still presupposes preliminary information and a trajectory of expectations [*Erwartungsrichtung*] against which to register the originality and novelty. This horizon of the expectable is constituted for the reader from out of a tradition or series of previously known works, and from a specific attitude, mediated by one (or more) genre and dissolved through new works. Just as there is no act of verbal communication that is not related to a general, socially or situationally conditioned norm or convention,[9] it is also unimaginable that a literary work set itself into an informational vacuum, without indicating a specific situation of understanding. To this extent, every work belongs to a genre—whereby I mean neither more nor less than that for each work a preconstituted horizon of expectations must be ready at hand (this can also be understood as a relationship of "rules of the game" [*Zusammenhang von Spielregeln*]) to orient the reader's (public's) understanding and to enable a qualifying reception.

The continually new "widening of the genre," in which Croce saw the supposed validity of definitional and normative genre concepts led ad absurdum, describes from another perspective the processlike appearance and "legitimate transitoriness" of literary genres,[10] as soon as one is prepared to desubstantialize the classical concept of genre. This demands that one ascribe no other generality to literary "genres" (no longer so called, indeed, except metaphorically) than that which manifests itself in the course of its historical appearance. By no means must everything generically general—what allows a group of texts to appear as similar or related—be dismissed, along with the timeless validity of the concept of an essence [*Wesensbegriff*] implicit in the classical genre poetics. One may refer here to the differentiation in linguistics as well of a generality that assumes a middle position between the universal and the individual.[11] Following this line of thought, literary genres are to be understood not as *genera* (classes) in the logical senses, but rather as *groups* or *historical families*.[12] As such, they cannot be deduced or defined, but only historically determined, delimited, and described. In this they are analogous to historical languages, for which it likewise holds that German or French, for example, do not allow themselves to be defined, but rather only synchronically described and historically investigated.

With the help of determinations that Kant developed for aesthetic judgment, one can likewise grasp the generality of literary genres that do not let themselves be reduced to an anterior, determinate, and invariable norm. According to Kant, the modality of a judgment of taste cannot be the "necessary consequence of an objective law," but rather can be called "merely exemplary," because it necessarily "demands the consent of all to one judgment, which can be considered as the example of a general rule that one cannot assert." This mediation of the general and the particular through the exemplary clearly also holds for the receptive and productive continuity of a literary genre that, as "an undetermined norm," is at once example and model, "the public meaning of which always only fulfills and determines itself in the particular judgment of taste and in the particular work of art." Thus understood, the category of the exemplary does away with the schema of rule-and-instance and makes possible a processlike determination of the concept of genre in the aesthetic realm. For "that which the exemplary indicates is *undetermined*, having dynamic character, that is, being further determined through each new concretization."[13]

Such a determination no longer applies the generality of literary genres normatively (*ante rem*) or in a classificatory manner (*post rem*), but rather historically (*in re*), that is, in a "continuity in which each earlier event furthers and supplements itself through the later one,"[14] and its advantages are self-evident. It frees the development of theory from the hierarchical cosmos of a limited number of genres, sanctioned by the pattern of antiquity, that do not allow themselves to be mixed or increased. Understood as groups or historical families, not only the canonized major and minor genres can constitute a group and be described in terms of the history of genres, but also other series of works that are bound by a structure forming a continuity and that appear historically.[15] The continuity formative of a genre can lie in the series of all the texts of one genre, such as the animal fable, or in the oppositional series of the chanson de geste and the courtly romance; it can lie in the succession of the works of one author, such as those of Rutebeuf, or in the cross-sectional phenomena of a period style such as the allegorical manner of the thirteenth century. But it can also lie in the history of a kind of verse such as the paired tetrameter, in the development of a "literary tone"[16] that overlaps with particular phenomena such as epic hyperbole, or in a thematic structure such as the saga-form of the medieval Alexander the Great. But a work can also be grasped according to *various* generic aspects, as, for example, the *Roman de la rose* of Jean de Meun, in which—held together through the traditional framework of the minne-allegory—satire and travesty, allegory and mysticism in the manner of the school of Chartres, the philosophical tractatus, and comedic scenes (the roles of Amis and of Vielle) all crisscross one another. But such a division does not relieve the critic from posing the question of the generic *dominant* within the relational system of the text (in our example it is the lay-encyclopedia, which forms of representation Jean de Meun boldly and ingeniously meant to broaden).

With the introduction of the concept of the *dominant*[17] that shapes the system, the so-called mixing of genres—which in the classical theory was the merely negative side-piece to the "pure genres"—can be made into a methodologically productive category. One would then further distinguish between a generic structure in an independent or constitutive function, and one in a dependent or accompanying function. Thus, for example, the satiric element in the Romance Middle Ages at first and for a long time appears only in a dependent function: in connection with the sermon, the moral didactic or "chastising" poem (for example, *La Bible Guiot*), the literature of rank (*Etats du monde*, the mirror of princes), the animal epic, the verse-farce, the *poesia giocosa*, or also the "conflict poem," the polemical lyric and all the forms that A. Adler counted as *historicum*. Where it then gains a constitutive function, as, for example, in the satiric works of Peire Cardenal, Rutebeuf, or Cecco Angiolieri, independent genres of satire arise, which however—in contrast to the ancient or Horatian tradition, with which the literature of the Renaissance first reestablishes contact—do not become absorbed in the continuity of a *single* overarching genre. But there are also cases in which a generic structure appears only in an accompanying function, as, for example, the so-called *gap*, or the grotesque, which in the Romance Middle Ages never arrived at the form of an independent literary genre.[18] Accordingly, a literary genre in the nonlogical, group-specific sense is determinable in that, in contrast to the wider sphere of dependent functions, it is independently able to constitute texts, whereby this

constitution must by synchronically comprehensible in a structure
of nonsubstitutable elements, as well as diachronically in a potential
for forming a continuity.

III

If, to begin with, we inquire into the determinability of literary
genres in a synchronic perspective, then one must proceed from the
fact that the delimitation and differentiation cannot be decided according to one-sided formal or thematic characteristics. There is
the old recognition, first formulated by Shaftesbury, that the prosodic form does not by itself alone make up the genre, but rather
that an "inner form" must correspond to the outer form, from out
of which the particular "measure," the unique "proportion" of an
independent genre first allows itself to be clarified.[19] This "inner
form" is once again not to be grasped by a single criterion. That
which constitutes a literary genre in its unique structure or "family
similarity" manifests itself at first in an ensemble of formal as well
as thematic characteristics; these must first be investigated in their
function in a ruled coherence, before their *dominant*, which shapes
a system, can be recognized, and thereby the delimitation from
other genres can be decided.

One means toward the establishment of constitutive genre distinctions is the test of commutation. Thus for example the different
structures of the fairy tale [*Märchen*] and the novella cannot be
grasped only through the oppositions of unreality and everydayness;
naive morality and moral casuistry; the self-evident wonder of fairy
tales and the "unheard-of event," but rather may also be understood
through the different significance of the same figures: "One puts a
princess in a fairy tale next to a princess in a novella, and one notices
the difference."[20] As a further example one could introduce the nonexchangeability of characters between the chanson de geste and the
courtly novel. Despite the gradual assimilation of the heroic epic to
the knightly romance in the French tradition, heroes like Roland
or Yvain, ladies like Alda or Enide, and lords like Charlemagne or
Artus were not brought from out of the one genre into the other; a
reception through another tradition, the Italian one, was first called
for, so that through a fusion of the two French genres into a new
one, the so-called romance epic, the originally distinct groups of
characters could be transposed into a single structure of action. The
original separation is repeatedly perceptible in Chrétien de Troyes,
once one recognizes signals of nonexchangeability behind the rhetori-

cal schema of the overcoming.[21] Another striking indication of structural distinctions is the contradictory application of procedure in cases where the author then corrects himself. Thus for example the author of the *Fierabras* uses two motifs of fairy tale-like wonder that are constitutive for the Artus-romance (a magic belt and a miraculous balsam); they would damage a rule of his genre, the chanson de geste—namely, the boundary of probability in an exemplary action, which is still to be maintained even in heroic hyperbole—and thus they are each immediately allowed to fall away, that is, simply to disappear from the action as inconsequential motifs.[22]

The synchronic determination of literary genres can today no longer avoid the question of their "universals." In the multiplicity of the artistic and utilitarian genres of a literature, is there not a limited number of recurrent functions, and thereby, something like a system of literary communication, withing which genres are desscribable as partial systems or as variations of a fundamental model? As regards this question, typological poetics, with its recourse to anthropological categories (such as temporal or spatial experience), has brought us less far than the tradition of Aristotelian poetics. The latter's norms and interrelations of rules obviously preserve so much of empirical observation that they retain heuristic value when one then moves along an inductive path from a period's fundamental model for particular genres to achieving the hypothesis of a literary system of communication. As a first step toward this goal, the following seeks to adduce a partial system of generic functions from the examples of the medieval epic (chanson de geste), romance (*roman arthurien*), and novella (the *Decameron*).

The fundamental model that the medieval genres of epic (= E), romance (= R) and novella (= N) have in common may be described in four modalities, which may in turn be differentiated through more narrow determinations, and which are filled by the three genres in different manners:[23]

1. *Author and Text* (Narration)

1.1 Rhapsode vs. Narrator vs. Absent Narrator

> E: Speaking poet (*jongleur*) and aural audience; the author retreats behind material, so that the occurrences seem to narrate themselves.
> R: Writing poet and unseen audience; the author steps forward as mediating narrator behind material.
> N: Writing poet and unseen audience; the mediating narrator for the most part conceals himself in that which is narrated.

1.2 Epic Objectivity vs. Fable to be Interpreted vs. Event to be Discussed

    E: Epic formulas, such as the assertion of truth, participation in the hero's fate, and epic forestalling, construct an emotional unity between jongleur and audience.

    R: Narrator's interpolations (*signes du narrateur*) serve the interpretation of the fable (*matière et sens* separate from one another).

    N: Narrator's commentaries often leave the meaning of the event uninterpreted; this remains left to the audience's discussion.

1.3 Epic Distance vs. Actuality; "How-suspense" vs. "If-at-all-suspense"

    E: From the epic distance the occurrence appears as a wholly past one; the epic forestalling makes possible the pathos of the "how-suspense."

    R: To be sure, it is narrated from epic distance in the "passé du savoir"; and yet an "if-suspense" draws into the fable, counterbalanced through the secure expectation of the happy ending.

    N: Also narrates the spatial and temporal distance, as if it were present; "if-at-all-suspense," without an expectable happy ending.

2. *Modus dicendi* (Forms of Representation)

2.1 Nonwritten (oral literature) vs. Written (book)

    E: Oral (improvising?) delivery for a nonliterate audience.

    R: A text composed in writing and intended for reading (or reading aloud) that also arises from a written tradition (*romanz*: rewritten in the vernacular).

    N: Whereas the *romanz* arises from a written (originally Latin) tradition, the novella—fixed in writing—comes from an oral tradition and enters back into it.

2.2 Verse vs. Prose

    E: Assonantal *lais*, the "formulaic style" of which also allows for improvisation.

    R: "Couplet" narrative form (paired octosyllabic lines).

    N: Colloquial prose, raised to an art form by Boccaccio.

2.3 Level of Style: sermo sublimis vs. medius vs. humilis

    E: Elevated style, in the paratactic syntax provided by the Bible.

R: Middle style; comfortably narrative; restrictive vis-à-vis everyday reality because of the filter of courtly speech.

N: Conversational tone, with a new license to say even things from the lower reality, in a suitable manner (Boccaccio: *con onesti vocaboli*).

2.4 Closure vs. Sequel; Length vs. Brevity

E: Epic breadth, neither first beginning nor definitive end (the formation of genealogical cycles).

R: Extract, singular series of adventures, and advance (the round-table) give the story of the novelistic heroes a closure that no longer refers to any before or after.

N: The brevity corresponds to temporal tension (running from an arbitrary beginning to a dissolving end, without a middle); the end of the novella as a "solution for this time" implies further novellas.

3. *Construction and Levels of Significance* (Unities of the Represented)

3.1 Action (*argumentum*): Epic Occurrence [*Begebenheit*] vs. Romance Happening [*Geschehen*] vs. Unprecedented Event [*Ereignis*]

E: The epic action, from an often minimal cause growing into a catastrophe, has its unity in an objective occurrence that encompasses the world-order; its hero is a representative of the fate of his community.

R: The romance happening—the adventure as a structure for the fulfillment of meaning arising by accident—has its unity in the singular character of the exemplary hero.

N: The events of the novella are neither part of a higher order nor a singular path of life, but rather an "unprecedented occurrence coming to pass" (Goethe) that raises a moral question.

3.2 Characters, Social Status: High vs. Middle vs. Low

E: Exclusively aristocratic (high-feudal); the peak of the heroic hierarchy includes the often-mythified king ("half-god"), followed by the circle of the best (twelve peers), surrounded by normal knights, for the most part nameless; the heathen opposition reflects the same hierarchy.

R: Exclusively aristocratic, the excluded lower order appearing in the contrasting figure of the ugly *vilain*; opposition between the inactive ideal king (Artus) and the knight who alone takes the field and whose adventure stands in relation to the winning of his lady.

N: The characters of the novella, encompassing all bourgeois roles and not excluding representatives of other classes, distance themselves from the heroic canon of the beautiful and noble.

3.3 Represented Reality: Symbolic vs. Exemplary vs. Descriptive

E: Only a few symbols for the outer world (*pin, olivier*) frame the portrayal of heroic acts; the latter are differentiated through symbolic gestures and elevated through typological references.

R: The exemplary, stylized courtly world forms the framework within which the excluded unideal reality is transformed into elements of a magical opposing sphere, and elevated through the fairy tale-like fortune of the "other world."

N: The novella is able to represent the outer world as an environment of a variety of things through its conversational tone as well as through a new circumstantial manner of description.

4. *Modus recipiendi and Social Function*

4.1 Degrees of Reality: *res gesta (historia)* vs. *res ficta* vs. *argumentum qui fieri potuit*

E: Claim to historical truth and the preservation of past acts for enduring memory; the substratum of the chanson de geste— the legend—clings to one place or to names made known through history.

R: To be sure, the romance follows the fictional principle of the fairy tale, that in the adventure no occurrence may be like reality; and yet the courtly narrator presents the claim of discovering a *sensus moralis* in the *res ficta*.

N: The novella does not inquire into the meaning of history and excludes the miraculous character of the fairy tale, because it always stands in the middle of time and space and therefore needs the probability of a societal event.

4.2 Mode of Reception: Admiration and Emotion vs. Entertainment and Instruction vs. Astonishment and Reflection

E: Heroic ideality, which excludes ineluctable tragedy as well as liberating comedy and implies an ethics of action worthy of imitation in the polarity of admiration and emotion (the hero's characteristics of the martyr).

R: The fairy tale-like ideality of the adventure not only allows the enjoyment of a literary fiction (already available for ironization), but also communicates the doctrine of courtly education [*Bildung*] through its ethics of the event.

N: The moral casuistry brought to light by the astonishing event in particular, and by the *plurale tantum* of novellas in collections in general, shows in tragedy as well as in comedy the problems inherent in the ethical norms of everyday life and demands the reflection of the educated reader.

4.3 Social Function: Interpretation of History (*mémoire collective*) vs. Initiation vs. Conversation (the formation of judgment)

E: Primary form of historical transmission for the nonreader, in which the national history of an ideal past (*le passé tel qu'il eût dû être*) is transposed and elevated into an epic-mythic system of world-explanation.

R: The later function as an entertainment for the private reader is preceded by the original function as the initiation into courtly life and courtly love: "the legitimate quest for a terrestrial happiness regulated by a social discipline and a lifestyle."

N: Conversation as a form of "passionate observation of secular life" and reflection of social norms. [24]

Such kinds of structural analyses, still lacking for many literary genres, could gradually lead to a synchronic cross-section in which the organization of the traditional and the noncanonized genres appears not as a logical classification, but rather as the literary system of a definite historical situation. But since "every synchronic system contains its past and its future as inseparable structural elements of this system," [25] a historical systematics of literary genres demands further cross-sections of literary production in the before and after of diachrony.

IV

If we inquire into the determinability of literary genres in a diachronic perspective, then we should begin with the relationship of the individual text to the series of texts that is formative of a genre. The limiting case when a text is the only known example of a genre only proves that it is more difficult—but in no way excluded in principle—to determine a generic structure without recourse to the history of the genre. What, for example, is generic in the genre of the *chante-fable*, handed down only through *Aucassin et Nicolette*, manifests itself with sufficient clarity from the structural difference vis-à-vis related genres such as the Latin *prosimetrum* or Dante's *Vita Nuova*, from which it distinguishes itself through the narrative running through the verse parts as well as the prose parts, to say nothing of its different level of style and form of delivery (miming?). On the other hand, its generic character also manifests itself in its relationship to the lyric and epic generic models that it cites, combines, and not infrequently parodies. The technique of allusion and montage unique to *Aucassin et Nicolette* may have rendered more difficult the reproducibility of the chante-fable, since it demands a greater knowledge of the contemporary forms from the author as well as from the public; but in principle the possibility that further exemplars of this genre existed is not to be disputed. On the other hand, the relationship between constant and variable structural elements that comes to light in historical change can be established only from a diachronic perspective.

The variability within historical appearance presented difficulties for the theory of genres as long as one depended on a substantialist notion of genre, or sought to grasp the histories of genres within the evolutionary schema of growth, flowering, and decay. How can a genre's historical change be described if the generically general [*Allgemeine*] is to understood neither as a timeless norm nor as an arbitrary convention? How can the structure of a genre transform itself without losing its uniqueness? How is the temporal process of a genre to be thought, if not as a development toward a masterwork and a decline in the phase of the epigones? If in place of the naturalistic concept of genre (the genre as an idea that appears in each particular being and, as genre, only repeats itself) one poses the historical concept of a continuity, "in which every earlier element extends and completes itself through the later one" (according to Aristotle, the ἐπίϑοος εἰς αὐτό that distinguishes mankind from the animal),[26] then the relationship between the individual text and the series of texts formative of a genre presents itself as a process of the continual founding and altering of horizons.[27] The new text evokes for the reader (listener) the horizon of expectations and "rules of the game" familiar to him from earlier texts, which as such can then be varied, extended, corrected, but also transformed, crossed out, or simply reproduced. Variation, extension, and correction determine the latitude of a generic structure; a break with the convention on the one hand and mere reproduction on the other determines its boundaries.

If a text simply reproduces the elements of a generic structure, only plugs some other material into the preserved model of representation, and merely takes over the received topics and metaphorics, it constitutes that stereotypical kind of literature into which, precisely, successful genres such as, for example, the chanson de geste in the twelfth century or the fabliau in the thirteenth soon sink. The limit that is thereby reached is that of mere use-value or "consumption-character." The more stereotypically a text repeats the generic, the more inferior is its artistic character and its degree of historicity. For it is also valid for literary genres that "they transform themselves to the extent that they have history, and they have history to the extent that they transform themselves."[28]

The historicity of a literary genre stands out against a process of the shaping of a structure, its variation, extension, and correction, which can lead to its ossification, or can also end with its suppression through a new genre. The nonsense-poetry can serve as an example here, which in France in the thirteenth century appeared in two independent genres, the *fatrasie* and the *resverie*.[29] Viewed genetically, the fatrasie can be defined as a derivation or, better, a transformation of a narrative genre, the "lying tale" [*Lügenmärchen*].[30] The new genre is characterized by the omission of the enveloping context that signals the artful lie; by the rupture (*brisure*) of every nexus of narration or meaning in the fatrastic plot; and by the strict, bipartite, asymmetrical construction of the poem, and the paradox arising therefrom of a structure of "the total cancelling of all real logic, outside of any rational context but within an absurd metrical-narrative 'unity.'"[31] The invention of the fatrasie as a fixed form of poetry is probably to be attributed to Philippe de Remi. If this hypothesis of W. Kellermann's is correct, then the *Fatrasies d'Arras* stemming from the same period already indicate the first variation and material extension: the atemporal motifs of Philippe are mixed in with satiric secondary intentions (degrading the sacred and the heroic) and with the comedy of the scabrous. This tendency is pushed so far in a further variation created by Raimmondin and Watriquet de Couvin that a new, parodistic genre—the *fatras*—splits off from the fatrasie as the pure form of nonsense-poetry. Here a proverblike refrain of mostly amorous content is placed before the fatrastic eleven-syllable line, and it provides the framework of the poem, which then parodies its possible utterance in the form of an impossible discourse. With this, the *fatras impossible* that develops away from the fatrasie becomes a "parodistic hybrid-creation of a gloss," to which Baudet Herenc later opposed the *fatras possible*, a serious counterpart with mostly spiritual thematics;[32] in the above-sketched process, the latter is surely to be considered as a correction of the nonsense-poetry.

Belonging to this nonsense-poetry is the genre of the resverie, which appears contemporaneously with the fatrasie and comes down to us in only three examples, and which only recently was recognized and described by W. Kellermann in its independent structures.[33] The resverie shows how the same intention — the language-game of the production of nonsensical utterances — can be transformed into another genre through the invention of a new "rule to the game." For here a dialogical situation is to be presupposed, in which a seven-syllable line recited by the poet must be answered by a four-syllable line that is to satisfy two conditions: "It must form a unity of meaning with the preceding verse, and provide the poet with a new rhyme-word for a new line that is, in its content, wholly different from the preceding one."[34] In this genre as well we bump into Philippe de Remi, who rendered its form more difficult through his rhyme-acrobatics; it appears to have expired with the so-called *Dit des traverces* (1303). But it returns a century and a half later in the *Sottie des menus propos* (1461), which cut the language-game of the resveries to fit the figure of the fool and reactualized it by connecting it with the idea of the foolish world.[35] The leaping character of this process, in which the later form of the *Coq-à-l'âne* is also to be included; the continual variations rendering it more difficult or more simplistic; the differentiation through new "rules of the game"; the conversion of the structure into the form of delivery of another (here, the dramatic) genre: all these elements characterize the historical life of literary genres and at the same time refute the organic schema, since in this nonteleological continuity "the result at the end" doubtless cannot be "made into the goal of the beginning."[36]

V

The example of nonsense poetry meanwhile indicates only the immanent process of a genre in its literary aspects, and not the — here scarcely determinable — historical or lived-world situations that might have conditioned this process in the interaction between author and society, the audience's expectations and the literary event. To inquire into such entanglements is indispensable if one is to be serious about the historicization of genre poetics and the temporalization of the concept of form. The methodological postulate that the new formation or the death of literary forms — ultimately, indeed, every turn in the history of genres — must have a correspondence in the sociohistorical situation, or at least an impulse arising from it, is no longer upheld by Marxist theory nor by literary sociology with the naïveté with which it was maintained by the classical theory of reflection [*Wiederspiegelungstheorie*].[37] Even proponents of these methods acknowledge today that the genres "represent to a certain extent an a priori of literary reality."[38] They emphasize the interdependence between the infrastructure of society and the superstructure of literature above all where changes in the basic economic and politicosocial relations "bear the character of a historical revolution," transform themselves into the structural elements of art, and then "[break through] the traditional, stabilized forms, styles and value-concepts of literature."[39] On the other hand, they see how literary genres, after the moment of their social formation "achieve a life of their own and an autonomy which reaches beyond their historical hour of fate."[40] They speak of an "often anachronistic afterlife" and of the historical death of literary genres,[41] most recently—under the influence of Brechtian aesthetics—even of the possiblility of "refunctioning" long-past genres and artistic devices independently of their original social determination, making them serviceable for a new aesthetic and social function.[42]

The latest work by Erich Köhler on the history of the genre of the *pastourelle* may be used as an example of this tendency in scholarship.[43] The point of departure is a decisive change in direction of the genre. In both his pastourelles, the troubador Gavaudan consciously (his shepherdess representing the sum of the experiences of all her predecessors) goes beyond the constitutive rule of the genre— the unsuppressible essential difference between "nobilitas" and "rusticitas." In this meeting of knight and shepherdess, high and lower love are mediated and reconciled, whereby Gavaudan refers to buried elements of the bucolic, to the representation of an earthly paradise before the fall of original sin. If, with Erich Köhler, one sees in the pastourelle more than a game with literary roles, then unresolved contradictions of social reality lie hidden in Gavaudan's utopian solution. Gavaudan's teacher Marcabru had called into question the matter-of-course manner in which the rising class of the lower knighthood had distanced itself from its origin in the medium of the pastourelle. Gavaudan had sought to bridge the gap between knighthood and folk through the new theme of friendship (*amistat*) between knight and shepherdess. The price was an elevation of the illusionary, so that Gavaudan's utopia of reconciliation already represents the limiting case of the pastourelle that anticipates the self-cancelling of the genre.

VI

A second example of literary-sociological scholarship will introduce the category of structural changes now to be considered, those that lead to the splitting off of a new genre. The existence of the *sirventes-songs* — a genre historically secured through forty-nine examples and its description coined by Folquet de Romans — was, because of their "mixed character," one of the oldest irritations for Provençal studies. For the *chanso-sirventes* ties the theme of love to that of politics. Meanwhile, as Erich Köhler demonstrated, with this double-thematics the genre once again presents the original unity of feminine praise and lordly service, which in the *vers* genre of the earliest troubador poetry were not yet separated thematically, but then separated into the genres of the chanso and sirventes that thereby arose. The historical system of this lyric poetry thus demonstrates first how, through a structural change (the separation of the thematics of love and moral satire), two new, "purer" genres arose; and second, how, from the need to again bring to consciousness the unity lost in the one-sided structures of the two genres, arose the antithetical structural law of an independent genre.[44]

The form of a new genre can also proceed from structural alterations that cause a group of simple genres already at hand to enter into a higher principle of organization. The classic case for this is the form of the Tuscan novella coined by Boccaccio, which would be normative for the whole later development of the modern genre of the novella. Considered genetically, an astonishing multiplicity of older narrative or didactic genres enter into Boccaccio's *Decameron*: medieval forms such as the *exemplum*, the fabliau, the legend, the miracle, the *lai*, the *vida*, the *nova*, love-casuistry, Oriental narrative literature, Apuleius and Milanese love-stories, local Florentine histories and anecdotes. As H.-J. Neuschäfer demonstrated,[45] Boccaccio transposed the given thematic and formal multiplicity into the unmistakable structure of a new genre through a determinable transformation, the rules of which may be defined formally as placing the plot-schemata in a temporal dimension, thematically as the calling into question of moral norms. The step from the older narrative and didactic forms to the new genre-structure of the novella that integrated them can be described through oppositions such as: the unipolar or bipolar nature of the characters; the plot as typical or as a singular case; the finality or ambivalence of moral norms; transcendental dispensation or human self-affirmation. Generic determinates from the later theory of the novella such as, for example, that of the "unprecedented occurrence" or the solution of a moral case-which by themselves would not suffice to characterize the genre—achieve their specific significance in connection with the structure formed by Boccaccio. Naturally this does not mean that all elements of this generic structure must from now on be found in all later novellas. Boccaccio's successors do not simply repetitively continue an initial structure: "It is much more the case that there one can, on the one hand, establish a certain return to the exemplary and flexible narrative forms of the Middle Ages that were in no way 'overcome' by Boccaccio once and for all, but on the other hand, also discover new and independent modes of narration."[46] In its historical appearance the novella accents the various forms that its polygenesis incorporates, sometimes in simplifying variants (for example, in the flexible *conte*), sometimes in complicating cases (for example, in the multifaceted casuistry of Mme. de La Fayette).

When the theories of the novella of particular authors are too narrow or too partial to be covered by the multiformed process of this progressive unfolding and correcting of the genre's system, one may not simply conclude from the discrepancy between poetic theory and literary production that there just is no generically typical form of the novella.[47] Rather the congruence between theory and practice that is never fully achieved—more specifically, the congruence between explicit theory, immanent poetics, and literary production—itself belongs among the factors that condition the process of the historical appearance of a literary genre. Thus, a canonical theory, or one canonized for a certain time, cannot immediately be contrasted as a generic norm with the series of works realized in practice. Rather, between the theory that posits the norm and the literary series, there mediates the immanent poetics that determines the structure of the individual work and is to be read out of it. And in cases where a theoretical norm lays claim to universally binding validity—as, for example, the Aristotelian poetics for post-medieval literature—the conflict between the authoritative generic norm and the immanent poetics can become precisely the motive force that keeps the historical process of the genre moving.

Since the vernacular genres of medieval literature did not develop from a pregiven canon and in conflict with it, their system can be read only out of the immanent poetics and verified in the constancy or variability of particular structural elements with the continuity formative of a genre. This method necessarily presupposes the hermeneutic circle, but not the organic circle of fulfillment. Where there is no initially posited and described generic norm, the establishing of a generic structure must be gained from the perception [*Anschauung*] of individual texts, in a continually renewed pre-conceiving [*Vorgriff*] of an expectable whole or regulative system for the series of texts. This preconceiving does not necessitate any telos of fulfillment. It presupposes an aesthetic principle that lends meaning to the "rules of the game," not their fulfilled state of being. The processlike appearance of a genre in time has, as Karl Viëtor has emphasized, "no goal at all; it will not come to rest in a fulfillment, but rather will be present in a continually renewed realization. There is only a historical end to the history of a genre, just as it has a beginning in time."[48] Since that which is generic in a tradition may not in itself establish the aesthetic value of its texts, the notion that the fulfillment of a text remains the same as the purity with which it fulfills the model or type of a genre is a specifically classicist expectation. In medieval literature, on the other hand, masterworks such as, for example, the *Chanson de Roland*, Chrétien's romances, the first Renart parts, Guillaume de Lorris's love-allegory, or the *Divina Commedia* demonstrate precisely that they far surpass the conventions of their genre. Here the preceding texts of the genre did not develop with foreseeable necessity toward its most perfect expression, nor did the masterworks provide a model of the genre, the reproduction of which alone already guaranteed success for the works that came later.

If one follows the fundamental rule of the historicization of the concept of form, and sees the history of literary genres as a temporal process of the continual founding and altering of horizons, then the metaphorics of the courses of development, function, and decay can be replaced by the nonteleological concept of the playing out of a limited number of possibilities.[49] In this concept a masterwork is definable in terms of an alteration of the horizon of the genre that is as unexpected as it is enriching; the genre's prehistory is definable in terms of a trying and testing of possibilities; and its arrival at a historical end is definable in terms of formal ossification, automatization, or a giving-up or misunderstanding of the "rules of the game," as is often found in the last epigones.[50] But the history of genres in this perspective also presupposes reflection on that which can become visible only to the retrospective observer: the beginning character of the beginnings and the definite character of an end; the norm-founding or norm-breaking role of particular examples; and finally, the historical as well as the aesthetic significance of masterworks, which itself may change with the history of their effects and later interpretations, and thereby may also differently illuminate the coherence of the history of their genre that is to be narrated. For in the dimension of their reception, literary genres as well stand under the dialectic of after-history and prehistory, insofar as, according to Walter Benjamin, because of their after-history "their prehistory also becomes recognizable as conceived in continual change."[51]

VII

The theory of literary genres cannot remain within the structures of self-enclosed histories of genres, but rather must also consider the possibility of a historical systematics. If for centuries no attempt has been undertaken to bring the totality of literary genres of a period into a system of contemporary phenomena, the reason may be that the normative doctrine of genres has been profoundly discredited and, along with it, any systematics decried as speculative. In the meantime, the modern theory of genres can proceed only descriptively, and not by definition; this insight in no way excludes the possibility that, along the path of synchronic description and historical investigation, one may arrive, though not at a generically determined system of communication, nonetheless at a historical sequence of such systems. Even the literature of the Middle ages is no arbitrary sum of its parts, but rather a latent ordering or sequence of orderings of literary genres. After all, several references by medieval authors and the (in this respect, still unevaluated) selection and arrangement of texts and genres in collected manuscripts point to this ordering. The Latin poetics, with its rhetorical categories and classifications of style, might well also be brought to bear heuristically on an establishing and delimitation of generic characteristics, even though for the most part it contains only traditional didactic material and was not normative for the vernacular literature.

From the transmission of ancient rhetoric and theory of poetry, there were in the Middle Ages basically four schemata of division at one's disposal that could, in varying degree, serve the explanation of genres: modes of discourse (*genus demonstrativum, deliberativum, iudicialis*), levels of style (*genera dicendi: humile, medium, sublime*), forms of delivery (*genus dramaticum, narrativum, mixtum*), and finally objects (*tres status hominum: pastor otiosus, agricola, miles dominans*).[52] The doctrine of the three modes of discourse, each with two submodes, is admittedly not developed into a system for the division of corresponding literary genres in the rhetorical handbooks; it remains to be investigated whether they provided anything for the oratorical literature that first appeared in Italy. In the ancient tradition the three genera dicendi were distinguished above all according to formal elements of the level of style (vocabulary, meter, imagery, ornamentation). Here the medieval reception took a step beyond the ancient theory. Twelfth- and thirteenth-century authors introduced the concept of "style" ("*sunt igitur tres styli: humilis, mediocris, grandiloqus*"), which they no longer defined solely according to the means of representation, but also according to its object (i.e., the social class of the represented characters and the elements of their environment).[53] The model for this system was the interpretation of Virgil's works going back to Servius and Donat, which had him in the *Bucolica, Georgica,* and *Aeneid* representing three stages of human society (shepherd, farmer, warrior) in the appropriate, that is, similarly leveled, style. Of the Virgilian genres, admittedly only the bucolic is cultivated in the Middle Ages, and not the georgic: and the *Aeneid* is also nowhere identified with the chanson de geste.[54] And yet the principle of classification according to the social class of the characters carried out by Johannes de Garlandia has its correspondence at least in the strictly class-ordered "rules of the game" of the Old French epic and romance, if one ignores the missing ordering in the levels of style.

The theory of the three forms of delivery according to the system of the grammarian Diomedes (*narrativum* when the poet himself speaks, *dramaticum* when the characters alone speak, *mixtum* when poet and characters alternately have the voice) achieved particular influence in the Middle Ages through Bede and Isidore. Diomedes' tripartite division, proceeding from the most superficial formal characteristics, did more to cause confusion concerning the function of ancient genres (for example, concerning that of the ancient theater, so that the structure of plays to be performed had to be sought and developed anew) than it did to establish productive new distinctions.[55] Johannes de Garlandia brought order into this transmission. His *Poetria,* a synthesis of the *Artes dictaminis* and the *Artes poeticae,* fit Diomedes' tripartite division into a new *summa* of literary genres, which is systematically arranged according to four perspectives: 1. according to the verbal form (*prosa* and *metrum*), the first arranged into four genres; the technographic or scholarly, the historical, the epistolary, the rhythmic and musical); 2. according to the form of delivery (*quicumque loquitor*: Diomedes' tripartite division); 3. according to the degree of reality of the narrative (three *species narrationis*: res gesta or *historia*, res ficta or *fabula*, res ficta quae tamen fieri potuit or *argumentum*); 4. according to the feeling expressed in the poetry (*de differentia carminum*, a fourfold arrangement that develops a differentiation of the *genera tragica, comica, satyrica,* and *mimica* that is mentioned by Diomedes and in the *Tractatus coi-*

silianus).[56] The system of genres of Johannes de Garlandia's *Poetria* did not arise purely deductively, but rather, in its richness in definitions related to content, perhaps sought to order the state of literary genres arrived at in the reality of the thirteenth century: this is a hypothesis for which at least two arguments seem to speak. A. Adler has pointed out that the *historicum* in Johannes's definition (that is, the satiric genre in the fourth rubric) quite precisely expresses the perimeters and the function of the thirteenth-century literary forms that one may distinguish as the beginnings of political satire. And the distinction, thematic as well as stylistic, between tragedy (*carmen quod incipit a gaudio et terminat in lucto*) and comedy (*carmen iocusum incipiens a tristitia et terminans in gaudium*) returns in the genre-theory of Dante's letter to Can Grande and corresponds to the structure as well as to the (later) title of the *Divina Commedia*.[57]

References by vernacular authors that bring to light synchronic relations or partial systems of literary genres have as yet not really been collected.[58] One of the most impressive examples is offered by the prologue to the oldest part of the *Roman de Renart*:

> Seigneurs, oî avez mainte conte
> Que mainte conterre vous raconte,
> Conment Paris ravi Elaine,
> Le mal qu'il en ot et la paine:
> De Tristan dont la Chievre fist,
> Qui assez bellement en dist
> Et fabliaus et chancon de geste
> Maint autre conte par la terre.
> Mais onques n'oîstes la guerre,
> Qui tant fu dure de grant fin,
> Entre Renart et Ysengrin.
> [Pt. II 1-11]

The jongleur, who boasts of his object as a totally new thing, distinguishes it from a series of well-known individual works and genres: *troja* (ancient romance), *tristan* (Breton romance), fabliau, chanson de geste, and then an unidentified animal-poem (perhaps a vernacular version of *Ysengrimus*?). This list of the works that were popular around 1176/77 allows one to grasp a literary system insofar as the genres that are specified are not just accidentally selected, but rather form the specific horizon of expectations before which the new and often parodistic conte about the beginning of the enmity between the fox and the wolf—running counter to the heroic poetry of the courtly conception of love—must take place.[59]

Toward the end of the twelfth century, Jean Bodel begins his *Saisnes* with the statement that there are only three great epic genres for connoisseurs, which he names according to content (*materes*) and then ranks according to degree of reality, so that the genre of his own work obviously appears at the top:[60]

> Li conte de Bretaigne sont si vain et plaisant.
> Cil de Rome sont sage et de sens aprendant.
> Cil de France sont voir chascun jour aparant.
> [vv. 9-11]

In this scale, chanson de geste and Breton romance correspond to the opposition res gesta and res ficta (here with the addition: "wonderful and pleasing") that we encountered in Johannes de Garlandia's species narrationis; the ancient romance "rich in teachings" can stand for the (probable) argumentum.

For the lyric one can refer here to Dante's *De vulgari eloquentia*, the second part of which is a poetics relating to vernacular poetry, and which refers to the *modus* of the *canzone*, the ballata, the sonnet, and other *illegitimos et erregulares modos* as genres of the lyric (II, 3). And as themes that are worthy of the high style, he introduces the public good (*Salus*), love (*Venus*), and ethics (*Virtus*). Yet this ordering springs not primarily from a division of genres, but rather once again from a poetics of the kinds of style. For such themes "are not viewed as the causes of the high style, but as means for its realization."[61] Nevertheless, this does not speak against the existence of generic structures. The new lyric genres created by the Provencal poets in the Romance vernacular certainly did not develop in isolation, but rather did so in reciprocal dependence and division of function. Such divisions and reshufflings within a lyric system may be grasped only when the history of all the established genres is written and investigated in connection with the later poetics: Raimon Vidal's *Razos de trobar*, the contemporaneous *Leys d'amor* appearing at the beginning of the thirteenth century in Toulouse, the *Dreita manera de trobar* of the *Consistorio del gay saver* founded in 1387 in Barcelona, Eustache Deschamps' treatise *L'art de dictier et de fere chançons*, which goes back to the canon of Toulouse, and Enrique de Villena's Spanish *Art de trovar*. From among these I might introduce the oldest stock-taking of Provençal poetry, which Guilhelm Molinier incorporated into his *Leys d'amors* between 1328 and 1355. He distinguishes between ten major genres and seventeen subjacent ones. The former include the canso, sirventes, *dansa, descort, tenso, partimen, pastorela, retroncha, planh,* and *escondig.* Among the latter some served as accompaniment for dances; for others, no examples are yet known, so that their identification is problematical.[62] This system of the major lyric genres was dissolved around the turn of the thirteenth to the fourteenth century through the new system of the so-called "genres à formes fixes." As D. Poirion has demonstrated,[63] this shake-up is connected with a change in the relationship between music and text: whereas in the thirteenth century the musical rhythm alone still determined lyric poetry, the poetic text and polyphonic melody now separate into heterogeneous developments. At first, lyric poetry threatened to disappear altogether: "Neither the *motets* layered upon the inaudible texts nor the *dits* which rhymed the long discourses retain the essential originality of lyric poetry." But then from the beginning of the fourteenth century onward, a new system of lyric genres developed: *rondeau* and *virelai, chant royal* and ballad, lai and *complainte,* which through Guillaume de Machaut's *Remède de Fortune* became typical for the courtly poets; and from the narrative *dit* a freer development toward that modern type of subjective poetry began, which is represented above all by Villon's work.

VIII

The question of the reality of literary genres in the historical everyday world, or that of their social function, has been ignored in medieval scholarship, and not because of a lack of documents. Resisting any insight into this question, there has long been the humanist overemphasis on the written and printed tradition, a Platonic aesthetics according to which past literature can really be "present" for us in a book at any moment,[64] and the naively objectivist equation of philological interpretation with the experience of the original reader or hearer. The necessary reorientation of scholarship was first introduced by Jean Rychner for the chanson de geste.[65] His programmatic slogan referring to the "oral style," the epic technique, and the oral dissemination of the Old French epic—"The *chanson de geste,* diffused under these conditions, ought to have been composed for these conditions."[66]—should also be emphasized for most of the other genres of vernacular literature, for which the problem of their conditions of influence [*Wirkungsbedingungen*] and social function still remains an open one. For this scholarly task, Romance philology can garner advice from a discipline that for more than fifty years has been developing methods for this, and testing them on a material that is furthermore exemplary for the literature of the Middle Ages: namely, theological research into literary criticism of the Bible.

During the same time that Romance philology stood under the spell of "work-immanent" methods, and Croce's suspicion of literary genres was rarely contradicted, a scholarly tendency blossomed within theology that made a philological principle into one of its own: namely, that "the literature in which the life of a community — thus, also the original Christian congregation — plays itself out arises out of very definite expressions and needs of the life of this community, which in turn present a certain style, certain forms and certain genres."[67] Literary forms and genres are thus neither subjective creations of the author, nor merely retrospective ordering-concepts, but rather primarily social phenomena, which means that they depend on functions in the lived world. The Bible is also a *literary* monument that bears witness to the life of a community; it can no longer remain withdrawn from historical understanding as "genus illud singulare, transcendens, nullam cum aliis comparationem ferens, quod est ipsa Scriptura sacra."[68] Accordingly, the understanding of the Bible is no longer thinkable without a literary-critical scholarship that takes account of the environment and its languages, the personality of the author, and the literary genres known to the original addressees of the books.[69] This literary-historical scholarship has been brought underway by the so-called "form-historical school" of Protestant theology (H. Gunkel, M. Dibelius, R. Bultman), and has since found its way into Catholic doctrine. The principle "that research into the author and the literary genre of a determinate work has as its goal the exact understanding of the message which the work contains"[70] also lies at the basis of the Catholic handbooks on Biblical scholarship,[71] which can draw support from the fact that Pope Pius XII, in the encyclical *Divino afflante spiritu* of 30 September 1943, recognized the modern theory of literary genres as an aid in Biblical exegesis.

It is instructive for the problems of genre arising in the face of texts from the Romance Middle Ages that theological scholarship has a concept of genre that is structural as well as sociological: at first such scholarship inquires into the generically conditioned form, and the function in the lived world, of a given literary product in order then to consider it in its historical dimension. The literary genre becomes defined as a "structural ensemble into which everything comes to insert itself in order to arrive at a particular meaning"; "each of these literary genres communicates a certain truth to the reader, but in different orders."[72] The recognition of such structures must meanwhile be preceded by "the question of the presupposed situation, of the speaker, his intention, his listeners, and of the whole disposition; in short, the question of the 'locus in life' " [Gunkel].[73] With the phrase "locus in life" one understands a typical situation or mode of behavior in the life of a community, such as, for example, the festival of a sacrifice at sacred sites for the literary form of the hymn, but also such noncultic situations as work, hunting, and war; it is from these situations that the presupposed motifs that were constitutive for the form and intention of a genre first become comprehensible. For "only the history of a genre proves whether the form of a literary work is not an accidental product, but rather a form capable of development which has its own life."[74] The form-historical method that developed from this concept first determines "the origin and affiliation of a specific literary genre in and to typical situations and behaviors of a community," and then follows the rise, alteration, and transition of the form so constituted in its history as a literary genre. As an example of this one may here cite Rudolf Bultmann's representation of the *apophthegmata*.[75]

IX

But the "literary history of the Bible" is also of great importance for medieval Romance philology from a thematic point of view. In recent decades one looked above all at the prototype of classical antiquity—its rhetoric and literary *topoi*, and its model authors—when asking about the origins of Romance literature. But the new literary genres of the Romance vernaculars in no way proceeded from this tradition in a linear development or an immediate "appropriative transformation of the ancient heritage." Concerning the "afterlife of antiquity," the scholarship on tradition, believing in continuity, intentionally ignored the question of how the literature of the Christian era might actually be compatible with ancient literary theory, and whether there was something like a Christian aesthetics. In opposition to this attitude, Erich Auerbach variously demonstrated that the new demands and contents of the Christian faith had to break through the ancient literary system with its practice of a hierarchy of styles related to objects: "humble everyday things . . . lose their baseness in the Christian context and become compatible with the lofty style; and conversely . . . the highest mysteries of the faith may be set forth in the simple words of the lowly style which everyone can understand. This was such a radical departure from the rhetorical, and indeed from the entire literary, tradition that it nearly signifies the destruction of its foundation."[76] The consequences of the formation of a new, Christian discursive art—a "low rhetoric in the sense of the *sermo humilis*" established in Augustine's *De doctrina christiana*—for the forms of literature in late-Latin Christian antiquity and, later, in the Middle Ages, are still scarcely investigated. This is especially the case for the new formation of tradition in didactic literature, the genres of which bear the imprint of Christian eloquence, "edifica- tion," and instruction. But the realm of *sermo humilis* also reaches into the epic and dramatic genres, which are determined by the model of the Bible not only thematically—through Christian dogma, through typology and the moral doctrine, as well as through the authority of the exempla—but also formally in manifold ways.

If one looks at the results of the "literary history of the Bible," then one can only wonder why medieval studies have not yet under- taken any systematic attempt to investigate the possible model that literary genres found in the Bible may provide for medieval literature. The abundance of literary forms and genres ascertainable in the Old and New Testaments is astonishing, and leads directly to the dis- covery of Romance parallels. The Bible contains worldly lyrics (songs of work, ridicule, drinking, burial, and war) as well as spiritual ones (the hymn or the lament). It developed the most varied forms of narrative prose: etiological, historical, and also heroic sagas (the leg- endary garland for Samson); legends of martyrs and novellas (the King's novellas, but also the Book of Ruth). It contains the model for various forms of historiography (tribal legend, genealogy, royal chronicle), historical prose (documents, letters, contracts, war re- ports), and biography (the self-disclosures of the prophets). All imagi- nable forms of wisdom literature (proverb, riddle, parable, fable, de- bate, allegory) and religious instruction (sermon, exhortation, epistle) are also found in it.

Finally, the method of the form-historical school also places the still-current distinction between the genres of "spiritual" and "world- ly" literature in a problematic light. With this distinction, a literary understanding that arises only with the emancipation of the fine arts from their ties to cultic and social functions is transferred to a period that did not yet feel any separation between religious life and literary culture, the contents of faith and the forms of art. In the Middle Ages, all literature is still functionally determined through its "locus in life." What is generic in it arises from such immediately realized, self-evident, and therefore (for the most part) unreflected functions; and thus, not from a reflected relationship with form as an aesthetic means, which can only appear with the developed generic conscious-ness of a literature that has become autonomous.[77] Two methodo-logical consequences are to be drawn from this, according to M. Waltz: the object of research is here "not the genre as it existed in the consciousness of contemporaries, but the function of the works"; but then a further object of study is the process, already beginning in the Middle Ages with the courtly lyric, in which a reflected generic consciousness appears with the problematization of the function, and leads in the Renaissance to the liberation of the autonomy of liter-ature.[78] The distinction between "spiritual" and "worldly," func-tional constraint and "literariness," has meaning in the Middle Ages only when it is understood as the *process* of a gradual literarization of genres that originally are tied to cultic, religious, and social functions.

For the application of the form-historical method to medieval literature, one can rightly claim that it is not satisfactory to explain the form of a genre directly from its "locus in life"—on the one hand, because the genre can just as well form the "locus of life" as the lat-ter can the former, and on the other hand, because the function of a genre depends not only on its relation to a real, lived procedure, but also on its position within a comprehensive symbolic system fa-miliar to contemporaries.[79] For the literary genre the question of the "locus in life" has a synchronic as well as a diachronic dimension: it implies its function within the comprehensive ordering of the sym-bolic forms of expression of a culture and, at the same time, its po-sition in the historical change of this symbolic system. For our per-iod, this latter aspect means the process of the beginning literariza-tion and individualization of generic conventions.

This process should not be misunderstood as an organic develop-ment, nor as secularization. Instead, the later, "profane" history of a genre originally tied to religious or cultic functions does not need to develop immanently and linearly *out* of its original structural charac-teristics, but rather can be brought underway through heterogeneous impulses. Thus, the process of literarization or subjectification can fulfill itself precisely *counter to* the original purposeful orientation of the genre, that is, counter to its spirituality or edifying convention. For example, although Guillaume de Lorris's *Roman de la rose* in many respects appears only to further develop—under "profane" symptoms—the spiritual traditions of the *bellum intestinum* (*Psy-chomachia*) and allegorical poetry in the mode of the *Roman de miserere* (of Reclus de Molliens, with numerous motivic analogies),[80] the structurally related first great worldly allegory nonetheless arises from an opposing process. Toward the end of the twelfth century the

separation of allegorical poetry from Biblical exegesis stood under
the aegis of the contradiction that connected the spiritual author
with the new allegorical form (*duplex sententia*) of the dit (from *ver-
itatem dicere*) but against the brand-new contes and fables of worldly-
courtly poetry. But now Guillaume de Lorris took up this challenge
in that he lay claim to the same allegorical truth for the poetry of
courtly love that the spiritual tradition of textual exegesis had re-
served for itself: "Faced with the absolute Book, at once model and
rival, poetry in search of its autonomy forces itself to bring forth a
word of authority (Love, for example) which it opposes to that of
the Bible."[81] The allegorization of poetry appearing in the thirteenth
century is neither an immanent generic development nor a mere secularization of religious content, but rather the ostentatious appropriation and conscious literarization of a method proper to the spiritual
tradition through poets like Guillaume de Lorris who sought an autonomous worldly literature.

The history of the development of the passion play offers a further
example. Its development, which can be traced *ab ovo* from the famous interpolation of the Easter mass (*Quem quaeritis in sepulchro
. . .*) in the tenth century up to the monstrous vernacular passion
mysteries of the fifteenth century, is commonly seen as the prototype of a homogeneous process of progressive secularization, in which
the originally liturgical event is increasingly secularized through
scenes of increasingly worldly content until it finally degrades into a
mere dramatic play. In opposition to this interpretation, Rainer
Warning has brought to light heterogeneous impulses in the history
of the genre that cannot be brought under the rubric of a process of
secularization.[82] It is not incidental that the passion play shifts the
sacred plot *extra muros*: as a "mass in the marketplace" it produces
ritual forms that distance themselves from church doctrine and finally even contradict it. Mimetic image-making already had brought
church criticism upon the liturgical play; with the beginning of the
vernacular tradition, the devil was introduced as a dramatic-dualistic
counterpart, which approaches a remythification of the dogma of
the incarnation when viewed against the background of Anselm of
Canterbury's doctrine of satisfaction. In consequence of this dualistic
structure, there finally arises the drastic arrangement of the martyr-
dom of the crucifixion, which brings the ostensible representation of
the incarnation into the theologically ambiguous light of an archaic-
magical scapegoat-ritual: "To the extent that play and reality fuse
together, God himself is ridiculed, spat upon, whipped and nailed to
the cross in the stage figure of Jesus."[83] In light of this interpreta-

tion, the history of the genre shows an opposing process behind the supposed secularization, which sprang from the latent protest of the dualistic-pagan folk piety against the monotheistic dogmatics, and explains the heretic tendency of the plays; this tendency may have led to the prohibition of further performances by the Parisian parliament's edict of 1548.

X

The last step in a theory of literary genres can proceed from the fact that a literary genre exists for itself alone as little as does an individual work of art. This fact is less self-evident than it may at first appear, if one retains an image of how genres commonly appear in literary histories; they are seen as a sequence of generic developments, closed within themselves, that for the most part are held together only through the outer framework of some general characteristics of the period. But the basic principle of a historicization of the concept of form demands not only that one relinquish the substantialist notion of a constant number of unchangeable essential characteristics for the individual genres. It also demands that one dismantle the correlative notion of a sequence of literary genres closed within themselves, encapsulated from one another, and inquire into the reciprocal relations that make up the literary system of a given historical moment. For the task of discovering diachronic and synchronic interrelations between the literary genres of a period, the Russian Formalists found methodological approaches that well deserve to be applied to the field of medieval literature.[84]

The Formalist conception of genre as a historical system of relations participates in the attempt to replace the classical notion of literary tradition—as a steady, unilinear, cumulative course—with the dynamic principle of literary *evolution*, by which they do not mean an analogy to organic growth or to Darwinian selection. For here "evolution" is supposed to characterize the phenomenon of literary "succession" "not in the sense of a continuous 'development,' but rather in the sense of a 'struggle' and 'break' with immediate predecessors through a contemporary recourse to something older."[85] In the historical evolution of literature thus understood, literary genres can be grasped in the periodic alternation of the dominating role as well as in a sequence of rivalries. At the basis of this idea lies the notion of a self-changing "hierarchy of genres": "For the Formalists the 'period' is also a system with a system-specific 'attitude' and its corresponding 'dominants.' On the basis of the general attitude or intention the genres—which to an especially large extent are able to give expression to this attitude—arrive at the top of the hierarchy of genres and become the 'dominating' genres of the period. These can be entirely new genres, but also richly traditional genres can become restructured in respect to the new basic intention."[86]

From a diachronic perspective the historical alternation of the dominating genre manifests itself in the three steps of canonization, automatization, and reshuffling. Successful genres that embody the "high point" of the literature of a period gradually lose their effective power through continual reproduction; they are forced to the periphery by new genres often arising from a "vulgar" stratum if they cannot be reanimated through a restructuring (be it through the playing up of previously suppressed themes or methods, or through the taking up of materials or the taking-over of functions from other genres).[87] In the realm of the Romance literature of the Middle Ages, the following examples offer themselves for an explanation in terms of the theory of the "high point": the new appearance of the courtly romance, which around the middle of the twelfth century struggles for the dominating position with the older chanson de geste; then the rise of the prose romance, which around the turn of the thirteenth century makes its way with a new claim to truth;[88] and finally the triumph of allegory, which around 1234/35 (as Huon de Méry in the prologue to the *Tournoiement de l'Antéchrist* testifies, along with Guillaume de Lorris) presents itself as *novel pensé* and as yet unknown *matire*, and replaces the courtly epic and Arthurian world of the models of Chrétien de Troyes, Raoul de Houdenc, and their epigones, which are now felt as past. But as distinguished from the examples of the Formalists, for the most part chosen from modern literature, the history of genres in the twelfth and thirteenth centuries lacks a comparable stratum of subliterature. The new genres of the courtly verse-romance, the first prose romances, and the allegorical epic are not canonizations of lower genres, but rather proceed from a shift of functions (the paired or, respectively, narrative eight-syllabic line was found in rhymed chronicles; the prose in historiography; and the allegorical form in spiritual poetry).

The shift or taking over of function from other genres allows one to see the synchronic dimension in the literary system of a period. Literary genres do not exist alone, but rather form the various functions of a given period's system, to which they connect the individual work: "A work which is ripped out of the context of the given literary system and transposed into another one receives another coloring, clothes itself with other characteristics, enters into another genre, loses its genre; in other words, its function is shifted."[89] This process may also be demonstrated with the "matière de Bretagne": since its significance within the system of the Celtic-Cymric mythology and legendary world was no longer understood by the French narrators and their audience, its fables received the other "tone" of the fairy tale-like miraculous. Through this fictionalization conditioned by reception, the Arthurian romance distinguishes itself most sharply from the chanson de geste which arises from the historical saga and the martyr legends. From the perspective of their rivalry, new aspects of the history of these two genres may still be gained. Similarly, the history of courtly poetry could surely still be enriched if it were sketched within the historical relational-system of the genres that surround and, above all, also negate it: the Renart parts with their laughing satire of the whole courtly-knightly world; the verse farces (fabliaux) with their drastic and not infrequently grotesque perversions of courtly mores; the dits, sermons, and moral treatises with the existential earnestness of their doctrine of virtue and their scattered anticourtly polemics. Especially desirable would be research into the functional divisions in the didactic "small genres" and the narrative "short forms"; here one could make a sidepiece to André Jolles's *Einfache Formen*, the system of which would surely receive richly explanatory historical variants and extensions within the Romance sphere.[90]

XI

The Formalist theory imposed upon itself the limitation of considering and describing the evolution of literary genres and forms as an unilinear process. It disregards the function of literary genres in quotidian history, and dismissed the questions of their reception by and influence on the contemporary and later audiences as mere sociologism and psychologism. The historicity of literature nonetheless is not absorbed into the succession of aesthetic-formal systems and the changing of hierarchies of genres. It does not suffice to set the "literary series" only in relation with language as the nearest "extraliterary series." Since literary genres have their "locus in life" and therefore their social function, literary evolution must also, beyond its own relationship between diachrony and synchrony, be determinable through its social function within the general process of history. Since the Thirties, Jan Mukarovský and the so-called Prague Structuralism have accomplished this further development of Formalist theory in ground-breaking studies, the reception of which is still lacking in

Western European scholarship.[91] This step from formalism to a dialectical structuralism is interesting for a theory of literary genres above all because here the work of art is understood as a sign and carrier of meaning for a social reality, and the aesthetic is defined as a principle of mediation and a mode of organization for extra-aesthetic meanings. On the other hand, a theory of genres grounded in an aesthetics of reception necessarily will add to the study of the structural relations between literature and society, work and audience, where the historical system of norms of a "literary public" lies hidden in a distant past; there it can most readily still be reconstructed through the horizon of expectations of a genre system that pre-constituted the intention of the works as well as the understanding of the audience.

The testimonies of older literatures often remain mute and the documents of social history also rarely give a direct answer to the questions that must be asked to obtain information about the function, reception, and influence of literary works and genres in their historical reality and social environment. Thus structuralism and hermeneutics are here related to one another to an especially great extent. Their mediation through the methods of an aesthetics of reception is necessary to enable one to become at all aware of the social function (by means of the synchronic system of genres, norms, and values) and—connected with this—the "answering character" (by means of an analysis of the history of reception) of works of past art.[92] Along this path our epistemological interest in the literature of the Middle Ages will also be grounded anew: the opportunity for a renaissance in medieval studies appears today to lie much less in the significance of the Middle Ages as a homogeneous member of our familiar Western tradition than in the fact that its monuments have preserved only a fragmentary picture of a historically distant culture and life-world that are often foreign to us.

If one looks back on the scholarship of recent decades, there is no longer any mistaking that the humanist faith in an unbreakable tradition of literary forms and in the timeless presence of masterworks has deceived us about the historical distance and otherness of medieval literature. No perceptible historical continuity exists between the forms and genres of the Middle Ages and the literature of our present. Here the reception of the ancient poetics and canon of genres in the Renaissance unmistakably cut through the threads of the formation of tradition. The rediscovery of medieval literature by romantic philology produced only the ideology of new continuities in the form of the essential unity of each national literature, but did not enable one to draw the medieval canon of genres and works back into a new literary productivity. The forms and genres of modern literature arose as a counter-thrust to the canon of classicist-humanist aesthetics: troubadour lyrics were as little an impulse for the *Fleurs du mal* as was the knightly epic for the *Education sentimentale* or the passion play for the modern "non-Aristotelian" theater.

But from this one should not now conclude that the theory and history of the literary genres of the Middle Ages can no longer contribute to the understanding of the literature of our present. What they may achieve, and wherein they may once again arrive at an actuality, can rather first emerge when our relationship to the Middle Ages is liberated from the illusion of beginnings, that is, from the perspective that in this period one might find the first stage of our literature, the beginning that conditions all further development. The literature of the Middle Ages can once again become an irreplaceable paradigm, not as a beginning that receives its significance only through an end that is distant from it—the developed national literatures—but rather through its "beginningness," significant in itself. Through the "beginningness" of a literature newly forming itself in the vernacular languages, its archaic genres provide testimony for the ideal *and* reality of a unique political as well as cultural historical-world closed in itself, and offer us elementary structures in which the socially formative and communicative power of literature has manifested itself.

Chapter 4
Goethe's and Valéry's *Faust:*
On the Hermeneutics
of Question and Answer

I

"Comparaison n'est pas raison": no independent method can be grounded in comparison alone. Even today, still, no critique strikes the naive self-understanding of comparative literary studies more sharply than Etiemble's ironic formulation does. How can a discipline lay claim to independence when its methodological procedure belongs to the everyday practice of many scholarly activities? The learned humanist who reconstructs an event of the past from many sources; the linguist who investigates the structure of a language via contrast or from various states of the language; the jurist who draws on a precedent to solve a question of law: all work comparatively now and then, without seeing there an ultimate methodological principle. Only the professional comparatist seems to have forgotten that something more than the mere comparison belongs to the methodological application of comparison. For even the most highly developed practice of comparison tells us neither what should enter into the comparison (and what not), nor to what end. The relevance and thereby the selection of the comparison cannot be drawn directly from the compared elements themselves; even when in the end significance apparently "springs out" on its own, it nonetheless presupposes hermeneutically a preconception [*Vorgriff*], however often unadmitted.

It would be idle to be reminded of all this if a glance at the present abundance of comparatist production did not confirm that in the normal course of its research, comparative literary study still largely holds to a naive, hermeneutically unenlightened objectivism. It does

110

not concern itself with the relevance of its comparison, and it therefore evidently lives by the messianic expectation that one day a genie of synthesis will arrive, who will be able to bring the flooded mass of comparatist knowledge back into a whole that with one stroke will return to the collected comparisons the significance that has become unrecognizable. In recent years this whole has fondly been called "world literature" [*Weltliteratur*], whereby the later Goethe as well as Marx and Engels can stand together as godfathers in a preestablished harmony.[1] It is admittedly a step forward when in this way the universality of literature frees itself from one last consequence of romantic thinking—the thought that "each nation has a special, separate history for itself, and therefore also possesses a literature which is independent from the others" (Träger, p. 23). Indeed, the older comparative studies also owed their scholarly-historical *ratio vivendi* to this beautiful romantic thought: this *ratio* had to be invented and legitimated as the method of comparison to bring back together the literatures or "voices of the peoples" [*Stimmen der Völker*], which were essentially different. Whoever believes that national literatures are separate histories—that is, that they are natures with their own laws of development—cannot arrive at the point of making comparison the ultimate methodological recourse. But today the romantic definition of literary history, as the ideal form of the individuality and history of a nation, belongs to the past. And an understanding of history has come to the fore in which literature and art can still be granted only relative autonomy within the real socio-historical process. Thus a new comparative studies faces the problem of its legitimation as well as that of its methodology.

The new legitimation—its object of study "world literature" and no longer the substantial dissimilarity of works and authors in the context of their national literature—does not at once also solve the methodological problem. When, according to Claus Träger, the task of literary studies from now on should be the investigation of national literary works in relationship to "world literature"—which cannot be done independently of their position in the national history and its relationship to the historical progress of world history (Träger, p. 31)—for him this does not raise the question of how this broadest panorama of possible relations is to be grasped at all be means of comparative observation. "World literature" is no objective, prefound greatness, no system of evaluation pre-given once and for all, within which everything can be compared with everything else. Before the coining of the term (around 1827), "world literature" already existed historically in the European history of education as the canon of exemplary works and authors. This canon of "world literature" is thoroughly conditioned historically and socially insofar as it presupposes a process of approval [*Anerkennung*] through the aesthetic judgment of historical subjects from the various periods, and thereby also a changeable *consensus omnium*. If "world literature" is to become the vanishing point of a post-national literary history, in relation to which the relevance and selection of all comparisons define themselves, then a new comparative studies must first arrive at the point of working out, from period to period, the history of that universal and yet not timeless canon in relation to which the "world literary" significance and influence of works and authors are decided. In the course of this it would be demonstrated that "world literature," like all formations of tradition, includes preservation, suppression, and omission—that its *consensus omnium* is not only historically universal and socially partial, but also a process of approval as well as disapproval in which the judgment of the particular present either takes over or gives up past experience, either renews it or rejects it.

We are today, and especially in universities that pedagogically mediate literature in a perfect departmentalization of national languages and periods, still far from paying our dues to such conceptual problems. But in addition to the historical problem of "world literature" as an axis of relevance that remains to be worked out, one may also bring the methodological inference of my introductory critique to bear on the traditional objects of comparative studies: hermeneutic reflection must be brought into the method of comparison so that the relevance of the comparison is not abandoned to mere accident, when not to a prejudice of the tradition. The following discussion is to serve this purpose, for which I have chosen a traditional theme of comparative studies. It is no longer a matter of the traditional question of what might be specifically German or specifically French in Goethe's and in Valéry's *Faust*, and thereby represent their literary-national traditions. Nor should the two versions of the Faust myth be investigated to recognize what is specifically "Goethean" in Goethe or "Valéryan" in Valéry. For even this latter object of interest, to inquire into the individuality of authors instead of the essence of national literatures, still stands under the spell of what one could call the illusion of the timeless comparision.

Whoever would thus compare Goethe's and Valéry's *Faust* directly with one another places their works on a timeless level of comparison, as if it were a matter of two variations of one and the same substance. Or, to use the metaphorics of literary history, as if it were a matter of a high-level dialogue between illustrious spirits, with the philologist only needing to eavesdrop in order to understand voice and countervoice and to interpret them comparatively. But on closer examination, it would soon be shown that the direct comparison remains exterior, that no overarching significance can be determined from shared and distinguishing features alone, indeed, that Goethe's voice and Valéry's voice clearly don't speak *to one another at all:* they remain two monologues as long as one only compares them. They only enter into a dialogical relationship—put another way, Valéry's new *Faust* only shows itself to be an answer to Goethe's *Faust*—when one recognizes the questions that, in Valéry's view, Goethe left behind. To formulate it methodologically, broadening the bipartite schema toward a *tertium comparationis* that is no longer timeless means a rehistoricization, such that one discovers the hermeneutic relation of question and answer, problem and solution, which mediates not only Goethe and Valéry, but also the different meanings of their similar works (as regards motifs) with the contemporary horizon of interest of the interpreter who is comparatively questioning them.

"Comparaison n'est pas raison": the comparative principle becomes reasoned to the degree that one brings to consciousness the question or series of questions that orients each controlled comparison. This preliminary question, often unanswered by the objectivism of the philological operation, can be more or less relevant. One can argue about it. But the argument may adjust itself toward the actual matter at hand when the question that the interpreter poses to the text is confirmed as a question relevant to the meaning of the text through the hermeneutic process of question and answer. The question we pose to *Faust* must lead to the knowledge of the question to which Goethe's *Faust* and, later, Valéry's *Faust* were the answer. At the end of the whole series of question and answer it remains to be examined whether it has satisfied the latest interpreter, or rather leaves new problems unanswered.

Here one must warn against a second substantialist illusion. Whoever has escaped from the illusion of the timeless comparison may still run the danger of falling into the illusion of the timeless question.[2] The literary work and, to an even greater degree, the literary myth have the character of an answer, the conclusiveness of which can cover over or cause one to forget the original question, so that it must be inferred in an ever-changing form in the process of the interpretations. It will be shown in our case as well that it was no longer the original question of the Faust myth that Goethe answered with his drama of humanity, and that Valéry took up another

question implied in the Faust myth when the answer of Goethe's
Faust no longer satisfied him.

It may still be noted, if only on the margin, that structuralist text-
theory and, more recently, the semiotic text-theory that has become
so modish are in no way freed from the abovementioned illusions,
especially when they consider hermeneutic reflection to be superfluous. For the logical combinations of structural anthropology as
well as the binary sign-systems of semiotics are dependent on relevan-
cies;[3] their descriptive models must answer to a preliminary question
if they are to be selective in a controllable manner, and not to be
absorbed into that *l'art pour l'art* of formalized metalanguages,
which no longer describe anything since they no longer answer to
anything.

II

In June 1940, when Paul Valéry began to write down the first scenes
of a *Comédie* that (according to the testimony of his *Cahiers*) for a
long time had been hovering before him under the title of a *III*[me]
Faust, it was not only that the world appeared to him sufficiently
altered since *Faust I* and *II* for the theme left behind by Goethe to be
taken up again.[4] There was also a concrete motive for seeing the
"German Faust" as a provocation for a French answer. Valéry wrote
during the days of the military catastrophe; he felt the defeat of his
country as most deeply shameful and wanted "so to speak to revenge
the events"[5] through stubborn writing. Even if the work that thus
arose quickly surpassed its historical occasion, the titles of partial
plays left unfinished—*Lust—La Demoiselle de Cristal (Comédie)* and
Le Solitaire ou les Malédictions de l'Univers (Féerie dramatique)—
still point back to a polemical point of departure. Valéry's *Faust*
does not enter peacefully into the illustrious series of his predecessors: it is written *against* two concretizations of the post-Goethean
myth and stands in the relation of a *tessera* vis-à-vis its entire modern
tradition. This is Harold Bloom's term, in *The Anxiety of Influence*,
for the opposing figure that the poet can fulfill as completion or
antithesis when he reproaches a traditionally powerful predecessor
for not having gone far enough, in order thereby to escape from his
spell at the same time.[6] The first of these two concretizations is the
affaire Marguérite, Goethe's Gretchen-tragedy in the trivial form
into which it declined during the nineteenth century in the opera
(Louis Spohr, Gounod) as well as in the dramatic burlesque.[7] The
other concretization does not stand in any direct literary filiation to

Goethe's *Faust*; it is Nietzsche's *Übermensch*, to which Valéry's *Solitaire* refers, that second fragment that would have given a purely negative closing to the "third Faust" if the last third of the text were not missing. The provocative deviation from the tradition is indeed already indicated by the subtitles. Since the *Malédictions de l'Univers* (which one can also read with the "Faustian" hubris of Hitler's dictatorship in mind) have already been excellently interpreted in reference to the myth of the eternal return by Ned Bastet,[8] our investigation concerns itself primarily with the question of how the first fragment, Valéry's *Demoiselle de Cristal*, is to be understood in relation to the Goethean myth of Faust's salvation through the "eternal feminine."

In the center of the first part of Valéry's *Faust III* stands the resumption of the *Affaire Marguérite*, and not an integral appropriation and reformulation of Goethe's *Faust I* and *II*. This can be quite irritating for the comparatists: the conventional comparison of the two literary texts produces more incorrect evidence here than it does parallels. Instead of beginning with the classical monologue in the study, Valéry's *Faust III* immediately begins dialogically, with a dictation of the memoirs of the urbane, learned man, which are taken down not by the "dried-up creep" Wagner, but rather by the female secretary *Lust*, as lovely as she is quick-witted. After the devil's wager (with an inverted meaning) the whole series of scenes is missing: *Auerbachs Keller, Hexenküche, Strasse, Abend, Spaziergang, Der Nachbarin Haus*, and later, *Wal und Hohle, Am Brunnen, Zwinger, Nacht, Dom, Walpurgisnacht*. In place of this, the garden scene (but without Marthe) is considerably enlarged and the plot of the students' scene is also complicated (with the insertion of a newly invented trio of devils). A single scene reminds one of the whole of *Faust II*: the *Intermède: Les Fées*, which only at the end of *Le Solitaire* forms a sidepiece to II, 1: *Anmutige Gegend*.

This sum total, which cannot exactly be encouraging for the comparative method, is especially appropriate for undoing the prejudice of those philologists who still cannot imagine an author's mode of production as being other than their own. Valéry's *Faust III* certainly did not proceed from a philologically impeccable textual study; one has reason to doubt whether he even ever really knew Goethe's *Faust II*. It is also possible—*horribile auditu*—that Gounod's opera, which may have made an impression on Valéry in his childhood, thoroughly conditioned the concretization of the *Affaire Marguérite* to which his first part is polemically related. Processes of reception are necessarily selective; they presuppose procedures of abridgment and transvaluation that may be simplifying but also recomplicating insofar as it is a matter of an independent reception with renovating power, and not just a dependent imitation that does not pose any new questions to the tradition. Such questions, which disclose the meaning of the selection, may in the present case already be reconstructed with the garden scene that Valéry surprisingly enlarged.

The beginning of Valéry's garden scene (II, 5) reminds one of the declaration of love "through the flower" in Goethe's *Faust* (v. 3180), only that it is a rose and that the new *Marguérite* finally has to take hold of another ruse to display the concealed understanding. Meanwhile, Valéry named the new Margarete "Lust." What does this rebaptism mean? Must the German meaning of the word be understood as Lucien Goldmann did, so that Valéry would have diminished the love that is still all-encompassing with Goethe into sensual lust to represent the dichotomy of rational thought and pure sensuousness, and thereby a historical phase in the dialectic of theory and practice?[9] How does the surname *Demoiselle de Cristal* enter into this interpretation?

In the garden scene, a lengthy monologue reminds one of the classical answer to the "Gretchen question" (v. 3415), yet with the ostentatious deviation that the new Faust dispenses with Goethe's pantheism ("the universe means nothing to me"), and opposes to the feeling of well-being an explanation of the presently fulfilled instant through the so-called CEM-formula (*corps-esprit-monde*). The beginning of Valéry's monologue—"Have I reached the summit of my art? I am alive. And I am only living. There's an achievement. . . ."—could be in reference to Goethe's formulation in the wagerscene: "I will say to the instant:/ But stay! you are so beautiful!" (v. 1699). Is then the fulfilled instant in the garden—obviously a reprise of the Biblical paradise and perhaps also an ironic reference to Voltaire's "We must cultivate our garden"—to be seen as Valéry's correction of the Goethean myth of the interminable Faustian striving?

In his fulfilled instant, Valéry's Faust totally forgets the presence of *Lust*, so that it takes an exceedingly amusing, even comic game of hands to help the pair to the expected happiness of union. With Goethe it was Faust who seduced Gretchen and then entangled himself in guilt with her; with Valéry it is Lust who, as a new Eve, reaches for the mythological fruit that she bites into (a peach instead of an apple, the *belle pêche* that in French associates *péché* [sin] with it!). How does the *jeu de la main* that Valéry's Faust then complicates into a long story relate to the preceding monological ecstasy? Does the character of the other in her corporeal presence interrupt or complete the *connaissance pleine et pure* of the Valéryan Faust? And what connection may it have with this that Valéry took hold once again of the oldest myth about the limits and consequences of human curiosity for his modern solution to the Faustian striving for redeeming knowledge (Mephisto's commentary—"Another affair of Frruit . . . All over again," II, 6—leaves no room for doubt)?

With this, the point has been reached where the questions that have opened up with Valéry's Faust-reprise demand a look back at the preceding process of a literary reception of myth. Hans Blumenberg has shown how the development and the change in meaning of the Faust figure is to be seen in the historical context of the problem of the "process of theoretical curiosity."[10] We are more narrowly interested in the renewal of the formulation of the question through Goethe and Valéry, something that articulates itself precisely in the literary reception of myth, and is comprehensible in the "answering-character" of the texts.

III

The rise of the Faust myth occurs in the post-medieval phase of the Christian-Augustinian discrimination against curiosity.

The original Faust figure of Johann Spies's *Historia* of 1587 still personifies the fear of a sinful craving for knowledge, which 'on its own took eagle's wings and wanted to explore all grounds of heaven and earth.' But the English translator already softened the epithets of moral reprehensibility, and Christopher Marlowe raised to tragic greatness the baseness of the drive for knowledge which was prepared to play for any stake. Damnation still remained as the final consequence, but the doubt had begun whether the spirit can be sinful when it gives itself over totally to its own most unique impulse. . . . Only Lessing's Faust was supposed to find a solution; Goethe's Faust did find it—but did the solution dissolve the question which gave the figure its epochal stature?[11]

Blumenberg left this question open, and he also did not actually pursue the problem implied therein, namely, how Goethe could still actualize the old *Volksbuch* at all after the question that had given the Faust figure its epochal stature since the Renaissance has rendered itself unnecessary. It is in this space that I can begin my attempt to interpret Goethe's *Faust* in reference to its position within the Faust myth's context of question-and-answer.

The question to which the Faust myth originally was the answer is not as easy to reconstruct as the unequivocal fable of Faust's punished (because sinful) craving for knowledge leads one to believe. For the answer that the modern Faust myth provides implies an official question desired by the churchly authority, but also one that at first is not posed, or perhaps is suppressed. The permissible question may be formulated as follows, which is how it can still be drawn out of the dialogue between Satan and the devils in Lessing's fragments: which is the passion that more certainly than any other leads man into corruption? The fate of the original Faust figure illustrates in the drastic manner of a woodcut why craving for knowledge is sinful and where it must lead when man dares to go beyond the limits of knowledge which are set for him. As with all outward-directed *curiositas*, which had been entered into the Christian catalogue of vices since Augustine, the striving toward knowledge of nature ("to speculate on the elements" in the Volksbuch; correspondingly in Goethe: "that I might know what holds the world together in its most inner reaches," vv. 382/3) counted as sinful or as "magic" within the still-medieval presuppositions of the Faust myth. The process of the Enlightenment gave theoretical curiosity its due as opposed to the Christian discrimination against it, and it not only cast doubt on the notion that man's striving for knowledge—precisely his most innate and noble drive—should be sinful. When, with Lessing, the process in favor of theoretical curiosity decided that Faust's damnation would be transformed into his salvation, the settlement of the question of dogma also liberated another question that the original Faust myth had left unposed, since for it the question had been decided in advance. It is the question whether human happiness can ultimately break out of man's striving toward knowledge, or rather remains dependent upon it.[12]

This question refers back to the ancient association of theory and eudaemonia. It first breaks up when it is no longer knowledge of nature and the world, but rather the other-worldly hope of Christian faith that is supposed to lead to the possession of truth that guarantees human happiness. With the beginning of the modern age, the separation between the claim to happiness and the path of knowledge of nature and the world is no longer maintained: the rehabilitation of theoretical curiosity also had to reawaken the ancient expectation that the possession of happiness might lie in knowledge of nature itself. If, in the formulation of Hans Blumenberg, this expectation characterizes the "ecstatic upswing of curiosity" of a real Faust figure of the Renaissance, namely, Giordano Bruno (p. 191), then it is also already recognizable in the example of one of his great contemporaries why the modern investigator of nature "had to reproduce the connection between the truth of knowledge and the finding of happiness in a new manner if, in Francis Bacon's new formula, the domination of nature could be the presupposition for the regaining of paradise" (p. 11). The new claim to knowledge could certainly dust off the old expectation of happiness, but it could not fulfill it. For no direct instructions toward the happy life can be derived from the new science; no "possession of truth" that could serve for orienting the lived praxis of each individual person, as the contemplative *theoria* once did, can be acquired from the triumphant achievements of the liberated theoretical curiosity (pp. 18, 19). To this extent Faust's salvation certainly solves the question of the legitimacy of the human drive for knowledge, but not that of the newly arisen antithesis between the claim to happiness and theoretical curiosity.

When Goethe took up the Faust material in 1773, the process of legitimizing theoretical curiosity—as Lessing's fragments already prove—had to be taken as complete. The medieval premise of ungodly curiositas had been overcome, and in the following years Kant took the last step of "sublating" [*aufheben*] the Augustinian disjunction between self-knowledge and the craving for knowledge.[13] If Goethe wanted to do more than merely treat an already historical object, then new questions had to be found and dramatically worked up for the myth's pregiven answer. These may be hypothetically subsumed under one question to which the reconstruction of the interest in the Faust myth has led us, the question of whether the world that has been given over to human knowledge is then at all capable of fulfilling man's drive for happiness.

To begin with, the monologue, with its refrain of "I have already . . . ach!", may, in its opposition to the Enlightenment triumph of theoretical curiosity, be read as a mode of actualization that is typical for the young Goethe. In this satire of the university it is not only the old pansophistic and nature-mystic spirituality that is opposed to the dead knowledge of scholastic learning; and in the Wagner-scene it is not only the new belief in inner form that is opposed to rationalism and pedantic rhetoric. The *Sturm und Drang* Faust figure equates the *famulus* Wagner with the Enlightenment concept of knowledge ("his clear, cold, scientific striving"),[14] and the doubt whether such knowledge could grasp "living," "active nature" (vv. 414-41) henceforth in no way excludes the experimental method ("my instruments certainly ridicule yours," v. 667). The Titanism of investigation of

Goethe's Faust does not personify the most progressive science of his time, compared with which his return to an intuitive knowledge of nature as a whole must appear much more as a relapse into a concept of knowledge dating from before Newton, Galileo, and Bacon. The actuality of new questioning thus also begins only *after* this return indicated in the story, when the new Faust is "cured of the [old] drive for knowledge" (v. 1768).

As if the traditional questioning of the old curiositas might be brought to an end with this line from the wager-scene, the following lines unmistakably (if nonetheless still only within implication) pose a new question, which in fact is entirely suitable for taking up the process of theoretical curiosity again:

> My breast, cured of the drive for knowledge,
> Shall in the future exclude no pain,
> And whatever is given to all mankind,
> I will enjoy within my inner self.

(vv. 1768-71)

If knowledge of undivided nature and world is no longer to be reached with the methods of knowledge [*Wissen*], can it not then be sought and, as the path to happiness, found in enjoyment [*Geniessen*]? The *Schema zu Faust* (1797-99?) sufficiently clarifies the central significance of this question, with which the interest of knowledge shifts from nature to the subject, from the world as a whole to "all mankind." According to this schema, the dramatic action is to be elevated from "the character's enjoyment of life" through "enjoyment of deeds" to "enjoyment of creation," the last of which was surprisingly still to be situated "on the way to hell." The high stature of *enjoyment* within the significance of a knowledge at once participatory and lustful needs only to be pointed out here.[15] But Mephisto's reply then immediately makes it clear that the newly posed question, the possibility of enjoyably knowing mankind as a whole, first demands an answer to the more far-reaching question of whether this world is made for the happiness of man at all. Mephisto's doubt—"Believe like me: this whole is made for a god alone!" (vv. 1780/81)—provokes a new theodicy: the possibility of human happiness is to be proved along Faust's new path of experience; the divine order of this world as regards good and evil is to be justified through the wager entered into, and its determination for the naturally good man tested. From the perspective of the history of the problem of curiositas, this means that the drive for knowledge was certainly reennobled and rejustified with Faust's salvation in

Lessing's fragments, but that the claim to happiness originally bound up with it was not guaranteed. If the justification of human knowledge was to be led all the way to autonomy, then it needed a proper, inner-worldly guarantee of a possible fulfillment of existence that could replace the compensatory, other-worldly happiness of the Christian faith.

That Goethe's attempt in his new *Faust*, to renew the old question of the connection between striving for knowledge and fulfillment of happiness, should have led to a contemporary form of theodicy was made possible through the transformation of the traditional devil's pact into a wager. If one considers the work as a refraction of the Mephistophelian doubt whether this world is arranged not only for a god but also for the happiness of man, then the nonbiased reader can arrive at the impression that Goethe actually shied away from the obvious consequences of his answer. This answer lies in the various formulations with which Goethe took up again Lessing's great phrase concerning the "ever growing completion" that is granted to man not by the possession of, but rather by "the search for truth": the happiness of human existence fulfills itself not just at a final goal, but already along the way, in the unending character of its "high striving."[16] But does this not also mean that man, in the figure of the new Faust, is capable of liberating himself through his striving, to say nothing yet of such liberation through the labor of the history for which he himself is responsible? Goethe obviously avoided this radical solution, which, according to Odo Marquard, was inaugurated at this very time by philosophic idealism in the form of the philosophy of history, with the result of a new theodicy relieving God of the responsibility for history.[17] Goethe's Faust is not yet a figure for the history of the emancipation of mankind. Far from liberating Faust through his "high striving" alone, Goethe reentangles him in guilt through his actions toward Gretchen and, later, toward Philemon and Baucis, so that salvation is needed "from above" (v. 11939) and, along with it, the transcendental resort to the medieval building of faith.

The answer of Goethe's *Faust* to the newly posed question of the myth, concerning whether striving toward knowledge is compatible with the desire for happiness, leaves new problems behind it. Why did Goethe bring a new motif of sinning into the drama with the newly invented Gretchen-tragedy, after the process of the Enlightenment had done away with the old motif of sinning through the ennobling of the craving for knowledge? Was it only a concession to contemporary taste (the tragedy of the infanticidal mother), or did the Gretchen experience itself stand once again within a hidden context of the Faustian striving for enjoyable knowledge? An answer to the last question may more easily be found if we look back upon the intentions and limits of his predecessor from the perspective of Valéry's new *Faust*.

IV

It is not just incidental that Valéry contrasted his new *Faust*, as *Comédie* and *Féerie dramatique*, with Goethe's *Tragödie*. As if he wanted to demonstrate how antiquated everything has become that had been earnest for his predecessor, Valéry appears at first simply to invert the traditional positions, with the provocative point that in the intervening time their inversion had become true. The old Faust was resigned because he could never know enough, whereas the new Faust is so because he always already knows everything. The aged Mephisto who formerly rejuvenated Faust is now to be rejuvenated and led astray by Faust. Far from needing a rescue "from above" as the old Gretchen did, the "demoiselle de cristal" promoted to be Faust's secretary rejects all faith in other-worldly fulfillment. What do these comic inversions mean for the meaningful questions that the Faust myth brings along with it?

Valéry's *Faust* is no mere reprise that only thematizes a renewed return of the immemorial form of the myth. The meaning of this work only discloses itself in its full historical concretization when one recognizes the opposing figure (the *tessera* in Harold Bloom's sense) that it cuts in relation to Goethe as well as to the entire modern Faust tradition: Valéry's secret ambition is with this myth to exhaust once and for all the circle of the eternal return of life (here I am following Ned Bastet's interpretation), to represent not just a new Faust, but rather a "final Faust."[18] Therefore Valéry immediately introduces the aged Faust as involved in a final activity on the far side of all investigative curiosity, in the dictation of his memoirs. And as one would not expect otherwise with Valéry, this motif serves here as well to ironize the false claim that the narration of his past might arrive at knowledge of himself. Thus *Mon Faust* leads Valéry's lifelong polemic against historicism to its conclusion: what was can claim no higher truth than what might be ("I've told you several times that these memoirs are not recollections, and that I consider what I imagine to be just as worthy of being ME as that which was, and of which I have doubts," II, 5). The question of the historicist school, "how it really was" ["*wie es eigentlich gewesen*," Ranke], is curiositas led astray.

If it is true that in the nineteenth century the process of theoretical curiosity took a new turn from knowledge of nature to knowledge of history, then according to Valéry the historical curiosity could be philosophically legitimated only on the condition that it reconstitute the possible as opposed to the factual: "The past is simply a matter of faith. A faith is an abstention of our mind's powers, which refuses to formulate all the conceivable hypotheses concerning the absent things and give them all the same force of truth" (I, 1). The memoirs of the new and last Faust, undertaken in opposition to the reified history-writing of his biographers, are to go beyond the circumference of all possible attitudes toward the factual, untying all the events of a life and reconnecting them. The formulation, "to make a complete circuit of possible opinions on all the points, to know in succession all the tastes and all the distastes, to make and unmake and remake all these knots which are the events of a life" (I, 1), could be taken as Valéry's variation upon Goethe's "And whatever is given to all mankind, I will enjoy within my inner self." Yet Valéry's reprise begins as drama with Faust's anti-memoirs only in order to present with them the end of all theoretical and historical curiosity. Thus in the student-scene (II, 1) the famous teacher shows himself to be a last Faust for whom, like the eternal Jew, the experience of the new has come to be lost. Whoever lives beyond the single cycle of a human life becomes not richer but poorer in experience, since for him all knowledge, in its repetition, congeals into mere reknowledge. The following garden-scene will then show how Faust nonetheless escapes this role of a "Sisyphus of life."[19] But first it is still to be observed how Mephisto is brought into this end of curiositas.

Goethe, who transformed the traditional devil's pact into a wager on account of his new theodicy, nonetheless left Mephisto with one essential function of the old theodicy. Mephisto's self-presentation as "part of that force which always wants evil and always does good" (v. 1336) is a pansophic-idealist justification of evil of the kind that Valéry's Mephisto must recognize as one of his obsolete prejudices ("evil is good for everything," I, 2): "You don't even doubt that there are many other things in the world besides good and evil." The roster of the devil's outmoded prejudices and behavior is a long one, as he remains the same and thus lags behind the "fearful novelty of this age of man"; it ends with the melancholy insight: "But you poor people! Evil was so beautiful, at one time." Since Goethe's age the world has so transformed itself that its condition and fortunes, its knowledge and possibilities, can no more be grasped with the old polarity of the humane and the inhumane than the new man may be understood with the old terms of soul, sin, and immortality.

After "the process of knowledge itself surpassed everything which magic could once make enticing" (Blumenberg, p. 90), the metaphysical necessity of a theodicy is also removed and there remains for the *esprit pur* of evil only the comic role of the seducer left sitting, who now, in an exchange of roles with Faust, is supposed to catch up with everything that mankind has anticipated. He suffers the final loss of his former greatness through his future sacrifice. The Gretchen who has become the "demoiselle de cristal" shows him why a pure spirit, regardless whether angel or devil, cannot understand anything of the happiness of human existence: "How do you suppose that eternal beings could feel the value of a glance, an instant, the gift of a moment's unyielding . . . the gift of a good which must be siezed between its birth and its dying. They are nothing but darkness. . . . But I, but we, we have our lights and we have our shades . . . I tell you, Hell, Eternity means little to me" (III, 3). Whether this also includes Valéry's answer to the question left behind by Goethe, whence the possibility of human happiness is to arise — if it can no longer be expected from a Faustian striving for knowledge, nor is it to be assigned to salvation through a transcendental authority — must be demonstrated by the interpretation of the central garden-scene.

V

Why did Valéry indeed call the new Margarete "Lust" and "Demoiselle de Cristal"? With this question one should not overlook the fact that nowhere did Valéry ridicule his illustrious predecessor so furiously as precisely with the reprise of the *affaire Marguérite*. He has Mephisto say, in agreement with Faust, "I certainly hope the genre is finished. We are no longer, neither you nor I (each according to his nature), going to combine a supplementary rejuvenation with a complementary virginity."[20] Such utterances render dubious in advance all attempts at seeing Faust and *Lust* as a symbolic pair of distinct "masculine" and "feminine" principles that at one moment is happily to overcome the opposition between mind and body, *animus* and *anima*, or abstract thought and conrete sensual pleasure, and at another moment is to overcome the dichotomy between rational thought and pure sensuousness, knowledge and beauty, or something similar. The result of such attempts at interpretation is often an unintended allegoresis, as, in a manner that can very nearly be called medieval, Lucien Goldmann demonstrates when he plays his Goethe —held to be dialectical—off against the traditional rationalist Valéry, whose thought has regrettably "alienated itself from praxis."[21] Valéry's *Lust* is initially devoted to sheer sensual pleasure, and thus may, to Goldmann's consolation, still symbolize that "connection with the outer world and reality" that the thinking of Valéry's Faust, estranged from praxis, lacks. The only disturbing thing is that Valéry's Faust embraces the quite practical *Lust*, flouting the maxim "prenez garde à l'amour!" And yet a dialectical-materialist allegoresis will do away even with this: precisely for this inconsequence would Faust be conquered by solitude in the end!

"Prenez garde à l'allégorie"—we should rather ask what significance *Lust* takes on in her new role as Gretchen promoted to secretary. This role begins with a departure from the dutiful role, namely, a fit of irresistible laughter, which brings upon *Lust* a reprimand from her strict boss. In her insubordinate behavior, however, *Lust* ironically only confirms a theory of Faust's: "laughter is a refusal to think." What goes out from Faust boomerangs back via *Lust* in a manner that he doesn't expect. That which interrupts the autonomous progress of his thoughts or, more precisely, the dictation of his memoirs—namely, the irritating *refus de penser* by another—becomes the condition for a new spontaneity, an event not only in the receptive realm of the senses but also in the productive realm of the intellect. We need not entertain the consideration of how differently Eckermann's *Gespräche mit Goethe* might have run if an insubordinate demoiselle de cristal had taken the place of the obedient scribe. In *Mon Faust*, in any case, the secretary enters from the beginning into a conversational role that evidently—as the present interpretation will show—corresponds to the function that Valéry assigned to *sensibilité* in the mental economy.[22] Karl A. Blüher already saw this, but concluded all too quickly therefrom that "the 'sensibility' stands at the side of the masculine 'mind' as its feminine partner."[23] Even if the two are to form a "symbolic pair"—something that Valéry, with his pronounced rejection of "symbolism," could acknowledge only with ridicule—everything still depends on how "mind" and "sensibility" enter into a relationship with one another here, since they are in no way so neatly divided into the allegorical halves of masculine and feminine sides.

At first Faust treats *Lust* no differently than as the secondary character of the secretary in the comedy, as the subordinate and object of his orders: "You are not here to understand, my child. You are here to write at my dictation" (I, 1). When he adds, "and in addition to that, you are here to be agreeable to look at when I'm not thinking," this indeed appears only to devalue her yet one step lower, toward functioning as an object. Yet the explanations that *Lust* increasingly brings forth lead progressively to her recognition as subject. The embarrassed gesture with which the thinker's distracted hand grasps any old object ("a knick-knack, a familiar piece of ivory") while awaiting his thoughts displays itself as the necessary condition of a thinking that would be false if it separated itself from life. The neutral object thus becomes an *objet de tendresse* for the thinker, for which *Lust* then slyly introduces a "beautiful kitty, very soft and warm." The next step, the sheet entitled *Erôs énergumène* smuggled in by Mephisto, takes up accidentality—the capability "of being sensitive to some chance event"—as precisely the definition of genius. Thus not interiority as the *natura naturans* of classical-individualistic aesthetics, but rather receptivity toward objects is what makes sensibility productive.[24] Only here does Faust indicate that this formulation can also serve at the same time as the key to the obscure meaning of the discovered title *Erôs énergumène*, with his paraphrase of it as "Eros as source of extreme energy." A further step—the play with the turn-of-phrase "your chaste ears"—compels the writer of the memoirs to admit his curiosity concerning the questions his partner might well have suppressed while only listening. Now *Lust* is not simply to do that which was initially forbidden her —*comprendre*—but also to earn the surname that ennobles her to a subject above the ironically noble title of "Lust de cristal." For the demand to "become transparent" in no way only means that *Lust* is to become transparent for Faust and thereby remain receptive; rather, she should not conceal her own thoughts and should present utterances and answers. With this, unnoticed by Faust, the character of the other has assumed the aforementioned role that is indispens-able for his thinking. That this substitution of the transparent presence of an other for the neutral object has as-yet unforeseen consequences for the thinking itself, comes to light only with the garden-scene. This much, however, is already evident: in no way can *Lust* in *Mon Faust* signify the simple reduction of the "all-encompas-sing love" of Goethe's Gretchen to sheer sensuality (*volupté*); nor may the German word consciously chosen by Valéry present a newly cleaned version of the Epicurean significance of εδογε (inner tran-quility of body and soul). Whatever *Lust* evokes for the German ear,[25] if one holds to the significance unfolded in the dialogue itself ("Lust de Cristal . . . devenez transparante"), then the name of the new Gretchen certainly cannot symbolize the perfect state of a self-pleasing Epicurian wisdom. Yet what does the original Gretchen signify in general for Goethe's Faust?

Even one who values as highly as did Bertolt Brecht Goethe's notion, "combining the highly contemporary material of the infanticidal mother with the old 'puppet-play of Dr. Faustus,' " should not overlook the fact that this "deepest and boldest love-story in German drama" could represent something like a "dialectic of the bourgeois class feeling its oats"[26] only at the cost of categories of sin and salvation that are in no way enlightened, but rather once again thoroughly medieval. After this same highly contemporary material had, on the one hand, been degraded to the most trivial level through its reception in the nineteenth century, but after Valéry, on the other hand, nonetheless found the *affaire Marguérite* worthy of a reprise in spite of all the ridicule, one finds oneself facing the question of whether Goethe could not have already appropriated a deeper interest from the theme of seduced innocence, an interest that might explain the enduring influence of this love-story on the higher as well as the lower level of its receptions. I see this kernal of crystallization dating from the first dramatic concretization, in that Goethe gave to the meeting of the resigned learned man with the naive and innocent young bourgeois woman the meaning of Gretchen's love revealing something of that nature to Faust that was denied to his Titanic drive for knowledge.

Let us recall that Goethe's Faust, no differently than his mythic predecessor, seeks to know "what holds the world together in its most inner reaches" (v. 382), has doubts about the science of the classical faculties, and turns to magic. His failing attempts describe a spiritual realm in declining gradations. The highest authority is the macrocosm, the "endless nature" that—"but ach! only a drama"— cannot be grasped (vv. 430-59). The next lowest authority is the world-spirit, which indeed shows itself but which as the face in the fire cannot be endured by Faust (vv. 460-513). The formulation of the rejection—"you are like the spirit which you comprehend, not me!"—leaves behind the suspense of whom this spirit might indeed be, and of which authority such that man, sent back within his boundaries, might be able to attain it. Should it simply be Mephisto? This explanation, offered by many commentaries,[27] is scarcely satisfactory. To be sure, Faust comprehends, even sees through the "comrade" to whom the wager binds him; but why should he then also be like him, the "spirit who always negates"? This is already shown in the relationship with Gretchen, into which he brings Mephisto as the seducer after his own rejuvenation. In the words of Erich Trunz, "Mephistopheles wants sensuality, but with Faust it's love; Mephistopheles wants 'shallow insignificance,' while with Faust it's all-encompassing bliss."[28] Opposing the seducer, Gretchen effects this change in Faust, and furthermore also embodies the role of antagonist to Mephisto within the larger dramatic intrigue. She thus appears in a representative function that need not therefore be less real, just because it is only named metaphorically. In the scene "Abend" (v. 2678 ff.), metaphors of exuberance of feeling in Faust's mode of discourse first indicate a higher level of significance, until the initially concealed function of the loved one then visually comes to light. The "small, clean room" of the absent young woman becomes a "shrine" for Faust, through which a "sweet twilight glow" is diffused. He discovers "fullness" in this poverty, feels "bliss" "in this prison." The leather chair becomes the "throne of the fathers" for him; the simple things refer to "your spirit of fullness and order," the traces of her activity to her "dear hand! so like a god's!" Finally, the sight of her bed unleashes an apostrophe to that authority which Margarete represents for Faust:

> Here I'd like to tarry whole hours.
> Nature! here in lightest dreams
> You shaped the native angel!
> Here lay the child, filled with the warm life
> Of the tender bosom,
> And here through holy, pure hovering
> The divine image realized itself.

(vv. 2710-16)

What Faust sought in vain to grasp in the macrocosm and then in the world-spirit, is offered for his recognition on the human plane, in Margarete's naive beauty and pure little world. Nature, which denies itself to him from authority to authority, reveals itself in the purest figure or innocence of the feminine. Put another way, in the formulation of a later authority who in this regard is entirely above suspicion: in love as the natural relation of man to woman, "the relationship of man to nature is immediately his relationship to man, as his relationship to man is immediately his relationship to nature."[29] If one accepts this interpretation, then the beginning of Faust's monologue in *Wald und Höhle* — "Sublime spirit, you gave me, gave me everything for which I asked" (vv. 3217/18) — can more reasonably be related to the world-spirit and the now-apparent meaning of his discourse: "You are like the spirit which you comprehend" (v. 512). For it is the love for Gretchen that "opens up the previously locked 'secret deep wonder' of outer and inner nature"[30] for him, and gives him the power "to feel, to enjoy them" (v. 3221).

Thus understood, the experience with Gretchen answers in the affirmative the question of the myth that Goethe newly posed—whether striving toward knowledge is compatible with desire for happiness—but only in a limited manner. In a theologically suspicious manner, Dante had preceded Goethe in seeing the epistemological function of love as access to nature; Goethe's rediscovery of this in the end reburdened it with a function of salvation, as a borrowing from theology with a view toward the outcome of the wager and thus toward the theodicy, remains equally suspicious. Gretchen's intercession (*una poenitentium*) with a transcendental authority (*Mater dolorosa*) is needed to make possible the final homage to the world-immanent authority ("The eternal-feminine draws us onward"). In this elevation of Gretchen, nature embodied in the pure feminine, to the eternal feminine as the authority of salvation, one can grasp the beginnings of a remythification that can also be discovered elsewhere in Goethe—one need only think of his *Iphigenie*.[31] The new myth of the *Ewig Weiblichen*, legitimated with Goethe's name, did more than preserve some remainder of the "aura" of the Gretchen-tragedy, otherwise degraded into the fate of all the world in the nineteenth century. It also disguised the epistemological function of Faust's love for Gretchen, originally realized in the claim to happiness, so that Valéry first had to rediscover it in his own way, as he went against the grain of the nineteenth century's reception, in order to return the *affaire Marguérite* to the status which it had achieved with Goethe.

VI

The garden-scene in *Mon Faust* is Valéry's answer to the question concerning the possibility of human happiness. But it is an answer that must satisfy the demands that are to be made after Goethe: it can no longer lie in the endlessness of Faustian striving after the absorption of the old *curiositas* into modern science; nor can it hope any longer for a transcendental goal, for "salvation" at the end, after the shattering of the final, idealist theodicy in the face of the unreason of history. Only one who overlooks this relationship of the answer could maintain along with Kurt Wais that Valéry's Faust here enjoys "the Goethean fulfillment . . . as delimitation (*l'infini est défini*), as breathing, as gazing, then . . . the finding of the thou [*Du*] through the sense of touch."[32] Valéry's concept of *plénitude* contradicts the Faustian happiness that is supposed to lie in never-satisfied striving and that nonetheless is rewarded with a final "beautiful instant." The great monologue in the course of which Valéry's Faust totally forgets the co-presence of *Lust* is as far from Goethian fulfillment of existence—such as Valéry had already ironically opposed to all Faustian *impatience* in his *Discours en l'honneur de Goethe* (1932)—as his CEM-formula is from classical cosmology. The lucid interpretation by Karl Löwith devoted to Valéry's philosophical thought leaves no doubt about this, even if one should add to this interpretation—which opens up a first penetrating glance into the *Cahiers*—that *Mon Faust* leads one step beyond Valéry's Cartesianism and skepticism about language.[33]

As already mentioned, in the fifth scene of the second act Valéry recalled the lovers' meeting between Faust and Margarete in Marthe's garden through various scenic and verbal echoes. "It's divine this evening": what *Lust* at first still takes for the beginning of the next dictation is already the instant that, with the hesitation of dictating further, effaces the past of the memoir-writer—the Valéryan version of the instant of the "Verweile doch, du bist so schön" ("This moment is of such a great value"). As such, for Valéry's Faust it neither redeems—as in Goethe's wager—an expectation or anything at all that no longer is, nor is it—like the last words of Goethe's striving Faust—the *Vorgefühl* of something which is not yet.[34] The "beautiful instant" in *Mon Faust* at once negates the Goethean feeling of happiness in the never-satisfied Faustian striving and the exceptional character of an eventful final fulfillment of existence. To lend highest value to the instant, it is not the project of an extraordinary action that is called for (like the conquering of a piece of "the newest earth," v. 11566 in *Faust II*), but rather only an everyday beautiful summer evening ("it's divine this evening," in an intentionally trivial phrasing). And such happiness, which allows all thought of the possible to be absorbed into the present,[35] can appear as soon as "one accepts oneself as the one one is, as *tel quel*" (Löwith, p. 80), or in Faust's words, when "my person is exactly wedded to my presence, in exchange with whatever comes to pass."

But Valéry's answer to Goethe's "presentiment of such great happiness" also negates the idealist notion that this experience of the I in the self's pure being might stand in harmony with the whole of the world. "Your eyes seem to contemplate the universe in the medium of this little garden"—what Lust here believes she understands with her inspired words is rejected by Valéry's Faust even more decisively than Goethe's question of Gretchen: "The universe means nothing to me, and I am thinking of nothing." For Valéry as for his Faust, the whole is not the universe: "It is not a god who creates and maintains the world and man. Nor is it the cosmos existing from nature onward, but rather the connection and distinction, the relationship and mis-relationship between *corps, esprit* and *monde* which in the *Cahiers* he formulaically denotes with 'CEM' and calls *his* whole" (Löwith, p. 59). *Mon Faust* takes up the critique of the idea of the universe in the following manner. The constitution of the whole is described as a function of the sensual perception of the particular, in accordance with the CEM formula. As an experience of the purity of the self's being (*Moi pur*), it is thus removed from the imprisonment of the empirical I. But then it is surprisingly corrected through an intervention by the forgotten *Lust*, and then at the end contrasted with the Faustian, natural science-like attitude of the student.

"Have I reached the summit of my art? I am alive. And I am only living. There's an achievement." Faust, who has set out to enjoy the "greatest instant," speaks of the exception. The Moi pur can attain the purity of the self's being only to the extent that it detaches itself from all givens, from the environment and shared world that are dressed up in the possessive pronoun as well as from the empirical I and its history. Concerning this, Karl Löwith remarks: "The pure I-itself that sees everything which is called thus-and-so and is already familiar . . . as if for the first time, and does not merely recognize it, is a function of the most extreme wakefulness . . . To be able to detach oneself at any time from everything that exists at that moment, in order to see oneself and all phenomena of the world in their original strangeness as if for the first time, may be considered to be the authentically philosophical motif of Valéry's system, for which he is indebted to Descartes" (Löwith, p. 65). As if for the first time, Faust here experiences the simplest function of life: "I breathe—I see—I touch." The function of the body, to breathe ("I am born from each instant for each instant"), the function of the mind, to see ("What does it matter, what one sees? It suffices to see, and to know that one sees. There's a whole science there"), and the function of the hand, to grasp an object ("And with a single stroke, I find and I create the real"), describe Faust's ecstasy as a state of perfection for which he claims the same dignity as for the ecstasies of religious experience.[36] If the description up to this point corresponds to a step-by-step interpretation of the CEM-formula, *Mon*

Faust then goes far beyond the conceptual argumentation of the *Cahiers* with a fourth step, which ironizes and overcomes the seemingly perfect self-satisfaction of the Valéryan Moi pur.

As if Faust is to have the double meaning of the description of the third function—"My hand feels itself touched as much as it touches. Real means that. And nothing more."—demonstrated for him, *Lust* softly lays her hand on his shoulder. This gesture does not exactly correspond to the line from Lucretius that Faust has just cited here, "Tangere enim et tangi, nisi corpus, nulla potest res." It is much more the case that it reveals a meaning in the materialistic principle that could scarcely have been intended by Lucretius, just as it also responds with an ironic excess to Faust's preceding question: "What could be more real? I touch? I am touched." There is something yet more real than the arm of the bench which one can grasp oneself, in order to feel touch and being-touched. *Lust*'s foreign hand has a greater degree of *présent dans la présence*, for it reaches out on its own and thereby grants the *être touché* the second, fuller meaning, unexpected by Faust. An unexpected subject has appeared in the place of the expected object, the body of the other as an autonomous thou in the place of the body as disposable thing: *Faust*: "Someone is touching me . . . Who? . . . Is it thou, Lust? . . ." *Lust*: "It's I . . . Why say 'thou' to me?" *Faust*: "Because you touched me." In this play of hands, the continuation of which scarcely needs a commentary, nothing less than the extension of the whole from *corps-esprit-monde* to *other* is achieved, thus a fourth function that breaks through the solipsism of the CEM-formula. Valéry's concept of the pure I-itself that negates all that is given in order to constitute a whole, receives an ultimate correction in *Mon Faust*: the state of perfection attainable by man ("la connaissance pleine et pure") needs the other in its corporeal presence to become truly whole.

But this whole ("that is therefore born of you and me, and not of you or of me") is now drawn out through an intermezzo that breaks through the celebratory tone in the paradisiac garden in a pronouncedly comic manner. What is the business with the "young widow, sad and ardent" supposed to mean, with which Faust continues the dictation of his memoirs at precisely this moment? Were it only superfluously to make *Lust* jealous, the cost would be decidedly too great. It only becomes comprehensible when one recognizes the philosophic position to which it is addressed. For the story, initially introduced so abstrusely, appears in the context of Faust's memoirs as a reply to a famous philosophic experience of awakening, and thus responds to the question—already implied in the first scene of *Mon Faust*, and no laughing matter for Valéry—of why philosophers do not also use their hands in thinking. It is "Descartes' dream," familiar to every French lycée student, according to which Faust stylizes his own great philosophic discovery. The scenery is the same: the whereabouts of a German neighborhood, a winter evening "in front of the big fire," the moment of a monumental discovery—only that the philosophizing Faust additionally needs the above-mentioned young widow to occupy his idle hand. Yet here begins the ironic reversal: whereas Descartes found his principle for a general method for all sciences in the abstraction from all sensual experience, Faust-Valéry discovers "the error common to all philosophers" in their failure to recognize the connection between the concrete presence of things and abstract thinking.

The idea came to me . . . that . . . between all these things that are present . . . this fire . . . this cold . . . this color of the daylight . . . this . . . tender . . . form of equilibrium in . . . in the most . . . lovely . . . abandonment . . . the vague . . . feelings which moved in the shadows . . . of my mind . . . and . . . on the other hand . . . on the other hand . . . my abstract thought . . . a profound . . . and fixed . . . relationship . . . which extended even into my past . . . and doubtless . . . to what might be to . . . to . . . come . . . to come. . . . (II, 5)

The certainty of the *cogito ergo sum* is the error of Descartes and all philosophers who as *philosophes sans mains et sans yeux* overlook the fundamental role of the body in their systems,[37] and thereby forfeit that certainty of present things as well as of present cohumanity, a certainty that is not only subjective and that alone can fulfill the instant (here along with past and future!) and make possible a "happiness" that is not only "spiritual." The motif of the cothinking hand begins in jest with Faust's "while I'm awaiting my thought . . . the distracted hand pets and caresses" and Lust's "a beautiful kitty, very soft and warm" (I, 1). It is then elevated through the unexpected interpretation of the line from Lucretius—"the hand which touches and which is touched" (II, 5)—to a highly serious significance ("to introduce into the arid story of a metaphysical discovery a little bit of truth . . . secondly, a nothing of life, of . . . live? . . . flesh" II, 5). Together, this gives *Mon Faust* an unmistakably anti-Cartesian turn. But perhaps it also allows one to think of a still more distant origin.

The philosophizing Faust who needs his hand and an *objet de tendresse* to escape, through *Lust*, from the illusions of abstract thought, is not lacking in analogy to the Old Testament creation myth, according to which God took a rib from the sleeping Adam and made woman from it to provide the lonely man with the missing *object de tendresse* ("adiutor similis eius," Gen. 2:20-22). The Biblical narrative implies the creating hand of God ("aedificavit . . . costam, quam tulerat de Adam, in mulierem") without actually referring to it, just as later in the iconographic tradition the creator stretches his hand toward the arising creation only as a sort of verbal gesture [*Sprachgestus*] (as with Michelangelo's creation of Adam). Yet there exists alongside this a literary tradition known to me from the Middle Ages, but also taken up by Milton, according to which it is the highest praise of female beauty to say that God himself created her "with the mere hand."[38] Even if the interpretation I am risking —that the co-thinking hand of the philosophizing Faust appears in the invented biographic-mythic narrative in the place of the co-creating (if already heterodox) hand of the Biblical god of creation— cannot be supported through any historically concretizable filiation, it would presumably not have displeased Valéry. This may also be concluded from the fact that he himself used the Biblical myth of the Fall to answer, with this reprise, in his own way the old question of the possibility of happiness that springs from the fullness of human knowledge—through a provocative inversion of the Satanic prophecy, "Eritis sicut Deus, scientes bonum et malum."

The Christian myth that is supposed to explain the illegitimate curiosity through which mankind itself forfeited its happiness, winds up grounding Faust's and *Lust*'s happiness at the end of Valéry's four-act play. The common consumption of the fruit gets the jump on the traditional seducer (II, 6); seals an understanding *inter pares* that already began with the hand-play ("that is therefore born of you and me, and not of you or of me"); and refutes the theology of original sin and salvation through the "transformation (in the scene) of the state of Eros into the state of Nous" that was foreseen for the fourth act.[39] Thus, after the process of theoretical curoisity had been exhausted, Valéry in *Mon Faust* concludes that older process that Goethe—as the album-verse, used only ironically for the student, shows (v. 2048)—did not yet dare to touch: the revision of the Biblical judgment on man's claim to be like God. The surviving drafts of a fourth act offer to the state of affairs after the eating of the fruit a meaning opposed to the Biblical tradition: "We would be like the Gods, the harmonious, intelligent ones, in an immediate correspondence with our sensual lives, without words—and our minds would make love with one another as our bodies can do."[40]

VII

"IIIme Faust. All that Goethe ignored"—this early note of Valéry's (*Cahiers* XII, 894) may be given still more weight by our consideration from the perspective of the connection between question and answer that constitutes the historical changes in the modern Faust myth. The role that Goethe played for Valéry, as the predecessor of the classical Faust drama as well as the world-literary figure of the poet, itself remythologized during the course of the nineteenth century, may be better grasped with the categories of Harold Bloom's "antithetical criticism" than with "organic" metaphors. Such metaphors suppose harmonious further developments when, in fact, the formation of a tradition achieves itself from author to author in a leaping, unorganic manner, and mostly in the forms of a "creative misinterpretation." This must be said above all with respect to Kurt Wais, who starts from Valéry's Goethe lecture (1932) in order to be able to salvage a "considerable agreement" between the two poets, even for their divergent versions of Faust.[41] It is with the categories of this supposed agreement that, in our consideration, Goethe's and Valéry's Fausts deviate most sharply from one another: Valéry's Moi pur and CEM-formula have virtually nothing in common with "Goethe's fullness of existence" ("the past within the present") and concept of nature, and Valéry's privileging of the possible over the actual contradicts "Goethe's discontentedness."[42] Similarly, those provocative inversions of the wager (rejuvenation), the role of Gretchen (salvation), the situation of the "Verweile doch!", and finally the "album-verse's" *Eritis sicut deus* scarcely allow one to locate *Mon Faust* historically other than as an anti-Faust (the *Mon* in the title and the date of 1940 also speak for this). I would have gladly spared myself this polemic, were it not that it served the methodological demonstration of what meta-levels of mystical continuities and harmonized poetic dialogues one can arrive at "comparatively"[43] when the process of reception between two authors is not hermeneutically explained. The six categories of "creative misinterpretation" (*clinamen, tessera, kenosis, daemonization, askesis, apophrades*) with which Harold Bloom has attempted to explain the literary formation of a tradition through the modalities of the father-son relationship show imaginable inner relationships between two "greats of world literature" other than the one-dimensional notions of influence, imitation, or "mid-wifery."[44] If my interpretation has correctly grasped the relationship between Valéry and Goethe as tessera, it might also explain that it is entirely possible to attain the intuitive results of antithetical criticism in a manner that is subject to hermeneutic control.

The unfinished shape of the text in the case of Valéry's Faust fragments leaves many a suggested solution unconfirmed in the end, even from my perspective. That Valéry might have completed the two fragments through, for example, putting *Solitaire* before *Lust*,[45] in a manner that is close to the sketch in *Cahiers* XXIV, 16 ("Lust must have a struggle within F[aust] which effects the transformation —in the scene—of the state of Eros into the state of Nous"), is probably too beautiful to be true. For this same sketch foresees in addition to this a "scene of well-being" that is evidently supposed to put an end to the restored paradise.[46] Is Ned Bastet right when he would conclude from several fragments of the third scene of the fourth act that Faust would refuse *Lust* in the end, when she implores him to share the future with him, with the argument: "Ah! Lust! You are one who comes too late. . . . I know only too well what will happen and what there is in the little coffer"?[47] Would the four-act *Lust* then already be nothing other than that which the three-act *Le Solitaire* seems to take up as its main theme: "Faust as victim of the eternal return, chastised for having wanted to begin again"?[48] Then both fragments would stand under the new problem, going back to Nietzsche, of how man can escape from the "eternal return," break out of the circle of the endless reproduction of life, or, put another way, invent a different death, one which would be fulfillment and not merely interruption.

Ned Bastet has shown that *Le Solitaire* can indeed be understood as Valéry's answer to this question: if Faust is man, then the "solitary" would be the consciousness that amid the "curses of the universe" arrives, via negation after negation, at the outermost possibility of the Moi pur, to think the "ultimate thoughts"—"the purity of non-being"—in suicide.[49] Yet this interpretation leaves unexplained that Faust, as surviving observer, cannot be identical with the *Solitaire*, even when for his part he refuses the fairies' offer of rebirth. Must one not also consider whether the *Solitaire*, as opposed to Faust, is supposed to take up the now-empty place of the antiquated Mephisto and thereby take on the role of a more contemporary experimenter?[50] But what remains to a "last Faust" who has turned down the seduction of a *caligulisme intellectuel* ("All knowledge in one head, and to cut it off, to cut off one's own")[51] and resisted the temptations of rejuvenated return along with everything else—except . . . to write his memoirs?

Linked to this new argument for a post-ordering of *Lust* after the

Solitaire is the fact that the problem of how man can escape from the circle of the eternal return is indeed replayed in Faust's encounter with *Lust*. Here a long description in the *Cahiers*, entitled *Faust III*, is especially instructive. It takes off from the maxim, "all experience already done is worth nothing," and then applies it to the problem of love, "to find its like, or rather the person with whom the relation of love will lead to that break with known conditions." This "higher degree of love" is then defined (XXIV, 374-75) in a way that can be refound in the dialectic of the CEM-formula and the other as well as in the reprise of the Garden of Eden. Faust's confession, that "I am your *maître*, Lust, and it is you who have taught me the one thing that neither knowledge nor crime nor magic taught me" (IV, 2), would then be the precarious instant of a convergence between knowledge and the feeling of happiness which fulfills itself in the *moi fini* of the other on the far side of exhausted knowledge and the mere reproduction of life.[52] Fulfills itself, and yet cannot obtain a duration, as the foreseen departure scene shows. Whether with this the explicit character of *Mon Faust*, which Valéry indicated in another note with *Final: Harmoniques* (*Cahiers* XXIII, 913), would have been attained cannot be proved. If I, along with many interpreters, prefer this ending, I am also conscious that *Le Solitaire* cannot be subsumed under *Lust* without a *reste* (as well as the inverse), probably because it was not by accident that Valéry left both plays unfinished: their contradictions lie in the matter itself, in the various attempts to escape from radical skepticism.

VIII

Hermeneutic reflection cannot and need not deny the horizon of contemporary interests that continually co-conditions the kind and manner of questioning, even if the selection and sequence of question and answer must be corrected and decided from the perspective of the object of investigation. If, in concluding, we look back upon this process, the question of the Faust myth renewed by Goethe — whether and how the world left to human knowledge might be able to fulfill the human claim to happiness — has certainly not lost any of its interest. For today's interpreter, Goethe's answer would be questionable less because of the idealistic formulation of happiness, which would already lie in striving, and not only in definitive possession, than because of its legitimation by means of a theodicy with obscure premises and consequences. Already in Goethe's time, salvation "from above" could no longer solve the question of whether "this whole" was not indeed "made only for a god"; even if, at the end of *Faust II*, one still only wants to see an instance of poetic justice, this aesthetic solution nonetheless lets the existence and fate of others fall back, unjustified, upon the secularized path to salvation of self-enjoying subjectivity.

For Valéry, the historical development since Goethe eliminated the interest in the question of a theodicy and thereby also the problem of the justification of evil and salvation. Meanwhile, the question of eudaemonia renewed by Goethe was, for Valéry, not overcome through the triumph of theoretical curiosity, but rather increasingly sharpened through the truth-claim of scientific knowledge. Valéry's new answer contains a renouncing of all Faustian striving, including the illusions of technological domination of the world, leads to the overcoming of the Cartesian idol of pure mind, and arrives finally at a formulation of happiness that promises to invert the mythology of the fall into sin. In this threefold regard, *Mon Faust* also always leads beyond positions that Valéry himself had adopted earlier. The student who, with his threefold key of KNOWLEDGE - POWER - WILL (III, 5), represents the concept of *poiesis* from the Leonardo essays from which the destructive capability of the positive sciences proceeds, stands in contrast to the ecstasy of the "maître" with the opposing functions of BREATHING - SEEING - TOUCHING. Thus explained, the system of the CEM-formula developed in the *Cahiers* is proved to be deficient in the "hand-play" as well as later in the discovery of the Cartesian error, so long as it can not become a whole through the co-presence of the other. And the love between man and woman, which Valéry often — as still cited at the beginning of *Mon Faust* — debunked as a "gross convulsion," arrives in the encounter between Faust and *Lust* at a "tenderness, which love always is in its state of being born and reborn," which was to redeem once again the promise of happiness of the denied paradise in the mythological reply of the planned fourth act. Admittedly, a no less poetic conclusion than that of Goethe's *Faust*, and surely still less a solution to the problematic of human society and history! But for that very reason one of the most beautiful and — for the poet of the Moi pur — most surprising justifications of poetry: "This harmonious agreement would be more than an agreement of thought; is there not as well there the fulfillment of the promise which poetry represents, which is, after all, nothing but the attempt at communion?"

Chapter 5
The Poetic Text within the Change of Horizons of Reading: The Example of Baudelaire's "Spleen II"

I. The Distinguishing of Various Horizons of Reading as a Problem for Literary Hermeneutics

The following study has the character of an experiment. I will attempt to distinguish methodologically into three stages of interpretation that which normally remains undistinguished in the interpretive practice of philological commentary as well as textual analysis. If it is the case there that understanding and interpretation as well as immediate reception and reflective exegesis of a literary text are at once blended in the course of interpretation, then here the horizon of a first, aesthetically perceptual reading will be distinguished from that of a second, retrospectively interpretive reading. To this I will add a third, historical reading that begins with the reconstruction of the horizon of expectations in which the poem "Spleen" inscribed itself with the appearance of the *Fleurs du mal*, and that then will follow the history of its reception or "readings" up to the most recent one, that is, my own.

The three steps of my interpretation—no methodological innovation of mine—are grounded in the theory that the hermeneutic process is to be conceived as a unity of the three moments of understanding (*intelligere*), interpretation (*interpretare*), and application (*applicare*). Hans-Georg Gadamer deserves the credit for having brought the significance of this triadic unity of the hermeneutic process back to light.[1] This unity has determined, in a manner more or less one-sidedly realized, all textual interpretation from time immemorial; it was explicitly formulated by pietistic hermeneutics during the Enlightenment as the doctrine of the three *subtilitates*; it became discredited with the victory of the historicist and positivist ideal of scholarship; and it took center stage in the development of theory with the renewal of theological and juridical hermeneutics. The obvious backwardness of literary hermeneutics is explainable by the facts that here the hermeneutic process reduces to interpretation alone, that no theory of understanding has been developed for texts of an aesthetic character, and that the question of "application" has been relegated to book reviewers' criticism as an unscholarly one. Gadamer's suggestion, "to redefine the hermeneutics of the human studies from the perspective of the hermeneutics of jurisprudence and theology," is thus an opportunity for literary hermeneutics,[2] for the sake of which I ask the question whether and how the hermeneutic unity of all three moments realizes itself in the interpretation of a poetic text.

I direct my hermeneutic experiment at this problem by dividing into three steps the interpretation of a poem that already has a history of reception. The steps might be described phenomenologically as three successive readings. In dividing the hermeneutic process into these steps, the distinction between the three readings must be fabricated to a certain degree; yet only in this manner is it possible to demonstrate what kind of understanding, interpretation, and application might be proper to a text of aesthetic character. If there is to be an autonomous literary hermeneutics, it must prove itself in the fact —as Peter Szondi correctly demanded—"that it does not just consider the aesthetic character of the text to be interpreted in an appreciation that only follows upon the interpretation, but rather that makes the aesthetic character the premise of the interpretation itself."[3] This premise cannot be fulfilled with the methods of traditional stylistics (in the sense of Leo Spitzer's "critique des beautés"), linguistic poetics, and "textual analysis" alone. Whatever may be recognized in the final texture of the text, in the closed whole of its structure, as a verbal function bearing significance or as aesthetic equivalency, always presupposes something provisionally understood. That which the poetic text, thanks to its aesthetic character, provisionally offers to understanding proceeds from its processlike effect; for this reason it cannot be directly deduced from a description of its final structure as "artifact," however comprehensively this might have construed its "levels" and its aesthetic equivalencies. Today, the structural description of texts can and should be grounded hermeneutically in an analysis of the process of reception: the debate between Roman Jakobson and Claude Lévi-Strauss, and Michael Riffaterre teaches as much.[4] The poetic text can be disclosed in its aesthetic function only when the poetic structures that are read out of the finished aesthetic object as its characteristics are retranslated, from out of the objectification of the description, back into the process of the experience of the text that allows the reader to take part in the genesis of the aesthetic object. Put another way, and using the formulation with which Michael Riffaterre in 1962 introduced the turn from the structural description to the analysis of the reception of the poetic text: the text, which structural poetics described as the endpoint and sum of the devices actualized in it, must from now on be considered as the point of departure for its aesthetic effect; and this must be investigated in the succession of the pregiven elements of the reception that govern the process of aesthetic perception, and thereby also limit the arbitrariness of readings that are supposedly merely subjective.[5]

With the experiment begun here, I go further and in another direction than Riffaterre, who recently developed his structural stylistics into a *Semiotics of Poetry* (1978), which is more interested in the pregiven elements of reception and in the "rules of actualization" than in the aesthetic activity of the reader who takes up or receives the text.[6] I, on the other hand, seek to divide this activity into the two hermeneutic acts, understanding and interpretation, in that I distinguish reflective interpretation as the phase of a second reading from immediate understanding within aesthetic perception as the phase of the first reading. This distinction was necessitated by my interest in making, once and for all, the aesthetic character of the poetic text expressly and demonstrably into the premise of its interpretation. To recognize how the poetic text, thanks to its aesthetic character, allows us to initially perceive and understand something, the analysis cannot begin with the question of the significance of the particular within the achieved form of the whole; rather, it must pursue the significance still left open in the process of perception that the text, like a "score," indicates for the reader. The investigation of the aesthetic character proper to the poetic text, in distinction to the theological, the juridical, or even the philosophical one, must follow the orientation given to aesthetic perception through the construction of the text, the suggestion of its rhythm, and the gradual achievement of its form.

In the poetic text, aesthetic understanding is primarily directed at the process of perception; therefore it is hermeneutically related to the horizon of expectations of the first reading—which often, especially with historically distant texts or with hermetic lyrics, can only be made visible in its shaped coherence and its fullness of significance through repeated readings. The explicit interpretation in the second and in each further reading also remains related to the horizon of expectations of the first, i.e., perceptual reading—as long as the interpreter claims to make concrete a specific coherence of significance from out of the horizon of meaning of this text, and would not, for example, exercise the license of allegoresis to translate the meaning of the text into a foreign context, that is, to give it a significance transcending the horizon of meaning and thereby the intentionality of the text. The interpretation of a poetic text always presupposes aesthetic perception as its pre-understanding; it may only concretize significances that appeared or could have appeared possible to the interpreter within the horizon of his preceding reading.

Gadamer's dictum, "To understand means to understand something as an answer,"[7] must therefore be limited in regard to the poetic text. Here it can only concern the secondary act of *interpretive* understanding insofar as this concretizes a specific significance as an answer to a question; it may not, however, concern the primary act of *perceptual* understanding that introduces and constitutes the aesthetic experience of the poetic text. To be sure, aesthetic perception also always already includes understanding. For as is well known, the poetic text as an aesthetic object makes possible, in contrast to everyday perception that degenerates into a norm, a mode of perception at once more complex and more meaningful, which as aesthetic pleasure is able to rejuvenate cognitive vision or visual recognition (*aisthesis*).[8] Yet this accomplishment of aisthesis, capable of meaningful understanding, is not already in need of interpretation, and thus it also does not necessarily have the character of an answer to an implicit or explicit question. If it should hold for the reception of a poetic text that here—as Gadamer himself, following Husserl, has formulated it—"the eidetic reduction is spontaneously achieved in aesthetic experience,"[9] then the understanding within the act of aesthetic perception may not be assigned to an interpretation that—by the very fact that something is understood as an answer—reduces the surplus of meaning of the poetic text to one of its possible utterances. In the eidetic reduction of aesthetic perception, the reflective reduction on the part of the interpretation that would understand the text as an answer to an implicit question, can for the time being remain suspended, while at the same time an understanding can be at work allowing the reader to experience language in its power and, thereby, the world in its fullness of significance.

The distinguishing of reflective interpretation from the perceptual understanding of a poetic text is thus not as artificial as it might at first have seemed. It is made possible throught the self-evident horizonal structure of the experience of rereading. Every reader is familiar with the experience that the significance of a poem often discloses itself only on rereading, after returning from the end to the beginning. Here the experience of the first reading becomes the horizon of the second one: what the reader received in the progressive horizon of aesthetic perception can be articulated as a theme in the retrospective horizon of interpretation. If one adds that the interpretation itself may in turn become the foundation for an application—more precisely, that a text from the past is of interest not only in reference to its primary context, but that it is also interpreted to disclose a possible significance for the contemporary situation—then what comes to light is that the triadic unity of understanding, interpretation, and application (such as it is accomplished in the hermeneutic process) corresponds to the three horizons of relevance—thematic, interpretive, and motivational—the mutual relation of which, according to Alfred Schütz, determines the constitution of the subjective experience of the life-world [Lebenswelt].[10]

In executing the experiment of a repeated reading that will seek to identify thematically the three acts of the hermeneutic process, I may take up and develop further notions that Michael Riffaterre, Wolfgang Iser, and Roland Barthes have introduced into the analysis of the processes of reception. Riffaterre analyzes the course of the reception of a poem as the play of anticipation and correction conditioned through the categories of equivalence of tension, surprise, disappointment, irony, and comedy. An "overdetermination" is common to these categories that demands attention through the respective correction of an expectation, thereby steering the reader's course of reception and, consequently, progressively determining the meaning of the text to be interpreted. In my experience, Riffaterre's categories are more appropriate to narrative texts than to lyric ones: the reading of a poem awakens not so much tension regarding its continuation, as the expectation of what I would like to call lyrical consistency—the expectation that the lyrical movement will allow one to grasp verse by verse a coherence at first hidden, and thus allow the spectacle of the world to arise anew from a particular situation. Innovation and recognition become complementary in lyrical aisthesis, so that the positive category of satisfied expectation may be placed alongside Riffaterre's negative categories of surprise and disappointment, in which he speaks of satisfied expectation only perjoratively, as if it were equivalent to the effect of a cliché.[11]

Finally, his model for the reception of a poem presupposes the ideal reader ("superreader") who is not only equipped with the sum total of literary historical knowledge available today, but also is capable of consciously registering every aesthetic impression and referring it back to the text's structure of effect. Thus the interpreting competence overshadows the analysis of the perceptual understanding, even though Riffaterre interprets within the open horizon of the syntagmatic unfolding and correction of the system. To escape this dilemma, I have not fabricated something like a "naive reader," but rather have transposed myself into the role of a reader with the educational horizon of our contemporary present. The role of this historical reader should presuppose that one is experienced in one's associations with lyrics, but that one can initially suspend one's literary historical or linguistic competence, and put in its place the capacity occasionally to wonder during the course of the reading, and to express this wonder in the form of questions. Beside this historical reader from 1979, I have placed a commentator with scholarly competence, who deepens the aesthetic impressions of the reader whose understanding takes the form of pleasure, and who refers back to the text's structures of effect as much as possible. (In what follows, this commentary is indicated through indentation.)

Since I still do not yet suffer from not having become an empiricist, I can calmly put up with the fact that my solution does not yet provide the model for the overdue empirical research into reception. I will probably bring upon myself the reproach of not being typical enough as a reader, and not being sufficiently versed in linguistics or semiotics as an analyst; and yet I hope to have tested practically the theoretical postulate of combining structural and semiotic analysis with phenomenological interpretation and hermeneutic reflection. To find a methodological starting-point capable of further development, it was for me above all a matter of separating more sharply than has been done before the levels of aesthetic perception and reflective interpretation in the interpretation of poetic texts. An initial methodological advance may already result from this separation, namely that with the help of the question-answer relationship, the textual signals may now be specified within their syntagmatic coherence as the givens of the course of the reception that establish consistency. The "structures-of-appeal," "offers-of-identification," and "absences of meaning" [*Appellstrukturen, Identifikationsangebote, und Sinnlücken*] that Wolfgang Iser has conceived as categories in his theory of aesthetic effect are most easily made concrete in the course of the reception as inducements toward the constitution of meaning when one describes the effective factors of the poetic text as expectations, and transposes them into questions that the text in such passages either produces, leaves open, or answers.[12] If Iser, in *The Act of Reading*—in contrast to Riffaterre, who views the process of reception under the dominant category of overdetermination and interprets it *nolens volens*—has rehabilitated the aesthetic character of fictional texts under the dominant category of "indeterminacy" (and "redeterminability"), it nonetheless remained to me to describe the course of the reception in the first, perceptual reading as an experience of accumulating evidence that is also aesthetically more convincing, which, in turn, as the pregiven horizon for a second, interpretive reading, at once opens up and delimits the space for possible concretizations.

Accordingly, the change of horizons between the first and the second readings may be described as follows: the reader—who performs the "score" of the text in the course of the reception of verse after verse, and who is led toward the ending in a perceptual act of anticipation, from the particular toward the possible whole of form and meaning—becomes aware of the fulfilled form of the poem, but not yet of its fulfilled significance, let alone of its "whole meaning." Whoever acknowledges the hermeneutic premise that the meaningful whole of a lyric work is no longer to be understood as if substantial, as if its meaning were pregiven and timeless; rather, it is to be understood as a meaning to be performed—whoever acknowledges this premise awaits from the reader the recognition that from now on he may, in the act of interpretive understanding, hypostasize one among other possible significations of the poem, the relevance of which for him does not exclude the worth of others for discussion. From now on, the reader will seek and establish the still unfulfilled significance retrospectively, through a new reading, from the perspective of the fulfilled form, in a return from the end to the beginning, from the whole to the particular. Whatever initially resisted understanding manifests itself in the questions that the first going-through has left open. In answering them, one may expect that from the particular elements of significance—in various respects still indeterminate—a fulfilled whole may be established on the level of meaning through the labor of interpretation, which whole is every bit as much on the level of meaning as on the level of form. This meaningful whole can be found only through a selective taking of perspectives and cannot be attained through a supposedly objective description—

this falls under the hermeneutic premise of partiality. With this, the question of the historical horizon is posed, the horizon that conditioned the genesis and effect of the work and that once again delimits the present reader's interpretation. To investigate it is now the task of a third, historical reading.

This third step, insofar as it concerns the interpretation of a work from the premises of its time and genesis, is the one most familiar to historical-philological hermeneutics. Yet there the historically reconstructive reading is traditionally the first step, to which historicism adds the injunction that the interpreter has to ignore himself and his standpoint to be able to take up ever more purely the "objective meaning" of the text. Under the spell of this scholarly ideal, the objectivistic illusions of which are evident to almost everyone today, the hermeneutics of the classical and modern philologies sought to privilege historical understanding over the aesthetic appreciation, which, for its part, was rarely attempted at all. Such historicism failed to recognize that the aesthetic character of its texts—as a hermeneutic bridge denied to other disciplines—is that which makes possible the historical understanding of art across the distance in time in the first place, and which therefore must be integrated into the execution of the interpretation as a hermeneutic premise. But inversely, aesthetic understanding and interpretation also remain in reference to the controlling function of the historicist-reconstructive reading. It prevents the text from the past from being naively assimilated to the prejudices and expectations of meaning of the present, and thereby—through explicitly distinguishing the past horizon from the present—allows the poetic text to be seen in its alterity. The investigation of the "otherness," the unique distance, within the contemporaneity of the literary text, demands a reconstructive reading that can begin by seeking out the questions (most often unexplicit ones) to which the text was the response in its time. An interpretation of a literary text as a response should include two things: its response to expectations of a formal kind, such as the literary tradition prescribed for it before its appearance; and its response to questions of meaning such as they could have posed themselves within the historical life-world of its first readers. The reconstruction of the original horizon of expectations would nonetheless fall back into historicism if the historical interpretation could not in turn serve to transform the question, "What did the text say?" into the question, "What does the text say to me, and what do I say to it?" If, like theological or juridical hermeneutics, literary hermeneutics is to move from understanding, through interpretation, to application, then application here certainly cannot dissolve into practical action, but rather instead can satisfy the no less legitimate interest of using literary communication with the past to measure and to broaden the horizon of one's own experience vis-à-vis the experience of the other.

The omission of the distinguishing of horizons can have consequences such as may be indicated with the analysis of the reception of a Poe story by Roland Barthes.[13] Its strength lies in the demonstration of how the structuralist description of the narrative principle —which explains the text as a variant of a pregiven model—can be transformed into the textual analysis of "significance" that allows one to understand the text as a process, as an ongoing production of meaning or, more precisely, of possibilities of meaning ("the forms, the codes according to which meanings are possible").[14] Its weakness lies in a naive fusing of horizons: according to its own intention, the reading is supposed to be unmediated and ahistorical ("we will take up the text as it is, as it is when we read it"[15]), and yet this reading only comes about through a "superreader" who brings a comprehensive knowledge of the nineteenth century into play and who, in the course of the reception, notes those passages above all where cultural and linguistic codes can be recalled or associated. One cannot speak of a joining of the interpretation to the process of aesthetic perception, for this, as the "code of the 'actants' " in combination with the "symbolic code or field," can itself only be one more code among others (the "scientific, rhetorical, chronological, destinatory code," etc.).[16] Thus, a reading arises that is neither historical nor aesthetic, but rather is as subjective as it is impressionistic, and yet is supposed to ground the theory that each particular text is a tissue of texts— the interminable play of a free-floating intertextuality in "the struggle between man and signs."[17]

Literary hermeneutics, which Barthes not accidentally views as a (for him) "aenigmatic code," is on the contrary surely no longer interested today in interpreting the text as the revelation of the single truth concealed within it.[18] Against the theory of the "plural text," with its notion of "intertextuality" as a limitless and arbitrary production of possibilities of meaning and of no less arbitrary interpretations, literary hermeneutics poses the hypothesis that the concretization of the meaning of literary works progresses historically and follows a certain "logic" that precipitates in the formation and transformation of the aesthetic canon. Furthermore, it postulates that in the change of horizons of the interpretations, one may distinguish absolutely between arbitrary interpretations and those available to a consensus, between those that are merely original and those that are formative of a norm. The fundamental aspect that supports this hypothesis can lie only in the aesthetic character of the texts: as a regulative principle, it allows for there being a series of interpretations, but that are also capable of being reintegrated with respect to the meaning made concrete. Here I may recall the attempt at a pluralistic interpretation of Apollinaire's poem "L'arbre," undertaken at the second colloquium of the *Poetik und Hermeneutik* group. On the one hand, the distance vis-à-vis the poem adopted by each reader itself allowed for a different aesthetic perception to arise, and each specific concretization of the significance necessarily had to ignore other, no less plausible interpretations. And yet, the surprising confirmation that the individual interpretations did not contradict one another despite their differences led to the conclusion that even this "pluralistic text" can provide a unifying aesthetic orientation for perceptual understanding within the horizon of the first reading.[19]

To be sure, one may object that, after Baudelaire, a modern poem cannot furnish the reader with this evidence of a compelling whole after only the first reading, but rather only in rereading. And one may object that, mutatis mutandis, a poem from an older tradition or from another culture often only discloses itself for aesthetic understanding when historicist understanding has removed the obstacles to its reception and rendered possible an aesthetic perception of the formerly unenjoyable text. I am also thoroughly of this opinion,[20] so that I can use these objections for precisely one last point.

The priority of aesthetic perception within the triad of literary hermeneutics has need of the *horizon*, but not the temporal priority, of the first reading; this horizon of aesthetic understanding may also be gained only in the course of rereading or with the help of historicist understanding. Aesthetic perception is no universal code with timeless validity, but rather—like all aesthetic experience—is intertwined with historical experience. Thus, for the interpretation of texts from other cultures, the aesthetic character of poetic texts from the western tradition can only offer heuristic advantages. Literary interpretation must compensate with the three achievements of the hermeneutic process for the fact that aesthetic perception itself is subject to historical exchange. It thereby gains the opportunity of broadening historicist knowledge through aesthetic understanding, and perhaps of constituting, through its unconstrained kind of application, a corrective to other applications that are subject to situational pressures and the compulsions of decision-making.

II. The Progressive Horizon of Aesthetic Perception (a Hermeneutic Reconstruction of the First Reading)

Spleen

J'ai plus de souvenirs que si j'avais mille ans.

Un gros meuble à tiroirs encombré de bilans,
De vers, de billets doux, de procès, de romances,
Avec de lourds cheveux roulés dans des quittances,
Cache moins de secrets que mon triste cerveau.
6   C'est une pyramide, un immense caveau,
Qui contient plus de morts que la fosse commune.
—Je suis un cimetière abhorré de la lune,
Où, comme des remords, se traînent de longs vers
Qui s'acharnent toujours sur mes morts les plus chers.
Je suis un vieux boudoir plein de roses fanées,
12   Où gît tout un fouillis de modes surannées,
Où les pastels plaintifs et les pâles Boucher,
Seuls, respirent l'odeur d'un flacon débouché.

Rien n'égale en longueur les boiteuses journées,
Quand sous les lourds flocons des neigeuses années
L'ennui, fruit de la morne incuriosité,
18   Prend les proportions de l'immortalité.
—Désormais tu n'es plus, ô matière vivante!
Qu'un granit entouré d'une vague épouvante,
Assoupi dans le fond d'un Sahara brumeux!
Un vieux sphinx ignoré du monde insoucieux,
Oublié sur la carte, et dont l'humeur farouche
24   Ne chante qu' aux rayons du soleil qui se couche.

I have more memories than if I were a thousand years old.

A large chest of drawers cluttered with accounts,
With poems, love letters, legal briefs, songs,
With thick locks of hair wrapped in receipts,
Conceals fewer secrets than my sad brain.
6   It's a pyramid, an immense vault,
That contains more dead than a communal grave.
—I am a cemetery abhorred by the moon,
Where, like remorse, long worms crawl
Who always work on my dearest dead.
I am an old boudior full of faded roses,
12   Where a whole jumble of outmoded fashion lies,

Where plaintive pastels and wan Bouchers,
Alone, breathe in the scent of an uncorked bottle.

Nothing equals the halting days in length,
When, under the heavy flakes of the snowy years,
Boredom, fruit of gloomy incuriosity,
18   Takes the proportions of immortality.
— Henceforth you are no more, O living matter!
Than a block of granite surrounded by a vague terror,
Slumbering in the depths of a hazy Sahara!
An old sphinx ignored by a careless world,
Forgotten on the maps, and whose ill humor
24   Sings only to the rays of a sun that sets.

"Spleen": A poem that announces itself with this title poses several initial questions for the contemporary reader. What does *spleen* mean, and what can the word mean precisely as the title to a poem? Does it hint at a condition like depression, or only at the eccentric mood of one person? Will someone speak of himself here, of the world, including our world, or only of his own? (Please remember: the indented passages represent the commentary of my "historical reader of the present.")

For the reader of our present time, the title "Spleen" discloses the horizon of an open, largely still-indeterminate expectation and, with this, initiates the suspense of a word's meaning that can only be clarified through the reading of the poem. For in today's German usage (and in French as well), "spleen" has sunk to the trivial significance of a "tick," a "fixed idea"; it scarcely still allows one to suspect what sort of aura of singularity could be fitting for a person who presented his "spleen" as an attitude of wanting to be different in the face of his world. Felt as an anachronism, and allowing one to forget its original significance, the word may still recall connotations of depression (as Stefan George translated it) or of an eccentric mood for the educated reader—connotations of a consciously adopted attitude, to distinguish it from the natural characteristics of a person. The average reader can scarcely understand more by the "spleen" of a fellow person than a behavioral tick that remains fundamentally harmless, that does not hurt anyone else, and that can express itself in a fixed idea that, for the person concerned, obviously determines his relationship to the world as a whole in a monomaniacal way. This everyday significance returns the placement of the word in the title to the condition of the mysterious—thanks to the expectation, established by all lyric poetry, that in the medium of poetry the everyday and the occasional can take on a new and deeper significance, or recover an older, forgotten meaning.

"J'ai plus de souvenirs que si j'avais mille ans" (l. 1): The voice of an unknown "I" speaks into the space of the expectation awakened by the title word of "Spleen." It names itself already with the first word, and with the first line it strikes a tone that surprises the reader through the overpowering claim "to possess more memories than a life of a thousand years could comprehend." The word-sequence as well as the rhythm of this first line, separated off like a preamble, heightens the general impression that the realm evoked by the memories stretches into the immeasurable. The comparative phrase, "More memories than," is redeemed in the second half of the line through the unexpectedly high number, "thousand"; and yet precisely this weighty magnitude (with the connotation of "millenium") is, in its naming, already surpassed, the number extending into the limitless through the preceding "plus de." Read as a line of verse, the following accents may be noted:[21] *J'ai plus de s̄ouvenirs que s̄i j'avais mīlle ans*: also noted is a rhythm that in the first half-line works harmonically with the regular ("pseudoiambic") sequence of weakly and strongly accented syllables, but that in the second half-line works in a troublesome way with the main accents suspended and bumping up next to one another through the four unaccented syllables.

The accents on the "strong words" *souvenirs, mille,* and *ans* could be supplemented through secondary verse accents: in the first half-line, on *plus* in the second syllable (to bridge the large distance to the sixth syllable with the main accent), and possibly also on the fourth syllable, But in the second half-line the first four syllables can, on grammatical grounds, scarcely support an accent, so that special weight falls on the last two words suspended through the four unaccented syllables.

With *mille,* the reader can scarcely miss hearing the echo of the main-accented *ī* of *souvenīrs,* which it's placement before the middle caesura accents even more, so that the repeating vowel renders even more conspicuous the delimitation of the memories to the number thousand and "more than a thousand," as well as the reversal of the harmony of the first half-line in the disproportion of the second.

Symmetry and asymmetry are peculiarly enfolded in the first

line. With the middle caesura, which seeks to guarantee metrical-
ly the equivalence of the two half-lines, Baudelaire composition-
ally opened the symmetrical construction of the classical alexandrine onto the asymmetry of the immeasurable: a phonetic
preponderance of the *ī*-sound in the second half-line, which re-
inforces the meaning (*souvenirs*, highlighted through the final
position of the syllable before the caesura, as opposed to a twofold repetition of the *ī* in *sī* and *mīlle*), corresponds to the semantic surpassing of *mille ans* through the *plus de* in the first
half-line, so that the hyperbolic number "thousand"—phonetically announced as the peak of the *i*-series—becomes the counter-
point to *souvenirs*. But as one retrospectively recognizes, *spleen*
(through the long *ī*) also already belongs to this signifying series
of sounds, so that between the title word and the first line equivalence of significance is suggested that recalls the reader's suspended questions at the outset, and allows one to concretize
them anew.

If the first line already states something about the *spleen* of the "I"
who speaks, is it a condition of the greatest happiness or the deepest
suffering? Is it self-presumption or doubt that speaks out of it? Does
a boldness encroach here, or an agony predominate?

Lines 2-5: The reading of the lines following the first comes to a
halt after line five.

The halt is syntactically marked by the end of the sentence; in
the ongoing continuation of the reading as well, the ends of
sentences will provide the most obvious subdivisions within the
two unequal strophes of the poem.

The beginning of line two, "Un gros meuble à tiroirs," is transitionless, and through a motivation that is at first unrecognizable, it arouses the tension of wondering whether and how the description of a
dressing or writing table—extending ever further through three lines
—might then hang together with the initial leading theme of the
memories of the speaking "I" that is struck up in line one. This tension only resolves itself—and explosively, as it were—at the end of
line five with the long-delayed figure of a scarcely awaited comparison: "Cache moins de secrets que mon triste cerveau."

The tension produced by the structure of this verse construction allows one to grasp once again the expectation of lyric
consistency that is essential for aesthetic perception. Here everything works together in the grammatical and phonetic organi-

zation to allow the shocking resolution of the thematic expectation posed with "un gros meuble" to appear as a decisive contrast: the surpassing constructed once again in a comparative "moins de secrets que" (after the "plus de" of l.1), and the fall from the stylistic heights and thing-filled plenitude of the bureau into the prosaic character of the technical medical term *cerveau* that is also already announced phonetically and then, as it were, exploded through a doubled series of *s*-alliterations and consonantal *r*-connections (*secrets . . . triste . . . cerveau*). One can also speak of an explosive effect of the rhyme-word on the semantic level, where the reversal appears in the middle of the tight combination of adjective and substantive (one would expect "soul" or "heart" after the poetic epithet "sad," and hardly "brain"!) and is heightened even more through the rhyme. If one follows the chain of rhymes, then through the equivalences of *a* with the transition from the simple to the complex rhymes (from *a* in ll. 3/4), the effect is produced of a steady growth heightened through the homonymy (from *ans-bilans* to *romances-quittances*), which the *o*-rhyme of line five then suddenly disrupts.

With the comparison between writing desk and brain, the reader is offered a solution to the question regarding the connection between the opening line and the next group of verses: isn't the old desk covered with a jumble of mementos also a place of memories, the sum-total of time used up, perhaps even a possession of that "I" who at the beginning gazed back on an immeasurable plenitude of memories? Is the chaotic state of the desk, with its unfathomed secrets, a sign for how the "I" possessed of "spleen" comes upon its plenitude of memories within its remembrance? Does "Spleen" as the title word mean precisely this view of the mute relics of a past ossified into chaos? Yet opposed to this solution is the fact that, in its comparison, the lyric "I" also once again already distinguishes itself from the compared term: the "remembrance" of the bureau conceals fewer secrets than its "sad brain," so that the disorder of the things in lines 2-4 is a different state of affairs. In lingering with one's first reading, the reader can already gain the impression that prosaic and poetic things contrast charmingly in the mess on the chest of drawers, and that the catalog peaks with the grotesque image of "locks of hair wrapped in receipts"—in brief, that it is a matter of a "beautiful disorder." Toward what might it be leading?

While the thematic trajectory as a whole allows the recounting of the leftovers of the past to develop symmetrically, the smaller imagistic units constitute symmetrical contrasts, also supported by the metrical system. In all the verses the regular middle caesura creates symmetrical half-lines that give a harmonious sense of division to the recounting of the contents of the chest of drawers. On closer inspection, the recounting itself allows one to recognize a semantic ordering principle: prosaic and poetic objects follow one another with beautiful regularity. In line two the series is begun with "accounts," upon which "poems and love letters" follow in line three. The counterweight to these is created after the middle caesura by "legal briefs," with which "songs" contrast once again in the same half-line. In the next line, this method of producing a beautiful disorder is driven into a kind of bottleneck: the succession of heterogeneous things turns into their admixture, when "locks of hair" appear that are rolled up in "receipts." Thus the poetic catalog of a past stored up in disorder culminates in the profanation of the beautiful, in a final grotesque image of sentimental love.

"C'est une pyramide, un immense caveau" (ll. 6/7): as if the "I" that speaks would not itself provide an answer to the implicit question of what its remembrance might then be, if it is to be still more and different than the desk in the comparison, the next pair of lines begins with a provocative utterance on the part of the self that is surprising in its immediacy and that strikes up anew the measured tone of the first line. Once again a movement toward the overly large comes into play that is not satisfied with the image of the pyramid, but that surpasses even the representation of the immense grave through the comparative construction of a further comparison: "qui contient plus de morts que la fosse commune." But the sequence of images that carries this movement toward excess also suggests a second line of significance that is striking in its contrast: the far-reaching movement of memory can evidently grasp only what is dead. It culminates in the past-become-stone of the pyramid, and in the heap of bones of the mass grave. Does the decay of memory into a remembrance that contains only what is dead accordingly allow us to understand what "spleen" can mean for the lyric "I"?

The provocative element in the renewed utterance on the part of the self lies not only in the reprise of the apodictic tone of line one, but also in the concealed synchronization of the newly appearing pair of lines with line five. Here the analysis can make note of the equivalences of the "strong words" as well as a syntactic countersymmetry between line five and lines six and seven. The strong accent before the ever-preserved middle caesura and at the line-ends establishes a positional ordering of significance of *secrets, pyramide,* and *morts* on the one hand, and of *cerveau, caveau,* and *fosse commune* on the other. Between the small secrets of the bureau and the large ones of the pyramid, as between the small container of the brain and the large one of the grave, a disproportion arises that sets the development toward the immeasurable into play for a third time (after the memories of line one and the relics of lines two to four). Only with *morts* does the third member of the two lines of significance bring the *tertium comparationis* to light, and then bring about (as previously with *cerveau* of line five in contrast to lines two to four) the fall from the stylistic heights: with *fosse commune* as the final member of the comparison for the abstruse remembrance, the crassest representation of a worthless gravesite destroys the aura that surrounded a pyramid as the most sublime sort of grave. The syntactic parallelism of the opposing comparative formulations *moins de* (l. 5) and *plus de* (l. 7) can serve various functions. It arranges *secrets* and *morts* with one another, so that one can ask oneself whether those secrets of the remembrance were to mean its dead. It heightens once again the movement toward excess through the figures of surpassing. And finally, it serves here as well to distinguish once again the "I" in its comparisons from the compared elements. To the extent that this view already holds for the comparative formulation *plus de* in the first line, as well as for all of the previous three utterances on the part of the self, the effect of a discontinuous movement arises.

The lyrical "I" undertakes again and again the attempt to identify itself, in that it poses one comparison after another and then takes them back. Will this movement come to an end, and will the "I" perhaps arrive at itself?

"Je suis un cimetière abhorré de la lune" (ll. 8-11): a dash is scarcely needed here as a typographical signal that would make the new beginning of the following group of lines unmistakable. For here, where the new line once again—as previously only at the poem's beginning—begins with "I" as the first word, the self-proclamation takes on the strangest form: "I am a cemetery abhorred by the moon." If a certain distance of observation had still been maintained in the series of comparisons of the self with the bureau, pyramid, and mass grave, then the movement now turns into a self-identification that demands of the reader that he step across a threshold into the unreal and the uncanny. The uncanny is rendered most strongly perceptible through the onomatopoetic *abhorré*, which introduces a series of graveyard thoughts that is once again more familiar. The reader, who [the scholarly analyst would point out] is led by the parallel line-openings, and looks back from the graveyard lines to the opening line, can ask himself whether the connection now brought to light might mean that the immeasurable collection of memories of which the "I" boasted in the first line has now passed into the uncanniness of the Golgotha that the same "I," after line eight, is or believes it is. Would this mean that the question of what "Spleen" means for the "I" that speaks is already answered?

The syntactic parallelism in the strong opening positions of "J'ai" (l. 1) and "Je suis" (l. 8)—which highlight the first and fourth sentences in front of the intervening ones through the "I" as a repeating subject—can hardly be missed. For the syntactic correspondence is furthermore also supported through phonetic equivalences: "Je suis un cimetière" (l. 8) repeats the signifying *i*-series of line one three times over. Lines nine and ten, with the imagery of the graveyard lyric that has become clichéd for us, would indeed fall into the category of the trivial, were it not that the *or*-syllable of the onomatopoetically uncanny *abhorré* is maintained in *remords* (l. 9) and *morts* (l. 10), and that the double-meaning of *vers* (worms or verses) gives a grotesque *pointe* to the familiar topos of *vanitas*.

"Je suis un vieux boudoir" (ll. 11-14): The expectation that the attempts of the lyric "I" to describe his state of mind had come to rest with the "graveyard of memories"—this expectation is not fulfilled. The unrest that, even in that imagery, had not been thoroughly pacified ("de long vers qui s'acharnent toujours," ll. 9/10) takes the upper hand once again. As if this "I," driven by an inexplicable motivation—is it doubt, anxiety, or a certain unnamed suffering?—must always seek its identity in a different realm of used-up time, it now reaches out toward a space that conjures up a new parade of memories. It is an old boudoir, with a decor within it that allows one to recall the old bureau; [the scholarly analyst adds that] even the distant but still audible internal rhyme *meuble à tiroir / vieux boudoir* encourages this retrospective comparison. Once again the things take on the shape of a beautiful disorder. But this time they offer not the view of an accidental heap of incompatible elements, but rather conjoin into the harmonious ensemble of an elegant lady's room.

The first impression of a finely tuned harmony, all the more strongly noticeable after the dissonant graveyard verses, arises above all from the effect of two rich rhyme-pairs that contrapuntally maintain the main accent of the vowel *e* in the end-rhyme for eight lines, in a willed monotony that allows for a delicate play with the minimal deviation within the alternation between feminine (*fanēēs/surannēēs*) and masculine (*Bouchēr/débouché*) rhymes. Baudelaire's concept of poetic language—which must correspond to "the immortal needs for monotony, symmetry and surprise" in man[22] —could scarcely be better illustrated.

On closer examination, the harmony of this beautiful disorder is nonetheless already bathed in the light of decay: the things of the decor are all accompanied by an adjective expressing decline ("roses fanées," "modes surannées," "pastels plaintifs," "pâles Boucher," "flacon débouché"), and in their solitariness ("seuls, respirent l'odeur d'un flacon débouché") they allow one to feel an emptiness, not to say the disappearance of an occupant (one of the "dearest dead" of l. 10?). Does this mean that the renewed effort by the lyric "I" to find salvation in a past has once again become lost in an empty world of things decayed within themselves?

The alliteration of three *p*'s in line thirteen, which then falls to a *b*, ironizes, as it were, a decrescendo ("Où les p̄astels p̄laintifs et les p̄ales B̄oucher") that turns the word play going on between the rhyme-word *Boucher* and *débouché* into the grotesque: the still harmonious representation of the last perfume escaping from the uncorked bottle overturns into the dissonant connotation of a "decapitated" rococo painter Boucher.

"Rien n'égale en longueur les boiteuses journées" (ll. 15-18): The transitionless beginning of the next group of verses, four lines long, is not only typographically marked through a second large strophic unit, but is also marked through the fact that the "I" has unexpectedly disappeared (the two preceding sentences began

158 □ POETIC TEXT

with "Je suis"). The voice that now begins to speak appears unimplicated in the experience it first portrayed in high lyrical tones, and then, as it were, allowed to appear on stage in personified form and thereafter commented on in a tone of definitional formality. Along with the disappearance of the "I," the theme of memory also appears to have been exhausted: the *ennui* steps forth not from out of the past, but rather as the shape of an endless present, from out of the "halting days" and the "snowed-in years." Already with the first reading, the staging of its appearance must strike one: in their extraordinary onomatopoetic beauty, the preceding two lines seemed to open onto the view of a winter landscape and did not yet allow one to anticipate that which only the delayed naming of the ennui allows one to perceive—the all-permeating power of that "gloomy indifference" that before our eyes grows to an infinite size (as also manifest in the monstrous rhyme-pair (*incuriosité/immortalité*). With this movement, whether the answer to the significance of "Spleen" is to be sought in the appearance of ennui is not the only question that poses itself. There is also the further question of what it might indeed mean that this foreign power evidently raises its head and rules the stage of the world that is, from now on, the present, precisely at the moment when the "I" has stepped off that stage and has ceased to speak as a subject.

With the beginning of this group of verses, the surprising change of subject, level of tone, and temporal dimension is nonetheless provided with a transition and a contrast in that lines fifteen through eighteen immediately continue the rhyme-scheme of the preceding lines eleven through fourteen. Thus the two four-line strophes, equivalently rhymed, constitute a symmetrical whole precisely at the break between the two large strophic units (ll. 2-14, ll. 15-25), a whole that immediately resynchronizes the strophic division, and suggests that one ought to discover lines of significance in the phonetic equivalences that had remained concealed at first glance. The symmetry of the feminine rhymes establishes a relation between *roses fanées* and *boiteuses journées*, then between *modes surannées* and *neigeuses années*. In the first case, the movement falls from the beauty of the withered roses into the negative temporal experience of the "halting days"; in the second case the passing character of yesterday's fashions is elevated up to the beautiful monotony of the "years that are like heavy snowflakes." The symmetry of the masculine rhymes allows one to expect and to recognize that the second group of four lines, as already with the first (with *Boucher/débouché*), also carries along with it an ironic significance in the background. It manifests itself in the change of tone, when first the two lines of beautiful monotony, so perfect in their onomatopoeia (as well as in the internal rhyme of the preciously placed adjectives *boiteuses/neigeuses*), delay the entrance onto the stage on the part of ennui (through enjambment and syntactic inversion), and then two contrary lines follow that gloss this appearance as if "painting with concepts." The appearance is elevated to personification, defined in terms of its origin (*fruit de*) in an allegorizing manner, and described in its effects, all with a display of learned words that fall out of the lyric rhythm through polysyllabic character alone. Along with this, the representation of the endlessly growing *ennui* takes on sensorial and audible form in the return of the ever more significant *i*-series and in the threefold *p*-alliteration ("p̄rend les p̄rop̄ortions de l'immortalité," l. 18).

The ironization culminates in that most striking rhyme-pair *incuriosité/immortalité*, and leaves behind it the question of whether in the end, if the *incuriosité* has achieved the proportions of *immortalité*, the immortality must not also fall to the "gloomy indifference."

"—Désormais tu n'es plus, ô matière vivante!" (ll. 19-24): Here the new beginning of a final group of six lines is so transitionless that it scarcely needs the dash as a typographical signal. *Désormais* turns the preceding scene around into the future, and seems to give the following lines the character of prophetic discourse. Who can speak in such a manner, and with what authority? Who is the "you" on whom this anonymous judge turns? Is it a matter of a self-address in the pathetic "you"-form, or does this "you" mean another person? What does "matière vivante" mean? Is it man as a living being, opposed to matter; is it a figure in the still unrecognized metamorphoses of the lyric subject; or is it the part of his corporeal appearance that stands opposed to the "I" in its spiritual existence? But now further surprising metamorphoses seem to fall immediately upon the "you" itself that is so mysteriously evoked: from out of "living matter," a granite block appears (the hardest stone, hard like the *k*-sound with which line twenty begins in its enjambment: "qu'un granit"); from out of the granite block, the old sphinx appears—but now, opposed to the expectation that it would be a silence-made-stone, it begins to sing, although invited by no one since no one knows of it any longer, thereby burdening the reader with the enigma of what it might indeed be singing of with its gesture of wild but sullen fury ("dont l'humeur farouche ne chante"). Along with this final, highly unexpected reshuffling of the role of the lyric subject, the external scene has also changed: in the place of the decor laden with the past, and the external world that was wintered and darkened yet nonetheless still homey, the fear-producing ("entouré d'une vague épouvante") no man's land ("oublié sur la carte") of a desert has appeared, in which only the sun—already setting and evidently indifferent (doesn't "qui se couche" respond ironically to "humeur farouche?")—remains to hear the sphinx's song.

The three rhyme-pairs give variation to the semantic contrast of *matière vivante* in such a way that the contradiction between matter and life is continually reformulated up to the end. After *vivante*, there follows—emphasized through the hiatus of the half-accented *e* from *vague* to the main-accented *é*—the pejorative word *épouvante* for the petrifying terror; in response to *brumeux* (dark), which with its connotation of "misty" still allows one to think of the life-giving element of water, there is the negative composite-word *insoucieux*. The power of negation is phonetically sharpened in line twenty-two through contrastive equivalences: the alliteration of *i* and *in* ("Un vieux sphinx ignoré du monde insoucieux") and the double recurrence of *s* (*sphinx . . . insoucieux*) have the effect that the rhyme-word —to the extent that it reuses nearly all the phonetic elements of *vieux sphinx* (even the *ö*-sound of the epithet returns in the last syllable)—not only semantically negates the existence of the old sphinx (the sign of negation *in* takes up the sound of *sphinx* and is further strengthened through the morphological equivalence with the prefix of *ignoré*); it also, as it were, literally refutes it sound by sound. On the syntactic level, the participial constructions of lines twenty through twenty-three, arranged as parallels, rather describe the progressive process of a materialization of the *matière vivante*: the series of past perfect participles *entouré-assoupi-ignoré-publié* increasingly removes the lyric subject from the life-sphere of the shared world. All the more astounding, then, the effect in line twenty-four of the turn around from the ossified condition of the past perfect into the present tense of *chante*. Delayed in the enjambment after *humeur farouche*, the active verb allows one to recognize that the gesture of revolt that was no longer expected actually already began with the ad-

versative *et*. The preceding rhyme-word *farouche* has an especially important poetic function in this turnaround. As the third
and last representative of life among the rhyme-words (after *vivante* and *brumeux*), it on the one hand deviates with its main-
accented vowel from the preceding series of *u*-sounds that, in
the words *entōūré-assōūpi-insōūcieux* and finally (the oppositive
at the beginning of the same line) *ōūblié*, supports the process of the threatening materialization. But on the other hand,
the final ironic *pointe* is constructed with the highest art: that
the sun indifferently "goes to sleep" on the side of the material
world emptied of man, whereas the sphinx gives voice to its
final song of revolt on the side of life. *"Qui se couche"* is expressed syntactically (as an uncommon attributive phrase) and
rhythmically (as an assymmetrical violation of the middle caesura that is otherwise maintained) in such a way that the semantic coincidentia oppositorum in the rhyme-pair *farouche/qui se
couche* can be said to explode.

III. The Retrospective Horizon of Interpretive Understanding (the Movement of an Interpretation in the Second Reading)

"I have found the definition of beauty — of my beauty. It is something
ardent and sad, something a bit vague, leaving free play to conjecture."[23] Baudelaire's definition of beauty via an indeterminacy that
leaves free play to "conjecture," while at the same time also already
being delimited by the coincidentia oppositorum of *ardent* and *triste*,
may here serve to begin the second movement of the interpretation.
The first movement was to follow the reader's aesthetic perception
step by step, until with the last line of the poem, its form — if not necessarily also its meaning — fulfilled itself as a whole for him. To find
the still unfulfilled meaning demands, as I already stated, the return
from the end to the beginning — so that, from the perspective of the
achieved whole of the form, the still indeterminate particulars might
be illuminated, the series of conjectures clarified in their contexts,
and the meaning still left open sought within the harmony of a coherence of meaning. The conjectures of, and questions left open by,
the first reading of the "Spleen" poem allow themselves to be brought
formally and thematically into a certain common denominator. The
perceiving understanding fell, from verse-group to verse-group, upon
gaps in the lyric consistency, upon new beginnings or transitions *ex
abrupto*, so that at first an overarching motivation remained imper-
ceptible. Thus one should ask whether a latent principle of unity, re-

cognizable only within the horizon of the second reading, lies in that manifestly fragmentary character of the lyric movement that makes itself felt as much in the irregular units of verse as in the unexpected representatives who stand for the lyric subject. And if the expectation of lyric consistency is fulfilled with the second reading, is the question then also resolved regarding the meaning of the title, the still unknown significance that spleen is supposed to have for the lyric "I"?

If one looks at the whole of the lyric form, then Baudelaire's poem is unique in that on the one hand the strict norms of the alexandrine are preserved and played upon with virtuosity, and on the other hand the symmetrical law of construction of this classical genre of poetry par excellence is continually violated by an asymmetrical unfolding and retraction of the lyric movement. If one recalls Baudelaire's definition of poetry—that it "responds with rhythm and rhyme to the immortal needs of man for monotony, symmetry and surprise"[24] — then the surprising feature of this "Spleen" poem lies in the power of the asymmetrical tendency that in the strophic-syntactic units of verse as well as in the boldness of the comparisons and self-identifications increasingly works against the harmonizing system of verse, rhyme, and syntactic parallelism, only to be brought to a standstill at the end, as if by command, in the final strophe that shoots across the rest ("—Désormais tu n'es plus, ô matière vivante!"). This manifests itself most strikingly in the irregularly developing length of the seven sentence units.

The lyrical movement passes from the smallest-verse-unit (one line, l. 1) to the largest (six lines, ll. 19-24), and within this tensional arc it heightens itself syntactically through a twofold start, as it were. That is, a sentence of four lines (ll. 2-5) follows upon the smallest sentence-unit of line one, whereupon the movement begins anew, this time with a sentence two lines long (ll. 6/7), and then develops asymmetrically according to a formula of acceleration: first three lines (ll. 8-10), then four (ll. 11-14), then four again (ll. 15-18), and finally six (ll. 19-24). The asymmetrical acceleration is itself unconstant: after the steady movement from two to three to four lines (ll. 6-14), the four-line sentence-unit reduplicates itself, so that amidst the impetuously developing asymmetry, a symmetrical structure of twice four lines unexpectedly emerges, which is also bound together most harmoniously through the sameness of the rhymes. The reader can nevertheless afterwards reperceive this configuration in the rhythm of the whole movement, as a reversal of the acceleration into a monotony that seems to grow into the immeasurable. This effect is similarly

produced through the rhyme sequence of the fourth and fifth sen-
tence-units, where first the rhyme-pair *vers/chers* follows upon *lune*,
then the doubled rhyme on *é/ée*, which extends itself monotonously
upon the twice four rhyme-words. When the asymmetrically developed total movement is then brought to a standstill at the end by
the final sentence-unit, once again harmoniously organized in three
rhyme-pairs, the whole of the lyric structure confirms what was also
to be discovered in its parts from the beginning onward. The first
five lines, through the chain of rhymes from *ans-bilans* to *romances-
quittances*, already led to the effect of a developing movement that
was then suddenly cut through by the explosively prosaic rhyme-
word *cerveau*. The formal principle that, as the composite figure of
an assymmetrical development and a sudden cutting off, organizes
the discontinuous total rhythm of the poem—this principle obviously corresponds to a thematic discovery on the part of the first reading: that the lyric "I" in the course of his self-comparisons continually distinguishes himself from the compared element, and undertakes new attempts at identification. Let us now see whether in the
recognized organization, the significance of spleen might also be discovered, which significance seemed to conceal itself from us in the
metamorphoses of the lyric "I" and of the world of things that it
evoked.

Through its being set off like a preamble, the first verse awakens
the expectation that memory could constitute the principle that establishes the unity of all the evocations, and further, that it could
prove to be the origin of the spleen, of that enigmatic state of mind
of the "I" who is speaking. At first the type and manner of the evocations does in fact seem to correspond to this expectation. For remembering here leads neither to the happiness of time refound nor
to the melancholy suffering of the "no longer." Remembering evidently begins here with a gesture of self-transcendence, which then
unquestioningly turns into doubt as the various and always fruitless
attempts of the lyric "I" to refind himself in a past then only present
him with the view of a world of things that is emptied of meaning.
Within this process, the lyric "I" as well can no longer remain self-
integral in the mode of a self-certain subject. This is indicated above
all by the progressive reshuffling of the grammatical person of the
subject and its predicates: the *j'ai*, the "I" that *has* its memory, is
followed by the distancing *il* for the first object with which it compares itself; then by a *c'est* that cancels the distance as it compares
the subject with the pyramid and grave; and thereafter by a distance-
less *je suis* that allows the *comparandum* and *comparatum* to become

indistinguishable within an "I" that is first the cemetery, then the boudoir. With the *il* of the personification, which then comes on the stage as ennui in the enjambment of the *quand*-sentence, the former lyric subject is effectively erased and at the same time the process of memory is broken off. And when the vanished "I" is finally apostrophised once again in the grammatical person of the *tu*, the lost identity is also apparent in the fact that the "I" that no longer has or is anything has one last and enduring identification imposed upon it by the anonymous and unrecognizable authority of this apostrophe — the identification with an *il*, the sphinx as third person. Accordingly we can no longer consider memory as the principle that establishes unity; it already succumbs to an obscure power that alienates all the forms of the recalled past times, the same power against which the lyric subject as well evidently cannot maintain the integrity of its consciousness of itself as an "I" — so that both memory and autonomous subject are at once destroyed. The inexplicable motivation that compels this "I" to seek its identity in the space of a memory that has become immeasurable, the motivation that immediately allows all of the past life that the subject would grasp, either to disintegrate chaotically or to ossify morbidly — what lies nearer at hand than to recognize this motivation in the power that Baudelaire, with allegorical exaggeration, expressly allows to take the place of the muzzled "I," and even names: ".'ennui, fruit de la morne incuriosité?" If ennui is in fact supposed to be able to uncover the sought-after meaning of spleen, then first of all the "definition" given it as "fruit of gloomy indifference" must be taken seriously, must be tested as the key to an interpretation that at this point is not yet to have recourse to whatever the history of the words *spleen* and *ennui* in Baudelaire's usage can tell us.

If one looks back from lines fifteen through eighteen to line one, one can become aware that the ennui enters into the same movement of a development into the immeasurable as memory did at the beginning. With the formulation "enters into," I intend to call into question the understanding that the ennui also *causes* the movement. For it is precisely this that the syntactic structure of these lines leaves entirely uncertain: the endless present of the "halting days" that can be compared with nothing, and the ennui that has developed out of the "snowed-in years" into the immeasurable, are temporally equated by way of the *quand*-phrase. The ennui that allows the beauty of a winter landscape, at first recalled *ex negativo*, to turn into gloomy indifference — is it itself perhaps supposed to be only one among the other views of progressive reification in which the lyric "I" experiences the loss of its world? In the first go-through, we already noticed that the ennui came forth not from the past, but rather as a figure of monotony from the present, and that it allowed this present to appear to last eternally. The aspect of "morne incuriosité" thus is also lacking to the evocations of the past that the first line produces. Quite the contrary: what begins with "J'ai plus de souvenirs que si j'avais mille ans" therefore precisely produces the further attempts at the search for identity, for this "I" is overpowered by memories that could not become a matter of indifference to it—since it is in terror of not being able to forget but at the same time not being able to rediscover itself in that which is remembered. What in the first reading we could have taken for a gesture of self-presumption, now announces much more a terror in the face of the limitless that opens up with the first comparative ("plus de souvenirs") and returns with the second one ("moins de secrets"). The terror renews itself when the "I" haphazardly recalls remembered or represented places in a hasty movement, as if it had to seek a halt to a growing emptiness, and yet in everything where it lingers—desk, pyramid, grave, cemetery or boudoir—can always grasp hold only of things from a dead time: emblems of a ceaseless reification that allows the past life to which they refer to become unknowable, and that in the end falls upon the autonomous subject itself.

In this interpretation, the formal discovery coincides with the thematic one: the compositional figure of the asymmetrical development of the rhythmic movement then suddenly being cut off again coincides with the fragmented continuity of an experience of self become ceaseless, in which the lyric "I" tries again and again in vain to rebuild the collapsed world within the imaginary. With this, the question of what spleen can mean as an experience of the lyric "I" finds an answer that can be quite simply stated. From now on spleen can take on the meaning of an unexpressed anxiety—the world-anxiety[25] that, as a principle establishing unity, is able to explain the latent origin as well as the manifest consequences of the spleen; the collapse of all ego-centered orientation, according to which space and time open up onto the unencompassable, as well as the vanishing path of the "I" seeking a halt, who objectifies himself in the relics of his vainly projected world. This hypothesis should first be strengthened by way of an external mode of argumentation, and then tested when we follow the interpretation through to the end.

In morality as in physics, I have always had the sensation of the abyss [*gouffre*], not only the abyss of sleep, but the abyss of action, dream, memory, desire, sorrow, remorse, beauty, number, etc. I have cultivated my hysteria with pleasure and terror.[26]

Contained in this famous note in *Mon coeur mis à nu* is the first premonition of the mental illness to which Baudelaire was to succumb four years later. The quoted text has been drawn upon above all for the interpretation of the "Gouffre" poem, and a noteworthy "poetics of the fall" has been derived from it that makes the double meaning of *la chute* — theological as well as psychoanalytic — useful for the understanding of Baudelaire's poetry.[27] But the note can also be read as a commentary that is surprisingly closer textually to our "Spleen" poem. Then it describes world-anxiety as a break in experience that tends to enter amidst the accomplishments and states of mind of the familiar world, in memory as well as in remorse or desire, in everyday activity as well as in the experience of beauty. One recognizes here without difficulty the stations along the vanishing path of the "I" in the "Spleen" poem ("le gouffre du souvenir, de l'action, du beau" in the turn to the past, the present, and the future; *regret* and *remords* are not represented, while *nombre* is to be related to memory, *désir* perhaps to beauty); except that in the poem the abyss of anxiety is objectified not as the undercurrent from a depth, but rather as terror in the face of the limitless, against which the enthralled "I" can at first still oppose representations of enclosure (the desk, pyramid, grave, cemetery, boudoir). In passing, I might refer to the fact that, if one takes spleen as the experience and poetic objectification of world-anxiety, Baudelaire's poem corresponds through and through to discoveries brought to light by the phenomenologically oriented psychiatry of anxiety-psychoses.[28] Anxiety is described there as the collapse of the primordial situation, that is, of the construction of the world from out of the "I"-body center; the consequence of this collapse is the destruction of the certainty our senses derive from our spatial and temporal experience. After the body has lost its anchoring in the world in the catastrophe of anxiety, the following symptoms appear: one's own space and alienated space collapse together; proximity and distance can invert themselves; in the middle of the world available for experience, a locus of corporeal emptiness can delimit itself that can no longer be disclosed by one's own body, but rather is experienced as the vertex of an infinite vanishing line; the fragmentation of the natural experience of time manifests itself in an emptied "time without forgetfulness"; and finally, the loss of orientation that is heightened to the point of world-catastrophe tends to be compensated for by the psychotic in seeking to rebuild his lost world in the imaginary, in producing delusive spatial images among which the prison has predominant significance.

If this biographic-psychological excursus serves to identify world-anxiety as a possible latent origin of "Spleen," then now it is a matter of pursuing the poetic objectification of such world-anxiety in the course of which—as is to be expected—the poem increasingly transcends its psychopathological substratum. In its literary representation, anxiety is always anxiety that has already been mastered in the achievement of form through aesthetic sublimation. Just as Baudelaire's poem knows how to bring into language the most extreme alienation of the consciousness that has been overpowered by anxiety, it in fact brings about its own catharsis. As ineluctably as the process of self-alienation progresses into a loss of the world, traces of rebellion are nonetheless indicated in the counterimages that are evoked. The recalled spaces of memory are not immediately handed over to chaos and ossification, but rather first take on a form of "beautiful disorder" before they succumb to the emptiness of meaning. Even in the terrible, the "I" filled with anxiety discovers unanticipated spectacles of beauty along its escape path. The first reading came upon a poetry of details in the imagery of the bureau's contents, the boudoir, and the wintery ennui, a poetry that can inject itself, as it were, into the catalog of the dead things (most beautifully in "avec de lourds cheveux roulés dans des quittances"). And even in the fear-inducing no-man's-land of the "Sahara brumeux," the highly poetic repertoire of slumbering granite, forgotten sphinx, unheard song, and setting sun is offered up in opposition to the space of anxiety presented by the petrification. Finally, in response to "farouche" as the epithet of savage doubt, "qui se couche" appears in the final couplet as an ironic gesture, reconciled in rhyme, of decline within beauty. The sphinx, in the evocation of which the "rêverie pétrifiante" is completed, is the ultimate form of the reification of the lyric "I," the place-holder of the fallen subject, and the origin of the song, the sublation of terror into poetry—all combined into one.

With what right can one in this manner interpret the sphinx as the last in the series of "metamorphoses" of the lyric "I"? Talk of "metamorphoses" presupposes the representation of organic transformation of a preserved, substantial identity of the subject, and it is therefore not appropriate to the experience of the lyric "I" in this "Spleen" poem, an "I" that precisely loses its substantial identity as a subject step by step. Its path of experience is therefore also not defined through a continuous transformation of forms of the alien world and of one's own person that, even in its fall, would leave the suffering self with the final refuge of an opposing or otherwise excluded standpoint. The path of experience under the spell of spleen is much more conditioned through a discontinuous reversal of the "I" into a non-"I," of the most proper into the most alien; the boundary between inside and outside collapses, and what was internally sublated can now return from outside as a foreign power in which the "I" can no longer recognize the alienation of itself.

Baudelaire found in allegory the poetic instrument that first and foremost allows this process of a destruction of the self to be made representable. This "Spleen" poem brings to view in an exemplary manner the new revival of the allegorical method that had been declared dead. At the beginning, in lines two through five, the classical form of the developed comparison is first still employed, but with the peculiarity that the comparatum ("mon cerveau"), delayed across the three lines, only retrospectively allows the greatly drawn-out comparandum ("un gros meuble") to become recognizable as such. Thus the effect arises that the real external scene of the decor—"un gros meuble à tiroir," etc.—unnoticeably reverses into the internal scene: "cache moins de secrets que mon triste cerveau." In the next step the classical boundary between comparandum and comparatum is annulled through the fact that the lyric "I" unnoticeably combines itself with the compared element in the act of comparison: "Je suis un cimetière . . . Je suis un boudoir." Here one can speak absolutely of allegorical identification (for which no precedent is known to me from the earlier Romance tradition), for with the cancellation of the comparison, the "I" posits itself as the same as what it is not.[29] The failure of this desperate and powerful attempt at identification immediately introduces a second attempt that demonstrates once again that the "I" in spleen can no longer master the alien world on its own. For the subsequent step, Baudelaire introduced the personifying allegory. If it traditionally allowed a state of mind such as ennui to come onto the stage in allegorical dignity—as well as to gloss its origin in a pseudo-learned way, and to elevate its effect into the realm of the cosmic—here it attains a new function, namely, to make visible the overpowering of the self through the alien, or (as one may now also put it) the ego through the id. The wintery world that has imperceptibly become the stage on which ennui alone still rules has at the same time excluded the "I" from the stage, even though the foreign power is nothing other than "gloomy indifference," than an alienation of itself.

The "I" excluded from the stage of the world appears distanced in a threefold manner in line nineteen: it has become a "you" that must cede the central place of the subject to another "I"; it is exiled out of the present into an unchangeable future beside the world, and it has evidently forfeited its corporeal as well as its spiritual form, since now it is addressed only as "matière vivante." Whatever is still living in it will succumb to a materialization that, at the stage of disappearance represented by the granite block, turns, as it were, the "hard core" of the innermost self toward the outside and threatens the lyric "I" with total ossification. The apodictic tone of a judgment being handed down and the ironically celebratory address of line nineteen—"Désormais tu n'es plus, ô matière vivante!"—suggest this interpretation. Does this mean that in the end, the world-anxiety inverts into an anxiety about being judged? In favor of this idea is the possibility of interpreting archetypally the authority of a super-ego that imposes this judgment and remains anonymous: according to Gaston Bachelard, the dream of being petrified can signify terror of God's worth.[30] There is even an archetypal meaning for the sphinx: it can stand for the figure of the fallen sovereign, into which the disempowered autonomous subject can be transposed.[31]

Yet the poem precisely does not end in such archetypal symbolism. In its final image, two secular myths—sphinx and pillars of memory—are brought together and employed against the tradition in a new way to prepare for the lyric movement's final reversal. The sphinx normally conceals a truth, especially for him who might solve its riddle, but here it has become a "remembrance for no one," an allegory of the forgotten. But as the sphinx itself now breaks its petrified silence and begins to sing, the mythological reminder of the statue of memory immediately indicates one final thing, and a first thing for a second time: the last hour of singing, since it sounds here not at dawn but at the setting of the sun; and the rising of beauty into song, which overcomes anxiety and atones for the loss of the "I." Thus, at the end the poem leads the reader back to its beginning: through the final form of its subject, which now becomes retrospectively recognizable in the first form (for who may say with greater right than the sphinx, "j'ai plus de souvenirs que si j'avais mille ans"?), and through the compositional figure of a "poetry of poetry" that describes its own coming into

being (for what is the sphinx to sing about, if not of that which
the poem already encompasses?).

IV. Baudelaire's "Spleen" within the Changing Horizon of the History of its Reception (Historical Understanding and Aesthetic Judgment)

To the extent that we decided to arrange the historical interpretation
according to a first, aesthetic one and a second, interpretive one,
the reconstruction of the primary literary-historical context within
which the poem was received must introduce the historical investigation of our example. Which expectations on the part of its
contemporary readers can this "Spleen" poem have fulfilled or
denied? What was the literary tradition, and what was the historical
and social situation, with which the text might have come to have
a relation? How might the author himself have understood his poem?
And what was the meaning given to it by the first reception, and
which meanings were only made concrete in the later history of its
reception? In such questions historical understanding is not only
directed toward the reconstruction of the past. It should at the
same time bring to view the temporal distance that was leapt over
in the first and second stages of our readings, and allow one to
recognize through the explicit separation of the past and present
horizons of understanding how the meaning of the poem has unfolded itself historically in the interaction between effect and reception—up to those very questions that guide our interpretation and
to which the text in its own time did not yet have to be the answer.

It must first be acknowledged that our poem can be the paradigm
for such a hermeneutic demonstration only with considerable qualification. In the nineteenth century, the contemporary criticism was
directed above all to works as wholes, which, after the obligatory
and for the most part only rhetorically intended praise or blame of
the style, were immediately seen within the relationship of the
author's work and life, and were rather judged morally than appreciated aesthetically. An exception is provided by Baudelaire's
reception through the following generations of poets, who, beginning with Gautier's famous foreword to the 1868 edition of
Fleurs du mal, elevated him to the position of godfather of the
postromantic moderns. But even there one rarely finds interpretations of individual poems; they are to be expected only when
Baudelaire began to make it into the academic literary canon.[32]
The theme of our poem nonetheless allows us to follow the footprints

of its immediate reception, for *spleen* was much discussed as a key word within Baudelaire's provocative aesthetics. Even the harshest attack, which G. Bourdin, the trend-setting *Figaro* critic, launched against the *Fleurs du mal* in 1857, culminates in a quotation from our "Spleen" poem: "One line of M. Baudelaire admirably summarizes his manner; why did he not make it the epigraph to the *Fleurs du mal?—Je suis un cimetière abhorré de la lune.*"[33] An extended analysis of the *Fleurs du mal*'s horizon of expectations and provocative effect could reconstruct the aesthetic and moral norms from out of the numerous documents of its misunderstanding, which precipitated above all in the trial against Baudelaire and his publisher—norms with which Baudelaire broke in a way that evidently struck at the self-satisfaction of the Second Empire's bourgeois society in its most sensitive area, and startled it from its easy belief in progress. For the purposes of our investigation the procedure can be abbreviated by appealing to an eyewitness of particular competence who, from a distance of ten years, gave one of the first great appreciations of the work and accurate defenses of his friend, and recognized more clearly than other contemporaries just what kind of horizonal change had unexpectedly been introduced here by a scant volume of poems.

Théophile Gautier's "Notice" of 1868 already saw Baudelaire's turning away from romanticism in its full literary, aesthetic, and social importance.[34] The *Fleurs du mal* were marked by a "final hour of civilization" (p. 29). They arose in opposition to the illusions of bourgeois democracy as well as to those of its reformers ("the philanthropists, the progressivists, the utilitarians, the humanitarians, the utopians," p. 19). And they had created a new "style of decadence" that for the first time at all could bring to light the *maladie de l'époque moderne* (p. 52), the hitherto unacknowledged suffering under the unnatural conditions of the contemporary society. The immorality that one attributed to Baudelaire would obscure the strength of his critique of the ruling ideologies and especially of materialism, a critique that was also publicly announced in his articles on Poe.[35] If Baudelaire's lyrics could descend into the ugly, the repulsive, or the sickly, they also know how—in opposition to the "realist school" (p. 52)—to raise themselves once again into the "bluest regions of the spiritual," so that the subtitle "Spleen et Idéal" might very well have stood for the book as a whole (p. 20). With this Gautier made recourse to an argument that Baudelaire himself had already used in defending the *Fleurs du mal*; his book would be misunderstood in its "terrible morality" if one did not judge it as a whole: "To blasphemy, I oppose flights toward heaven; to obscenity, Platonic flowers . . . [It is] a book destined to represent the spirit's state of agitation within evil."[36] Thus, the individual poem can and should thoroughly offend the moral sensibility of the contemporary reader again and again; its provocative amorality is nonetheless balanced out within the conception of the cycle of poems, and only then would it be understood in accord with Baudelaire's intention, as a critique of the present age, of the ideology and the morality of appearances of the society of the Second Empire—as a critique of its time in the medium of a pure poetry that is supposed to surpass in its moral rigor the mimetic realism of the novel as well as the direct complaint of satire and caricature.

The testimonial value of his interpretation is raised precisely by the fact that Théophile Gautier recognized and praised the latent function as social criticism of the *Fleurs du mal*, even though it contradicted his doctrine of *l'art pour l'art* or at least gave a meaning to it that could scarcely have been expected. In its explanation of the misunderstanding that precipitated in the reactions on the part of the literary public of 1857, his interpretation already specifies everything that the ideological research of our time might know how to investigate, regarding the social expectations and illusions, the material conditions of the life-world, and the residue of the failed revolution of 1848 in the historical consciousness of Baudelaire's contemporaries. Within the confines of my historical reading, Gautier's interpretation can therefore stand for the analysis of the *Fleurs du mal*'s horizon of expectations within the lived world, which analysis cannot be carried out here. A materialist interpretation might not be satisfied with the discovery of this perceptive eyewitness, and might want to find in Baudelaire's work more concrete reflections of the social-historical process within the Second Empire, or traumatic traces of the defeat of 1848; but it would have to do so through purchase of the method of allegoresis, without which an interpretation of the literary superstructure from the conditions of the economic infrastructure is seldom to be had. Walter Benjamin, for example, saw in "Rêve parisien" "the phantasy of the forces of production having been shut down"; O. Sahlberg sees suppressed memories of 1848 in the versions of anxiety of the "Spleen" poems as well as in wishful erotic images such as "Moesta et Errabunda" or "Les Bijoux"; Wolfgang Fietkau sees in the negative Platonism of *Andromaque, je pense à vous!* Baudelaire's poetic as well as political effort to come to grips with the coup d'état of

2 December 1851; D. Oehler sees in "Correspondances" an "attack upon official nature; i.e., upon the order of the ruling class."[37] Whoever would acknowledge such findings cannot do without compensating for the lack of an objective mimetic relation through the subjective mediation of an allegorical meaning. In my opinion, such allegoresis in its modern usage is not to be flatly dismissed, but rather is thoroughly legitimate hermeneutically when it recognizes its subjective heuristics and therefore its partiality, and consequently no longer makes the dogmatic claim of having achieved the true and—now, finally—"objective" reading. Another question is the one first posed by Walter Benjamin: whether the "view of the alienated" in the *Fleurs du mal* might not have been the view of an allegorizer of modernity; I shall return to this question later.

Gautier explains spleen through a description of the alienated life of metropolitan civilization: "He [Baudelaire] loves to pursue the man withered, shrivelled up, contorted, convulsed by the artificial passions and the real *ennui* of modernity, to pursue him across the sinuosities of this immense madrepore of Paris in order to surprise him in his unhappiness, his anguish, his misery, his prostrations and his excitements, his nervousness and his despair" (p. 21). The "flowers of evil" grow there where the "forget-me-nots, roses, daisies, and violets" of romantic nature surely can thrive no more. Spleen, as suffering from modern reality, is accordingly as sharply distinguished from the indeterminate *Weltschmerz* of the romantic poets as the "black filth of the pavement" is from the "spring-like green of the rural suburbs."[38] But Gautier also recognizes that there is a "philosophy and metaphysics" at the bottom of the antinaturalism of the *Fleurs du mal* (pp. 53, 56): the thesis of fallen nature, applied to aesthetics from the theology of original sin, which has as its consequence for the modern concept of art the fact that the beautiful may no longer owe anything to nature.[39] Gautier therefore praises the "Rêve parisien" as one of the poems in which Baudelaire had driven nature completely out of a landscape (p. 39). His preference for the artificial, which his imagination often allows to extend to the border of the hallucinatory (p. 40), is for Gautier the appropriate attitude for the poet to adopt toward his time, the nineteenth century that can no longer return to naiveté (p. 16). The poet of the *Fleurs du mal* is therefore either unintentionally mannered or, as it were, born already mannered (*naturellement maniéré*), in the same way that in other times one simply and naturally began to live (p. 15). Among the necessarily artificial features of Baudelaire's modern lyrics belongs above all a provocative depersonalization of poetry that Gautier recognizes in the rejection of the romantic doctrine of the unconscious creativity of the inspired poet (pp. 24 and 72), as well as in the renunciation of immediate expression of individual feeling (p. 35). In the place of romantic subjectivity, the necessarily divided consciousness of the modern poet has come upon the scene: "All sensation becomes for him the motif of an analysis. Involuntarily, he doubles himself and, lacking any other subject, becomes the spy of himself" (p. 12).

With this, Gautier sketches the new aesthetic canon that explains several things historically: the public uproar and the prosecution of the *Fleurs du mal* in the name of bourgeois morality; the refusal of reception on the part of the majority of contemporary readers; and its first concretization as a trailblazing work of *décadence* by the approving literary avant-garde. If we now ask which expectations on the part of a reader educated in romantic poetry would have allowed one to reject a poem like our "Spleen" poem, then the norms of the "lyrics of experience" [*Erlebnislyrik*] stand wholly in the foreground: the correspondence between nature and soul, the communication of general human feelings, and the transparence of self-expression in the medium of poetry. On the other hand, in the continual inversions of outer and inner reality, Baudelaire's poem no longer allows one to recognize the harmony of nature, landscape, and psyche. In the unforeseeable changes of shape of the lyric "I," the continuity of a meaningful experience can no longer be recognized. And in the worlds projected by consciousness, the expressions of an integral self are no longer recognizable. Here the poet no longer presupposes the most familiar feelings and moods, in which the reader could find himself confirmed; rather, he demands that the "hypocrite lecteur, mon semblable, mon frère" recognize himself in everything that his poetic alter ego knows how to bring to light in the unfamiliar, terrifying, or shameful from out of the "deepest and ultimate hell of the soul."[40] For this Gautier also coined the formulation, "an unedited side of the soul and things" (p. 19); if one adds the already quoted "spy of himself" to the "unedited side of the soul," then these phrases testify to the still groping attempt to describe something for which the theory of the unconscious was not yet available. Here one can grasp the threshold that Baudelaire stepped across as the poet of modernity: the provocative effect of his *Fleurs du mal* arose finally from his rendering romantic interiority asubjective, or, put another way, from the attempt to make poetry into the medium of a return of the repressed and the tabooed, an attempt before which even the "black romantics" had still remained inhibited.

This manifests itself above all in the poetic method that Baudelaire put to use as the first poet to do so for a long time—allegory. "One of the most primordial and natural forms of poetry"—thus did Baudelaire, in the *Paradis artificiels* (1858), name this "so very spiritual genre"[41] that had been brought into disrepute in the nineteenth century, particularly through painting. He renewed its function in that he made it into an instrument for the depersonalization of poetic expression. I have investigated elsewhere how Baudelaire, in the course of grounding his "supernatural" theory of modern poetry, came to rehabilitate the literary form of allegory, upon which he had stumbled in describing the heightened perceptions under the influence of hashish, and how thereafter the allegorizing personification achieved an unexpected resurrection in the *Fleurs du mal*.[42] There, as the exuberant use of capitalized substantives already shows, Baudelaire helped the discredited personification toward a new "substantial majesty" in that he opposed it to the immediate expression of feelings on the part of romantic poetry. He thereby won back for the modern lyric a new means of rendering abstractions sensible, and he created the poetic model of a modern *psychomachia* that—as with Freud's psychoanalysis shortly thereafter—puts into question the supremacy of the self-conscious "I" within the psychic economy.[43]

The historical interpretation of our text has thus led to a reconstruction of its counterposition within the horizons of expectations of romantic poetry, a reconstruction that is now to be secured through the hermeneutic method of widening the context. For this I can refer the reader to the already mentioned study in which I commented on Baudelaire's recourse to allegory poetologically as well as in an interpretation of the four "Spleen" poems.[44] The context provided by this group of poems confirms the historical reading of our "Spleen" poem in a twofold manner: there as here, Baudelaire had recourse to the allegorical method, to undo the romantic expectation of a harmony between nature and psyche, and to call the powers of the unconscious into play against the self-mastering subject. There as here, he deepened the received theme of weariness with life or Weltschmerz—which romantics had cultivated as ennui—into that of world-anxiety; and the new, key word *spleen*—elevated from pathology into poetry—can be considered the reification of this anxiety. Around this time, the word's history expressly registers this change in meaning from the "English disease" to that of a key word for modern French poetry.[45] The definition given in the *Dictionnaire universel du XIXème siècle* of 1875[46] even applies a theory of decadence to this "new word for an old thing" that could have been drawn from Thèophile Gautier's "Notice." Gautier himself had there actually distinguished spleen in the new sense of Baudelaire's poetry of *décadence*, from ennui as a shop-worn aesthetic norm now considered typical for "bourgeois cravenness." He did this as he glossed the introductory poem of the *Fleurs du mal*, and found that Baudelaire had not spared his reader, "accusing him, despite his hypocrisy, of having all the vices that he condemns in others, and of nourishing in his heart that grand modern monster Ennui; the reader who, with his bourgeois cravenness, tamely dreams of Roman debauches and acts of ferociousness—a bureaucrat's Nero, a shop-keeper's Heliogabal."[47]

In the chapter of Paul Bourget's *Psychologie contemporaine* (1883) devoted to Baudelaire, the group of "Spleen" poems is especially emphasized. Bourget believes himself able to ground on these pieces his thesis that Baudelaire's nihilism (now named as such!) arose from the loss of Catholic faith. First is a description of the "universal nausea" from which contemporary society suffers, in a continuation of Gautier's theory of décadence that Bourget allows to culminate in a prognosis that has since become highly contemporary: "But slowly, surely, the belief in the bankruptcy of nature unfolds itself, which promises to become the sinister faith of the twentieth century if science, or an invasion by barbarians, does not save humanity which has become too reflective of the lassitude of its own thought."[48] Baudelaire, as the contemporary of decadence, is said to have made himself into its theorist, and as poet, to have combined three persons within himself in the most modern manner: he is at once mystic, libertine, and the analyst of both. This *coincidentia oppositorum* is most easily explained psychologically when one refers the "analyzing libertine" back to a "disabused Catholic." Baudelaire's spleen would not be so abysmal, and his nihilism would not be so sharply distinguished from romantic lamentations of lost happiness, were it not that his poetry presupposed a *horror vacui* left behind by the abandoned faith.[49] Since in the group of "Spleen" poems there is no trace of this tendency to be found, it is not surprising that Bourget must have recourse to "Madrigal triste" and to a strophe of "Le Voyage"[50] to bring to light within the manifestations of spleen the still pulsing conscience and the unquenchable desire for God on the part of one who is fundamentally a "mystical soul." The weaknesses of this interpretation are certainly more evident today than in Bourget's time: if, in the tension between *spleen et idéal*, one wanted to find only an unintentional secularization of Christian beliefs, then the modernity of the *Fleurs du mal* would not be essentially different from the experience of "empty transcendence" already discovered long before by the romantic poetry of solitude. But contrary to this view, Baudelaire not only consciously and provocatively profaned mystical experiences (as in "A une Madonne") and liturgical models (as in "Les litanies de Satan"); he also radicalized the Christian theology of original sin itself when he legitimated the antinaturalism of his aesthetics against the nature religion of romanticism with an interpretation of Genesis 3, according to which all of nature was corrupted along with the fall of Adam and Eve into sin.[51] Only with this "provocative secularization" does the deromantization of romanticism begin, and the *Fleur du mal*'s threshold to modernity become recognizable.[52]

Bourget's thesis of secularization was almost epochal in the history of Baudelaire's reception. The concretization of the meaning of the *Fleurs du mal* as a decadent modern's poetry of nihilism was taken up shortly thereafter by Huysmans and elevated to an aesthetic cult in *A rebours* (1885): Des Esseintes takes Baudelaire's work, printed and decorated in a private edition in the most expensive fashion, and places it on a private altar as a missal, opened to the poem "Anywhere out of the world." Yet Huysmans offers another reason for spleen: it is no longer the backlash of lost Catholic faith, but rather the unintentional return of repressed drives that Baudelaire was supposed to have been the first to decipher in the "hieroglyphs of the soul." The interpretive model for this psychological concretization would predominate for a long time, and later enter into the psychoanalytic interpretation. In this it is striking that the cathartic side of the *Fleur du mal*'s "moral psychology"—and, together with it, the sublimation of spleen into "the beautiful within the terrible"—did not come into the picture at all. The aesthetic appreciation of Baudelaire had its ground broken only slowly by his reception through Verlaine, Rimbaud, Mallarmé and Valéry—the later classicists of the epoch of the modern lyric that was initiated by him.[53] In the reception on the part of these poets, there is no direct testimony for the history of the interpretation of our "Spleen" poem. In his essay of 1942, which demonstrates why Baudelaire has now reached the peak of his fame, Valéry introduces only the poem "Recueillement." It is, let me note in passing, the only poem in the whole cycle in which the method of allegorical personification is employed not for alienation, but for the transfiguration of a situation.[54] When Valéry praises Baudelaire for having understood "how to construct a language within language," and thereby having rejuvenated the French lyric,[55] this formulation also includes the compositional figure cut by our "Spleen" poem—a "poetry of poetry" that describes its own coming into being, and that Valéry himself perpetuated in his "Cimetière marin" and elsewhere.

"*Spleen* exhibits experience in its bare essentials. With terror, the melancholic sees the world fallen back into a bare state of nature. No breath of pre-history surrounds it. No aura."[56] These lines from the unfinished body of Walter Benjamin's Baudelaire studies read like an interpretation of our "Spleen" poem. Although Benjamin left behind no finished interpretation of this poem, his name nonetheless may not be left absent from this history of reception. For it was Benjamin who, in the Thirties, recognized the "modern allegorist" in Baudelaire and thereby laid the ground for a concretization of the "Spleen" poems that even today is still unexhausted. To him we owe the insight that brought to light the buried connection between the older tradition of allegory that declined after its last flowering in the baroque, and its reawakening in the *Fleurs du mal*: "The allegorical mode of intuition is always built upon a devalued world of appearances. The specific devaluation of the world of things that lies in the commodity is the foundation of the allegorical intention in Baudelaire."[57] What has radically changed between the baroque and the modern because of the social and economic process may be read out of the transformed experience of nature: whereas the melancholy of the baroque allegorist responds to an experience of transience, "which values history as natural history or, more precisely, as the 'Passion story of the world',"[58] the spleen of the modern allegorist responds to a condition of the commodity-producing society that—in view of a ceaseless technical development—no longer allows one to still experience the thoroughly reified world *as* nature. What distinguishes Baudelaire's spleen from the age-old *taedium vitae* is the consciousness of this self-alienation that has appeared,[59] a feeling "that corresponds to a permanent catastrophe,"[60] a "naked terror" wholly different from Victor Hugo's "cosmic horror."[61] The allegorical intention that, according to Benjamin, has always laid to ruin the coherence within life, in order to appropriate for things—against their appearances—a significance within an emblematic context: in the nineteenth century, this intention comes upon a world of things transformed through the commodity-form and in itself already emptied of meaning; "the devaluation of the world of things in allegory is, within the world of things itself, surpassed by the commodity." The return of the old emblem that modern allegorists recognize under the cover of the new commodity-form[62] customarily remains concealed from their contemporaries through the fetishistic character of the commodity, through the price that allows its use-value to vanish into purely quantitative exchange-value, as well as through the advertisement that lends the beautiful semblance of the poetic to the world of commodities; while in the work of art the commodity-form is expressed more strongly than before.[63]

In light of this attempt to justify a materialist genesis for Baudelaire's recourse to allegory, one can see the destructive tendency of the allegorical intention at work in our "Spleen" poem, and interpret what is struck by it as the "experience of a world in a state of rigor mortis."[64] Elsewhere Benjamin remarked about the poem that it is "oriented through and through toward an empathy with a material that is dead in a double sense. It is anorganic [material]. . . . The image of the sphinx with which the poem closes has the obscure beauty of the stalls of shops as one still comes upon them in the arcades [of Paris]."[65] In my opinion, neither the "empathy" with the anorganic nor the "commodity-character" of the sphinx—if one takes this interpretation, admittedly only made in passing, at its word—appear to measure up to Benjamin's insights into the modern function of allegory in the *Fleurs du mal*. The aesthetic revaluation of nature, with which Baudelaire seals the break with romanticism's idealistic image of the world, does not stop even at the anorganic; in the desert landscape of our "Spleen" poem, this image appears every bit as emptied of meaning as the dead material into which all the products of human labor in the old boudoir had decayed. On the other hand, the allegorical intention pursued to the final rigor mortis of the world can revert from the external alienation into an appearance of the beautiful; this cannot arise from any "natural correspondence," for it can be produced only by the cathartic effect of the poem that the sphinx's singing thematizes. With its singing, the spell of materialization is broken and the sphinx is immediately withdrawn from the reified world: having become the allegory of uncomprehended beauty, it redeems what was already said of *La beauté* in the cycle—"Je trône dans l'azur comme un sphinx incompris."

The "poetry of poetry" is not the only resource that Baudelaire summoned in the *Fleurs du mal* against the experience of self-alienation in a reified world. Benjamin sought to anchor this "salvation" in a "theory of natural correspondences" that nonetheless could not be united with Baudelaire's famous renunciation of "natural nature." [66] Here Gerhard Hess has been more insightful as he interpreted the landscape of the *Fleurs du mal* within the cyclical contrast of upswing and degradation, glimpses of paradise and then falls, and described the formation of worlds of ecstasy and of ennui within a progressive development of everyday reality and natural surroundings. The neutral experience of the world of the quotidian now appears as a transitional phase or a place for the reversal between the lighting up of the *beauté fugitive* and the fall into the timeless monotony of spleen: "Ecstasy, the experienced and fantasized participation in the world, is only momentary. The fantasy in images seeks to hold on to a weak reflection of this ephemeral experience of the *profondeur de la vie*. It can only project it as a memory into the past, or as an expectation into the future. Compared to the charm and the profit of the images of the landscapes, which announce only their most fleeting possession, the *ennui* has its own 'depth.' Monotony filled with anxiety is not experienced as momentary, but rather as an unlimited condition. The time of its representation is the present." [67] Thanks to the "spiritual," "eternal" character of the personified abstractions—as Hess acknowledges independently of Walter Benjamin—allegory is the genuine poetic medium for rendering perceptible the reversal from outer into inner landscape and from the melancholic ego into the ungraspable and changeless id, as well as for achieving the most concrete effect with the highest degree of abstraction. [68] In his interpretation of our "Spleen" poem, Hess shows above all how the derealization of natural experience of the world goes together with a progressive emptying-out of time. Already in the first line the fullness of the rememberable becomes a gigantic space of a thousand years; the further attempts at self-identification lead without fail to the representation of enclosed spaces, then to the timeless monotony of the all-filling ennui, and finally to the "I" that has itself become material, as the final object of allegorical space: "As a granite block in the desert, as the forgotten sphinx, it has even lost the gift of concealment. The monotony is ossified." [69]

Judd Hubert, who did not yet have the hermeneutic key of the allegorical method at his disposal, works with the formal principle of "poetic ambiguity." This methodological operation allows him to repeatedly make his way to general antitheses similar to those of Geistesgeschichte (like Bergson's *matière et mémoire*, or

Pascal's *fini et infini*), and with our "Spleen" poem it seduced him
into a moralizing kind of allegoresis.[70] Poetic ambiguity is here seen
and pursued in the variations of the "image of the casket," which,
altogether, are supposed to symbolize the "skull," until with line
fifteen an inexplicable event occurs that unexpectedly inverts the
relationship between container and contained, and allows the skull
to move inward, the ennui outward—which latter in the end is
nothing other than the *Sahara brumeux*. Thus the sphinx can incarnate at once material, secret, and humanity, and beyond this, can
"symbolize" the poet's activity as a "metaphor for the skull."
The talk of everything that a word can "symbolize" betrays the
hermeneutically inadequate application of a universal code of symbolic meanings, meanings that could be decided only within the
consistency of the succession of perceptions and the structure of
meaning in the poem—to say nothing of the allegoresis, as arbitrary
as it is edifying, that allows for the conclusion regarding the biographical element that itself tells us nothing.[71] My critique nonetheless would not exclude the recognition that, in particulars, Hubert
has also discovered poetic ambivalences that—as above all with his
interpretation of the end as the "setting of the romantic sun" or as a
death-wish—in an overarching concretization could have achieved
a more specific significance than simply the confirmation of the
formal principle of poetic ambivalence. For this one might suggest
that which Hubert says elsewhere about ennui: that with Baudelaire
it presents a "satanic equivalence between things and ideas," that
as *spleen poétique* it becomes the poet's critical weapon, and that
finally it can provide a kind of catharsis.[72] But since the hermeneutic
step to the integration of the discovered ambiguities within a sin-
gularizing meaning that establishes consistency is not taken, it must
appear as if the formal principle must itself also be equal to the
meaning of the poem.

The singular meaning and individual shape of the poem also not
infrequently becomes lost in interpretations that appropriate for
themselves the stricter descriptive demands of linguistic poetics.
Thus Karl Blüher has interpreted our "Spleen" poem in its contrasts with Paul Eluard's "Le Mal," in order to show the differing
realizations of the poetic function in "symbolist" and surrealist
lyrics.[73] In contrast with Jakobson and Lévi-Strauss, his analysis
of levels begins with the thematic one, because it ultimately determines the organization of the other textual levels and guides the
aesthetic perception. But since the interpreter always knows in advance what spleen means in this poem, and does not first ask how

the reader learns through the poem what spleen might mean precisely here, even the perfect (if unrecognizedly selective) analysis of the semantic, morpho-syntactic, and phonological levels of expression can only wind up confirming the initial grasp of the content-level. The analysis of the poetic function of the language leads to the conclusion that "the morpho-syntactic and phonological levels, thanks to the symmetry of the meter, the well-proportioned character of the sentence constructions, and the gradual coherence of the sound structure, offer a harmonization that seeks to neutralize verbally what is negative and unharmonious in the thematics. The dissonance of the expression is aesthetically compensated for through the assonance and measure of these textual levels."[74] To this there corresponds the foreknowledge derived from literary history that Baudelaire's state of ennui is, beyond romanticism, actually "the extreme fascination of the negative-satanic character of *spleen*, combined with a dandy-like and playful moment that seeks to enjoy aesthetically the negativity, and especially the ugly."[75] *Quod erat demonstrandum*. I do not need to fence with the rigor of this structural analysis, and I can even bring the recognized effect of aesthetic sublimation into harmony with my interpretation of the ending to our "Spleen" poem, even if on the other hand I must doubt whether Blüher's initial grasp of the poem — which conceals essential aspects of the establishment of the theme of spleen — could withstand a historical critique. The *proton pseudos* of his initial grasp lies in the expectation of a "symbolist" poem, which allows him to misjudge *what* is actually harmonized in the passage through the negative experience of the lyric "I." The world-anxiety objectified in spleen can no longer be enjoyed in a "dandy-like and playful" manner by the lyric "I" when, together with the world-catastrophe, it loses the reassuring middle position of the autonomous subject. The variously and unexpectedly renewed shock of this experience — which even the reader cannot avoid within the horizon of the first reading — is not simply neutralized through the opposing harmonizing means provided by the construction of the lines, so that the aesthetic sublimation is only arrived at and recognizable in a final counterthrust, the concluding line with the sphinx's singing. The historically novel medium of the rediscovered allegory, which Baudelaire introduced to render perceptible the reification and depersonalization of the experience of the world, distinguishes the *Fleurs du mal* most sharply from late romanticism. The *Fleurs du mal* also stand askew vis-à-vis what a dubious literary-historical convention calls "symbolism" — even if sometimes with this name one understands the old symbolic art-form that Blüher's analysis fundamentally presupposes, as the classicist harmony of form and content.

In a further structuralist analysis, Sebastian Neumeister undertook the experiment of giving up altogether on an interpretation of the meaning of spleen in Baudelaire's poem, in order to be able to work out more purely his "poetic idea" from out of the movement within the text's web of relationships.[76] This movement, which linguistic poetics—as Neumeister rightly criticizes—often ignores in favor of a description of the static structure and its architechtonic equivalences, may be understood in the case of our "Spleen" poem as a play around the axis of symmetry, which then produces the figure of a spiral. Once again, one could judge the formal analysis as already decided in itself and move on to a semantic interpretation, were it not that the former depends on a problematic initial assumption that remains unconsidered hermeneutically. For Neumeister blithely separates the first line from the body of twenty-four lines (leaving the rhyme-chain unnoticed) as "a kind of second title," and brings symmetry into the formal structure of the poem only through this approach, which cannot be grounded philologically either. Thus the point becomes totally lost that our "Spleen" poem— as was demonstrated above—is quite unmistakably oriented toward an asymmetrical development and breaking-off of the lyric movement, in its strophic-syntactic verse-units but also in its far-reaching comparisons and discontinuously appearing identifications. To be sure, the mirror symmetries that Neumeister knows how to bring to light are not a purely arbitrary projection. They can often enrich our aesthetic perception, if one introduces them into the intended course of the lyric movement and its perspectives on the poem's meaning.[77] Neumeister missed the poem's direction and successive unfolding in that his pseudotitle elevates the memory to being the first theme, from out of which the ennui is then supposed to proceed "without effort," one minute constituting the axis of the movement, the other running through the whole poem as a "red thread." Thus the impression of a consistency on the level of the lyric subject is awakened, which consistency resubstantializes the subject against the intention of the poem. From which the conclusion may be drawn that in structural analyses one evidently cannot dispense with the question of the meaning concretized in the poetic structures, without having to suffer the consequences.

Laurent Jenny's most recent interpretation of our "Spleen" poem is especially interesting for our hermeneutic demonstration, since it makes use of the same discovery of the syntactic-forward structure to arrive at a different concretization of the meaning. Jenny as well recognizes the discontinuity of the syntactically unbound conditions or spaces, and refers this discontinuity back to a "narrative skeleton" conditioned by a play of the grammatical persons of the lyric subject. On the semantic level, this grammatical play is elevated to the level of an "adventure of the subject" that follows a metaphoric law, the identification that is always sought and continually fails;[78] its abstraction would be poetically compensated for through a fullness of metonymic references—the four fields of the objective world in which the "I" seeks its identity. Only the final image, the sphinx singing at dusk, makes the teleology of the poem (the "orientational process") recognizable: "The petrified 'I' who sings to the light arrives at its whole meaning only because it has been preceded by an 'excavated I,' an 'I' who portrays in himself the abyss of memory. That which leads from memory to song is what one is accustomed to call an itinerary, an itinerary that is not only intellectual but also charnel, since it is also the passage from one sort of death of the body to another: from putrefaction to mineralization."[79] The unnamed hermeneutic premise for this concretization as the "swan song of the subject" is obviously the theory of the "death of the subject" (*"décentrement du sujet"*) that in recent years has been brought to high honor by the *"semanalyse"* of the Parisian avant-garde. This is not meant as a rebuke, particularly since Jenny's interpretation enriches this theory with an application that restores value to the aesthetic function of the text that is otherwise neglected there. What is not posed is the question why this last adventure of the subject is advertised precisely as "Spleen" by Baudelaire. Interpreted as the "path from memory to song" and so titled, does the poem still at all need the title "Spleen"?

What is different in my interpretation takes off from a different reading of the first line. In it the "real I" compares itself with an "imaginary I" (imaginary because introduced in an if-clause: "si j'avais mille ans") in order to find in it its measure as a subject—and precisely with this it enters into a vicious circle. In the division of the self-doubling "I" there nestles the fiction in the shape of a memory that unflinchingly produces images and appears before the "I" like an inner abyss. In the face of this threatening abyss of memory, the movement of the search for identity begins, in which the "I" measures itself against objects that prove altogether to be either hollow, closed off, or themselves threatening. After ennui's triumph, the triumph of the third person over the first person that has now vanished, the reversal appears that can scarcely still be expected: the apostrophe of the second person makes the doubling of the "I" final; the limitless open space of the desert opposes itself to the empty enclosed spaces, the fate of petrification to that of decomposition; and the place of the feverishly searching memory is taken by the song that has produced its own stage.[80] Jenny's interpretation converges with mine not only in the interpretation of the final line, where he puts the emphasis more strongly on the "death in song," while I recall La beauté as the "uncomprehended sphinx." Both interpretations also enter into a possible relation of supplementarity where Jenny recognizes the "abyss of memory" in the beginning line as the cause of the "I"'s self-division, while I would inquire further into what this abyss might well mean—and would find in the world-anxiety an answer that contains the beginning of a new interpretation of the text.[81]

Questions left unposed are opportunities for the subsequent interpreter. They must not lead to the point of completely abolishing the answer that the predecessor found in the text to his questions. The coherence of question and answer in the history of an interpretation is primarily determined by categories of the enrichment of understanding (be they supplementation or development, a reaccenting or a new elucidation), and only secondarily by the logic of falsifiability. When a preceding interpretation can be falsified, for the most part this indicates neither historical errors nor objective "mistakes," but rather falsely posed or illegitimate questions on the part of the interpreter. In reference to literary works, questions are legitimate when their role as initial comprehensions for the sake of interpretation is borne out in the text; put another way, when it is shown that the text can be understood as a new response—and not just an incidental one. A nonincidental response demands that the text be consistently interpretable as the meaning of this response. When different responses within the history of interpretations of works of art do not reciprocally falsify one another, but rather testify to the historically progressive concretization of meaning in the struggle of interpretation, to what else would one attribute this, if not to the unifiability of legitimate questions, manifest at least in the experience of art.

Notes

Introduction

1. H. R. Jauss's first full-length book is a study of the narrative structure of Marcel Proust's *A la recherche du temps perdu*, well ahead of its time and all too little known outside Germany: *Zeit und Erinnerung in Marcel Proust 'A la recherche du temps perdu': Ein Beitrag zur Theorie des Romans* (Heidelberg, 1955).

2. The term was coined by Stanley Fish in an article that goes back to 1970 published in *New Literary History*. Fish later stated that it was "not the happiest of designations" for reasons, however, that have little to do with the point stressed here. For a good brief survey of reader-response criticism in the United States, see Leopold Damrosch, Jr., "Samuel Johnson and Reader-Response Criticism," in *The Eighteenth Century, Theory and Interpretation* XXI, 2 (Spring 1980), pp. 91-108), who quotes Fish. Anthologies of reader-response criticism such as, among others, *The Reader in the Text. Essays on Audience and Interpretation,* ed. Susan Suleiman and Inge Crossman (Princeton University Press, 1980) have recently been published in this country.

3. Rainer Warning, *Rezeptionsästhetik. Theorie und Praxis* (Munich, 1975).

4. The sequence of volumes containing the proceedings of the yearly meetings of the research group have appeared since 1963 under the general title *Poetik und Hermeneutik.* At this date, eight volumes have been issued.

5. See, for example, Martin Heidegger's introductory statement in *Erläuterungen zu Hölderlins Dichtung* (Frankfurt a. Main, 1951), p. 8.

6. Aristotle, *Rhetoric*, p. 4.

7. Rainer Warning, "Rezeptionsästhetik als literaturwissenschaftliche Pragmatik," in *Rezeptionsästhetik,* p. 25.

8. Jauss directly refers to Bloom in the essay on Valéry and Goethe, included in this volume.

9. See, for instance, Edmund Husserl, *Ideas: General Introduction to Phenomenology,* trans. W. R. Boyer Gibbon (London/New York, 1969) § § 27, 28, 44, 47.

10. The German "ungedacht" or the French "inpensé" would be better terms, not available in English.

11. "Silhouetted" approximately translates the Husserlian term "Abschattung."

12. Walter Benjamin, "Die Aufgabe des Übersetzers" in *Illuminationen* (Frankfurt, 1961), p. 56. English translation in *Illuminations*, trans. Harry Zohn (New York, 1968).

13. Warning, *Rezeptionsästhetik*, p. 9.

14. See Husserl, *Logical Investigations*, trans. J. N. Findlay (London, 1970), Vol. II; also J. P. Schobinger, *Variationen zu Walter Benjamins Sprachmeditationen*, (Basel/Stuttgart, 1979), p. 102, and Jacques Derrida, *La Voix et le phénomène* (Paris, 1967), especially chapter VII, "Le supplément d'origine," pp. 98-117.

15. Warning, *Rezeptionsästhetik*, p. 89.

16. Jan Mukařovský, *The Word and Verbal Art*, trans. John Burbank and Peter Steiner, with a foreword by René Wellek (Yale University Press, 1977), p. 68.

17. Friedrich Nietzsche, "Nachlass," in *Werke in drei Bänden*, ed. Karl Schlechta (Munich, 1956), III, p. 683.

18. *Ibid.*, III, p. 685.

19. Benjamin, *Illuminationen*, p. 62: "Damit ist allerdings zugestanden, dass alle Übersetzung nur eine irgendwie *vorläufige* Art ist, sich mit der Fremdheit der Sprachen auseinanderzusetzen."

20. H. R. Jauss, *Ästhetische Erfahrung und literarische Hermeneutik I* (Munich, 1977).

21. Friedrich Schlegel, "Über die Univerständlichkeit" in *Kritische Schriften*, ed. Wolf-dietrich Rasch (Munich, 1970), pp. 530-42.

22. H. R. Jauss, "The Poetic Text Within the Change of Horizons of Reading: The Example of Baudelaire's 'Spleen II'" (Chapter 5 of this volume).

23. In "Über einige Motive bei Baudelaire," *Illuminationen*, p. 210, Benjamin quotes the lines from another of the *Fleurs du Mal* poems:

Je vais m'éxercer seul à ma fantasque escrime,

Flairant dans tous les coins les hasardes de la rime, . . .

(Le Soleil)

24. *Vorlesungen über die Ästhetik* (Werkausgabe), I, p. 512.

25. *Ibid.*, I, p. 512.

26. *"Erscheinung des Schönen"* is, of course, the traditional Hegelian vocabulary for the aesthetic experience. The "umkippen" of Jauss's earlier, corrosive observation on Baudelaire's play on *Boucher/débouché* (157), which suggests the demolition of the aesthetic idol as if it were the *colonne Vendôme* or any monument honoring a tyrant, is now replaced by the more dignified "umschlagen." Taken literally, however, *schlagen* (to beat) in the cliché *umschlagen* is rather more threatening than *kippen* (to tilt).

27. The use of "tradition" in this context is one of the numerous occasions in which one can share Rousseau's naive regret that we have no diacritical mark at our disposal by which to indicate irony. It also indicates that, try as I may, when I seem to be reproaching Jauss for not freeing himself from classical constraints, I am not more liberated from them than he is.

28. A complete text of "Spleen II" appears on pp. 149-50.

29. "Poesié der Poesie" is a concept frequently developed in connection with Paul Valéry, whose authority as a poetician is, for various and complex reasons, overrated in Germany. The "Valérization" of Mallarmé and of Baudelaire is a case in which Harold Bloom's notion of belatedness would have a salutary effect.

30. *Enzyklopädie der philosophischen Wissenschaften* (Werkausgabe), III, § 453, p. 260.

31. *Ibid.*, III, § 458, p. 270.

32. *Ibid.*, III, § 464, p. 282.

33. That the coincidence may be due to common occult sources in Hegel and Baudelaire obscures rather than explains the passage. It distracts the reader from wondering why the use of this particular emblematic code can be "right" in a lyric poem as well as in a philosophical treatise.

Chapter 1. Literary History as a Challenge to Literary Theory

1. In this critique I follow M. Wehrli, who most recently wrote on "Sinn und Unsinn der Literaturgeschichte" (in the literary supplement of the *Neue Zürcher Zeitung* of 26 February 1967) and from another perspective similarly predicted the return of literary studies to history. Of the earlier work on the problem of literary history (henceforth cited only with the date), I am aware of: Roman Jakobson, "Über den Realismus in der Kunst" (1921), in *Texte der russischen Formalisten* I, ed. Jurij Striedter (Munich, 1969), pp. 373-91 (Eng., "On Realism in Art," in *Readings in Russian Poetics: Formalist and Structuralist Views*, eds. Ladislav Matejka and Krystyna Pomorska [Cambridge, Mass., 1971]); Walter Benjamin, "Literaturgeschichte und Literaturwissenschaft" (1931), in *Angelus Novus* (Frankfurt, 1966), pp. 450-56; René Wellek, "The Theory of Literary History," in *Études dédiées au quatrième Congrès de linguistes - Travaux du Cercle Linguistique de Prague* (1936), pp. 173-91; Wellek, "The Concept of Evolution in Literary History," in *Concepts of Criticism* (New Haven, 1963); U. Leo, "Das Problem der Literaturgeschichte" (1939), in *Sehen und Wirklichkeit bei Dante* (Frankfurt a.M., 1957); Werner Krauss, "Literaturgeschichte als geschichtlicher Auftrag" (1950), in *Studien und Aufsätze* (Berlin, 1959), pp. 19-72; J. Storost, "Das Problem der Literaturgeschichte," in *Dante-Jahrbuch* 38 (1960), pp. 1-17; Erich Trunz, "Literaturgeschichte als Auslegung und als Geschichte der Dichtung," in *Festschrift J. Trier* (Meisenheim, 1954); H. E. Hass, "Literatur und Geschichte," in *Neue deutsche Hefte* 5 (1958), pp. 307-18; Roland Barthes, "Histoire ou littérature," in *Sur Racine*, Paris, 1960, pp. 145-67 (Eng., "History or Literature," in *On Racine*, trans. Richard Howard [New York, 1964], pp. 151-72); F. Sengle, "Aufgaben der heutigen Literaturgeschichtsschreibung," in *Archiv für das Studium der neueren Sprachen* 200 (1964), pp. 241-64.

2. Thus above all René Wellek, 1936, pp. 173-75, and Wellek and Austin Warren, *Theory of Literature*, 3rd ed. (New York, 1962), p. 253: "Most leading histories of literature are either histories of civilization or collections of critical essays. One type is not a history of *art*; the other, not a *history* of art."

3. Georg Gottfried Gervinus, *Schriften zur Literatur* (Berlin, 1962), p. 4 (in an 1883 review of recent literary histories): "These books may have all kinds of usefullness, but of historical usefullness they have almost none. They trace chronologically the various kinds of literature [*Dichtung*], they set the writers in chronological order one after another, as others do the titles of books, and then characterize the writers and literature, respectively. But that is no history; it is scarcely the skeleton of a history."

4. "Was heisst und zu welchem Ende studiert man Universalgeschichte?," in *Schillers Sämtliche Werke*, Säkularausgabe, Bd. XIII, p. 3.

5. First published in 1837, under the title *Grundzüge der Historik*, in *Schriften*, pp. 49-103.

6. *Schriften*, p. 47.

7. "Über die Aufgabe des Geschichtsschreibers," in *Werke in fünf Bänden*, ed. A. Flitner and K. Giel (Darmstadt, 1960), Bd. I, p. 602: "Greece thereby displays an idea of national individuality that was never present either before or since, and as the secret of all existence lies in individuality, so does all world-hisotrical progress of humanity depend upon the degree, the freedom, and the uniqueness of its reciprocal influence."

8. *Grundzüge der Historik*, secs. 27/28.

9. *Schriften*, p. 48.

10. *Ibid.*

11. *Grundzüge der Historik*, sec. 26.

12. *Wahrheit und Methode—Grundzüge einer philosophischen Hermeneutik* (Tübingen, 1960), pp. 185-205, esp. p. 187; Eng., *Truth and Method—Fundamentals of a Philosophical Hermeneutics*, no trans. (New York, 1975), pp. 173-92, esp. p. 176: "Even the 'historical school' knew that fundamentally there can be no other history but universal history, because the unique significance of the detail can be determined only from the whole. How can the empirical researcher, to whom the whole can never be given, manage without losing his rights to the philosopher and his *a priori* arbitrariness?"

13. *Grundzüge der Historik*, sec. 32.

14. *Geschichte der poetischen Nationalliteratur der Deutschen*, Bd. IV, p. vii: "Our literature [*Dichtung*] has *had* its time, and if German life is not to stand still, then we must attract the talents that now lack a goal toward the real world and the state, where new spirit is to be molded in new material."

15. In the Advertisement to his *Geschichte der poetischen Nationalliteratur der Deutschen* (*Schriften*, p. 123), where Gervinus—there still the champion of Enlightenment historicism against romantic historicism—contradicts this fundamental rule and decisively distances himself from the "strictly objective manner of most of today's historians."

16. "Über die Epochen der neueren Geschichte," in *Geschichte und Politik—Ausgewählte Aufsätze und Meisterschriften*, ed. H. Hofmann (Stuttgart, 1940), p. 141.

17. "But if one wants . . . to assume that this progress subsists in the fact that in each period the life of humanity reaches a higher level, that each generation thus completely surpasses the preceding one, with the last always being the favored one, while the preceding one would only be the carrier of the following one—then that would be an injustice to the godhead" (*ibid.*). One may speak of a "new theodicy" because the idealist philosophy of history rejected by Ranke could, as O. Marquard has shown, already raise the hidden claim of a theodicy insofar as it discharged God and made man the subject responsible for history, and understood historical progress as a process of law or, alternatively, as progress in human legal relationships (cf. "Idealismus and Theodizee," in *Philosophiches Jahrbuch* 73 (1965), pp. 33-47).

18. *Sämtliche Werke*, p. 528; cf. p. 526 ff., where Schiller defines the task of the universal historian as a method with which one can at first suspend the teleological principle, that is, the goal of finding out and solving the problem of world order in the course of world history—"because a world history of the final order is only to be expected in the latest of times." The method itself describes historiography as a kind of "history of influence": the universal historian "turns from the latest world situation upward toward the origin of things" as he draws out from amongst the various givens those that have had an essential influence on the form of the world today; then he turns around along the path that has been thus found, and can report on the relationship of the past to the present constitution of the world as "world history" "along the guiding thread of these indicated facts."

19. The consequence of the principle that the historian ought first to empty his head of everything that he knows of the later course of history when he wishes to represent a past period (Fustel de Coulanges) is the irrationalism of an "empathy" [*Einfühlung*] that does not know how to give any accounting for the predeterminations and prejudgments of its historical standpoint. Walter Benjamin's critique of this position, delivered from the standpoint of historical materialism, leads unnoticed beyond the objectivism of the materialist conception of history; see his "Geschichtsphilosophische Thesen," No. VII, in *Schriften* I (Frankfurt a. M., 1955), p. 497; Eng., "Theses on the Philosophy of History," No. VII, in *Illuminations*, ed. Hannah Arendt, trans. Harry Zohn (New York, 1968), p. 256.

20. Wilhelm von Humboldt, *Werke*, p. 586.

21. *Ibid.*, p. 590: "The historian who would be worthy of this name must represent each given as part of a whole, or what is the same thing, the form of history itself in each given."

22. Characteristic of this division of literary history and literary criticism is the definition of the concept of philology in Gustav Gröber's *Grundriss der romanischen Philologie* [*Outline of Romance Philology*], Bd. I, 2nd ed. (Strasbourg, 1906), p. 194: "The appearance of the human spirit in language that can only be understood through mediation, and its achievement in the artistically used discourse of the past constitute the unique object of philology."

23. On this see Werner Krauss, 1950, p. 19 ff., and Walter Benjamin, 1931, p. 453: "In this swamp the hydra of scholarly aesthetics finds itself at home with its seven heads: creativity, empathy, timelessness, re-creation, shared experience, illusion, and aesthetic pleasure."

24. On this, cf. René Wellek, 1963, p. 271.

25. Werner Krauss, 1950, p. 57 ff., shows with the example of Ernst Robert Curtius how greatly this scholarly ideal is bound up with the thought of the George circle. [The German poet Stefan George (1868-1933), through his considerable personal and literary influence, gathered around him many of "the best and the brightest" of Germany's young writers, critics, and historians between the late 1890s and the 1920s, including Friedrich Gundolf, Ernst Bertram, Max Kommerell, Norbert von Hellingrath, Ernst Kantorowicz, and, briefly, Hugo von Hofmannsthal. The Nazis later tried to appropriate George's complex historico-mythopoetics, something he steadfastly refused. (Tr.)]

26. *Europäische Literatur und lateinisches Mittelalter* (Bern, 1948), p. 404; Eng., *European Literature and the Latin Middle Ages*, trans. Willard R. Trask (New York, 1953), p. 400.

27. "Work-immanent" [*Werkimmanente*] interpretation, perhaps best represented in Wolfgang Kayser's *Das sprachliche Kunstwerk* [*The Verbal Work of Art*] (Bern, 1948), was the rough analogue in postwar German literary criticism to American New Criticism. (Tr.)

28. Marx and Engels, *Die deutsche Ideologie* (1845-46), in Karl Marx and Friedrich Engels, *Werke* (Berlin, 1959), Bd. 3, pp. 26-27; Eng., *The German Ideology*, in *Collected Works*, trans. Clemens Dutt, W. Lough, and C. P. Magill (New York, 1976), vol. 5, pp. 36-37.

29. Werner Krauss, "Literaturgeschichte als geschichtlicher Auftrag" (1950), in *Studien und Aufsätze* (Berlin, 1959), pp. 26-66.

30. Karel Kosík, *Die Dialektik des Konkreten* (Frankfurt a.M., 1967) (*Theorie 2*), pp. 21-22.

31. Margaret Harkness's *Franz von Sickingen*, a political, prosocialist drama, aroused discussion among the Marxists. The portion of Engel's famous letter of April 1888 to Harkness (referred to in note 38 below) concerning the play can be found in *Marxism and Art*, ed. Berel Lang and Forrest Williams (New York, 1972), pp. 51-54. (Tr.)

32. The documents relevant to this debate—the watershed in Western Marxist literary theory both before and since the war—are now available in English in Ernst Bloch, Georg Lukács, Bertolt Brecht, Walter Benjamin, and Theodor Adorno, *Aesthetics and Politics*, ed. Ronald Taylor (London, 1977). (Tr.)

33. Hans Blumenberg, "Nachahmung der Natur: Zur Vorgeschichte der Idee des schöpferischen Menschen," in *Studium generale* 10 (1957), pp. 267, 270.

34. *Ibid.*, p. 276.

35. Cf. Blumenberg, *ibid.*, p. 270: "The antinaturalism of the nineteenth century is borne by this feeling of the narrowing of mankind's authentic productivity through a tiresome horizon of conditions. The new pathos of labor directed itself against nature: Comte coined the expression 'antinature," and Marx and Engels speak of 'antiphysis'."

36. Gyorgii Plekhanov (1856-1918), activist, theorist, and revolutionary exile, was one of the founders of Russian Marxism, and a colleague of Lenin and the Bolsheviks until he broke with them shortly before the revolution. He authored 26 volumes of Marxist theory, including *Art and Society* (1912). (Tr.)

37. Kosík, *Die Dialektik*, p. 116.

38. The leading example for this is Engle's interpretation of Balzac in his letter to Margaret Harkness (April 1888), which concludes with the argument "that Balzac thus was forced to be against his own class-sympathies and political prejudices, that he *saw* the necessity of the decline of his beloved nobles, and depicted them as men that did not deserve any better fate; and that he *saw* the real men of the future there when alone at that time they were to be found—I consider that as one of realism's greatest triumphs." (Karl Marx and Friedrich Engels, *Über Kunst und Literatur*, ed. M. Kliem [Berlin, 1967], Bd. I, p. 159.). The mystification that Balzac was "forced" into objective representation against his interests by social reality endows hypostasized reality—similar to Hegel's "cunning of reason"—with the power itself indirectly to produce literature [Dichtung]. In this "triumph of realism," Marxist literary theory found a carte blanche for appropriating conservative authors such as, for example, Goethe or Walter Scott, into the process of emancipation.

39. "Einleitung zur Kritik der polischen Ökonomie," in *Werke*, Bd. 13, p. 640; Eng., "Introduction to the Critique of Political Economy," in *Selected Writings*, ed. David McLellan (Oxford, 1977), p. 359.

40. "Einführung in die ästhetischen Schriften von Marx und Engels" (1945), "Literatur und Kunst als Überbau" (1951), in *Beiträge zur Geschichte der Asthetik* (Berlin, 1954).

41. *Ibid.*, p. 424.

42. *Werke*, Bd. 13, p. 641; Eng., *Selected Writings*, p. 360.

43. "The 'classical character' thus follows not from the observance of formal 'rules,' but rather precisely from the fact that the work of art is in a position to give the maximum expression of symbolization and individualization to the most essential and all-typical human relationships" (*Beiträge*, p. 425). On this see Peter Demetz, "Zwischen Klassik und Bolschewismus. Georg Lukács als Theoretiker der Dichtung," in *Merkur* 12 (1958), pp. 501-15, and Demetz, *Marx, Engels and the Poets*, trans. Jeffrey Sammons (Chicago, 1967).

44. Brecht ironically criticized this canonization of the "form of a few bourgeois novels of the last century" as the "formalist character of the theory of realism"; cf. his statements in the Brecht-Lukács debate in *Marxismus und Literatur*, ed. F. J. Raddatz (Hamburg, 1969), Bd. 2, pp. 87-98. [See note 32. (Tr.)]

45. Eng. in *Marxism and Linguistics* (New York, 1951). (Tr.)

46. *Beiträge zur Geschichte der Ästhetik*, p. 419.

47. Cited in Lukács, *Beiträge*, pp. 194-96.

48. On this see the Introduction ("Le tout et les parties") to *Le dieu caché: Étude zur la vision tragique dans les Pensées de Pascal et dans le théâtre de Racine* (Paris, 1959); Eng., *The Hidden God: A Study of Tragic Vision in the Pensées of Pascal and the Tragedies of Racine*, trans. Philip Thody, (New York, 1964); and *Pour une sociologie du roman* (Paris, 1964), pp. 44 ff.; Eng., *Toward a Sociology of the Novel*, trans. Alan Sheridan (London, 1975), pp. 10 ff..

49. On this see W. Mittenzwei's critique, "Die Brecht-Lukács-Debatte," in *Das Argument* 10 (1968), p. 31, which reproaches Lukács's overemphasis on this unity as a lack of dialectics: "But Marxist dialectics begins with the contradictory character of the unity of essence and appearance."

50. Thus in Lukács's theory of reflection, the concept of intensive totality has its unavoidable correlative in the "immediacy of reception": the objective reality is said to be correctly known in the work of art precisely when the "receiver" (reader, hearer, viewer)

recognizes himself in it (cf. *Probleme des Realismus*, Berlin, 1955, p. 13 ff.). According to this, the influence of the work of art already presupposes the correct collective experience in its public, from which experience it can only gradually differ, as ever truer and more complete reflection.

51. Kosík, *Die Dialektik*, p. 123.

52. *Studien zur deutschen und französischen Aufklärung* (Berlin, 1963), p. 6, and "Literaturgeschichte als geschichtlicher Auftrag," p. 66.

53. "Statt eines Nachwortes zu 'D'un Réalisme sans rivages' ", in *Marxismus und Literatur*, p. 227.

54. *Die Dialektik*, pp. 138, 139; here one can remember Marx, "Einleitung zur Kritik der Politischen Okonomie," p. 624; "The art object—like every other product—creates a public of artistic taste and capable of enjoying beauty. The production thus produces not only an object for the subject, but also a subject for the object."

55. Kosík, *Die Dialektik*, p. 140.

56. *Ibid.*, p. 148.

57. I refer to Marx's well-known statement, "The formation of the five senses is a labor of the whole preceding world-history"; cf. *Ökonomisch-philosophische Manuskripte* (1844), in Marx and Engels, *Über Kunst und Literatur*, p. 119; Eng., *The Economic and Philosophic Manuscripts of 1844*, ed. Dirk J. Struik, trans. Martin Milligan (New York, 1964).

58. Editions in German translation are: Boris Eichenbaum, *Aufsätze zur Theorie und Geschichte der Literatur* (Frankfurt a.M., 1965); Jurij Tynjanov, *Die literarischen Kunstmittel und die Evolution in der Literatur* (Frankfurt a.M., 1967); Viktor Sklovskij, *Theorie der Prosa* (Frankfurt, 1966); in French translation: *Théorie de la littérature. Textes des formalistes russes*, ed. and trans. Tzvetan Todorov, Paris, 1965. [In English translation the leading anthologies are *Readings in Russian Poetics: Formalist and Structuralist Views*, and *Russian Formalist Criticism: Four Essays*, ed. and trans. Lee T. Lemon and Marian J. Reis (Lincoln, Neb., 1965). (Tr.)] The most relevant critical evaluation of the Formalist school is Jurij Striedter's "Introduction" to the *Texte der russischen Formalisten* I (Munich, 1969), to whom I owe a great deal for his advice and suggestion with the writing of sections 4 and 10.

59. This famous formula coined by Viktor Shklovsky in 1921 was shortly thereafter improved upon with the concept of an aesthetic "system" in which each artistic device had a definite function to fulfill; cf. Victor Ehrlich, *Russian Formalism* (The Hague, 1955), p. 90.

60. "Der Zusammenhang der Mittel des Sujetbaus mit den allgemeinen Stilmitteln" (*Poetik*, 1919), cited in Boris Eichenbaum, *Aufsätze*, p. 27. Among the other early signs of the "evolution of genres," Ferdinand Brunetière already held the "influence of works on work" to be the most important relation in literary history; cf. Wellek, 1963, p. 44.

61. Eichenbaum, *Aufsätze*, p. 47.

62. *Ibid.*, p. 46; Tynjanov, "Das literarische Faktum" and "Über literarische Evolution." [Eng. of the latter in *Readings in Russian Poetics*. (Tr.)]

63. Tynjanov and Jakobson, "Probleme der Literatur- und Sprachforschung," in *Kursbuch* 5 (1966), p. 75; Eng., "Problems in the Study of Literature and Language," in *Readings in Russian Poetics*.

64. Tynjanov, *Die literarischen Kunstmittel*, p. 40, opposes the "succession of systems" as the main concept of literary evolution to "tradition" as the fundamental concept of the old literary history.

65. In linguistics this principle is represented above all by E. Coseriu, cf. *Sincronía, diacronía e historia* (Montevideo, 1958).

66. "Bedenken eines Philologen," *Studium generale* 7 (1954), 321-23. The new approach to literary tradition that R. Guiette has sought in a series of pioneering essays (partly in *Questions de littérature* [Ghent, 1960]), using his own method of combining aesthetic criticism with historical knowledge, corresponds almost literally to his (unpublished) axiom, "The greatest error of philologists is to believe that literature has been made for philologists." See also his "Eloge de la lecture," *Revue générale belge* (January 1966), pp. 3-14.

67. This thesis is one of the main points of the *Introduction à une esthétique de la littérature* by G. Picon (Paris, 1953); see esp. pp. 90 ff.

68. Correspondingly, Walter Benjamin (1931) formulated: "For it is not a question of representing the written works in relation to their time but of bringing to representation the time that knows them—that is our time—in the time when they originated. Thus literature becomes an organon of history and the task of literary history is to make it this—and not to make written works the material of history" (*Angelus Novus* [Frankfurt a.M., 1966], p. 456).

69. *The Idea of History* (New York and Oxford, 1956), p. 228.

70. Here I am following A. Nisin in his criticism of the latent Platonism of philological methods, that is, of their belief in the timeless substance of a literary work and in a timeless point of view of the reader: "For the work of art, if it cannot incarnate the essence of art, is also not an object which we can regard according to the Cartesian rule 'without putting anything of ouselves into it but what can apply indiscriminately to all objects.'"; *La Littérature et le lecteur* (Paris, 1959), p. 57 (see also my review in *Archiv für das Studium der neueren Sprachen* 197 [1960], 223-35).

71. Picon, *Introduction*, p. 34. This view of the dialogical mode of being of a literary work of art is found in Malraux (*Les voix du silence*) as well as in Picon, Nisin, and Guiette—a tradition of literary aesthetics which is still alive in France and to which I am especially indebted; it finally goes back to a famous sentence in Valéry's poetics, "It is the execution of the poem which is the poem."

72. Peter Szondi, "Über philologische Erkenntnis," *Hölderlin-Studien* (Frankfurt a.M., 1967), rightly sees in this the decisive difference between literary and historical studies, p. 11: "No commentary, no stylistic examination of a poem should aim to give a description of the poem that could be taken by itself. Even the least critical reader will want to confront it with the poem and will not understand it until he has traced the claim back to the acts of knowledge whence they originated." Guiette says something very similar in "Eloge de la lecture" (see note 66).

73. Note also J. Storost (1960), who simply equates the historical event with the literary event ("A work of art is first of all an artistic act and hence historical like the Battle of Isos").

74. René Wellek (1936), p. 179.

75. In *Slovo a slovesnost*, I, p. 192, cited by Wellek (1936), pp. 179 ff.

76. G. Buck, *Lernen und Erfahrung* (Stuttgart, 1967), p. 56, who refers here to Husserl (*Erfahrung und Urteil*, esp. § 8) but who more broadly goes beyond Husserl in a determination of the negativity in the process of experience that is of significance for the horizonal structure of aesthetic experience (cf. note 114 below).

77. Wolf Dieter Stempel, "Pour une description des genres littéraires," in *Actes du XIIe congrès international de linguistique Romane* (Bucharest, 1968), also in *Beiträge zur Textlinguistik*, ed. W. D. Stempel (Munich, 1970).

78. Here I can refer to my study, "Theory of Genres and Medieval Literature," Chapter 3 in this volume.

79. According to the interpretation of H. J. Neuschäfer, *Der Sinn der Parodie im Don Quijote*, Studia Romanica 5 (Heidelberg, 1963).

80. According to the interpretation of Rainer Warning, *Illusion und Wirklichkeit in Tristam Shandy und Jacques le Fataliste*, Theorie und Geschichte der Literatur und der schönen Künste 4 (Munich, 1965), esp. pp. 80 ff.

81. According to the interpretation of Karl Heinz Stierle, *Dunkelheit und Form in Gérard de Nervals "Chimères"*, Theorie und Geschichte der Literatur und der schönen Künste 5 (Munich, 1967), esp. pp. 55 and 91.

82. On this Husserlian concept, see Buck, *Lernen und Erfahrung*, pp. 64 ff.

83. Here I am incorporating results of the discussion of "kitsch," as a borderline phenomenon of the aesthetic, which took place during the third colloquium of the research group "Poetik und Hermeneutik" (now in the volume *Die nicht mehr schönen Künste— Grenzphänomene des Ästhetischen*, ed. H. R. Jauss [Munich, 1968]). For the "culinary" approach, which presupposes mere entertainment art, the same thing holds as for kitsch, namely, that here the "demands of the consumers are *a priori* satisfied" (P. Beylin), that "the fulfilled expectation becomes the norm of the product" (Wolfgang Iser), or that "its work, without having or solving a problem, presents the appearance of a solution to a problem" (M. Imdahl), pp. 651-67.

84. As also the epigonal; on this, see Boris Tomashevsky, in *Théorie de la littérature. Textes des formalistes russes*, ed. T. Todorov (Paris, 1965), p. 306, n. 53: "The appearance of a genius always equals a literary revolution which dethrones the dominant canon and gives power to processes subordinated until then. . . . The epigones repeat a worn-out combination of processes, and as original and revolutionary as it was, this combination becomes stereotypical and traditional. Thus the epigones kill, sometimes for a long time, the aptitude of their contemporaries to sense the aesthetic force of the examples they imitate: they discredit their masters."

85. R. Escarpit, *Das Buch und der Leser: Entwurf einer Literatursoziologie* (Cologne and Opladen, 1961; first, expanded German edition of *Sociologie de la littérature* [Paris, 1958]), p. 116.

86. K. H. Bender, *König und Vasall: Untersuchungen zur Chanson de Geste des XII. Jahrhunderts*, Studia Romanica 13 (Heidelberg, 1967), shows what step is necessary to get beyond this one-sided determination. In this history of the early French epic, the apparent congruence of feudal society and epic ideality is represented as a process that is maintained through a continually changing discrepancy between "reality" and "ideology," that is, between the historical constellations of feudal conflicts and the poetic responses of the epics.

87. The incomparably more promising literary sociology of Erich Auerbach brought these aspects to light in the variety of epoch-making breaks in the relationship between author and reader; for this see the evaluation of Fritz Schalk in his edition of Auerbach's *Gesammelte Aufsätze zur romanischen Philologie* (Bern and Munich, 1967), pp. 11 ff.

88. See Harald Weinrich, "Für eine Literaturgeschichte des Lesers," *Merkur* 21 (November, 1967), an attempt arising from the same intent as mine, which, analogously to the way that the linguistics of the speaker, customary earlier, has been replaced by the linguistics of the listener, argues for a methodological consideration of the perspective of the reader in literary history and thereby most happily supports my aims. Weinrich shows above all how the empirical methods of literary sociology can be supplemented by the linguistic and literary interpretation of the role of the reader implicit in the work.

89. In "*Madame Bovary* par Gustave Flaubert," Baudelaire, *Oeuvres complètes*, Pléiade ed. (Paris, 1951), p. 998: "The last years of Louise-Philippe witnessed the last explosions of a spirit still excitable by the play of the imagination; but the new novelist found himself faced with a completely worn-out society—worse than worn-out—stupified and gluttonous, with a horror only of fiction, and love only for possession."

90. Cf. *ibid.*, p. 999, as well as the accusation, speech for the defense, and verdict of the *Bovary* trial in Flaubert, *Oeuvres*, Pléiade ed. (Paris, 1951), I, pp. 649-717, esp. p. 717; also

198 □ NOTES TO PP. 27-31

about *Fanny*, E. Montégut, "Le roman intime de la littérature réaliste," *Revue des deux mondes* 18 (1858), pp. 196-213, esp. pp. 201 and 209 ff.

91. As Baudelaire declares, *Oeuvres complètes*, p. 996: "for since the disappearance of Balzac . . . all curiosity relative to the novel has been pacified and put to rest."

92. For these and other contemporary verdicts see H. R. Jauss, "Die beiden Fassungen von Flauberts *Education sentimentale*," *Heidelberger Jahrbücher* 2 (1958), pp. 96-116, esp. p. 97.

93. On this, see the excellent analysis by the contemporary critic E. Montégut (see note 90 above), who explains in detail why the dream-world and the figures in Feydeau's novel are typical for the audience in the neighborhoods "between the Bourse and the boulevard Montmartre" (p. 209) that needs an "alcool poétique," enjoys "seeing their vulgar adventures of yesterday and their vulgar projects of tomorrow poeticized" (p. 210), and subscribes to an "idolatry of the material," by which Montégut understands the ingredients of the "dream factory" of 1858—"a sort of sanctimonius admiration, almost devout, for furniture, wallpaper, dress, escapes like a perfume of patchouli from each of its pages" (p. 201).

94. Examples of this method, which not only follow the success, fame, and influence of a writer through history but also examine the historical conditions and changes in understanding him, are rare. The following should be mentioned: G. F. Ford, *Dickens and His Readers* (Princeton, 1955); A. Nisin, *Les Oeuvres et les siècles* (Paris, 1960), which discusses "Virgile, Dante et nous," Ronsard, Corneille, Racine; E. Lämmert, "Zur Wirkungsgeschichte Eichendorffs in Deutschland," *Festschrift für Richard Alewyn*, ed. H. Singer and B. von Wiese (Cologne and Graz, 1967). The methodological problem of the step from the influence to the reception of a work was indicated most sharply by F. Vodička already in 1941 in his study "Die Problematik der Rezeption von Nerudas Werk" (now in *Struktur vývoje* Prague, 1969) with the question of the changes in the work that are realized in its successive aesthetic perceptions.

95. See H. R. Jauss, *Untersuchungen zur mittelalterlichen Tierdichtung* (Tübingen, 1959), esp. chap. IV A and D.

96. A Vinaver, "A la recherche d'une poétique médiévale," *Cahiers de civilisation médiévale* 2 (1959), 1-16.

97. Gadamer, *Wahrheit und Methode*, pp. 284, 285; Eng., p. 268.

98. *Ibid.*, p. 283; Eng., p. 267.

99. *Ibid.*, p. 352; Eng., p. 333.

100. *Ibid.*, p. 289; Eng., p. 273.

101. *Ibid.*, p. 356; Eng., p. 337.

102. Wellek, 1936, p. 184; *ibid.*, 1963, pp. 17-20.

103. *Ibid.*, p. 17.

104. *Ibid..*

105. *Ibid..*

106. *Wahrheit und Methode*, p. 274; Eng., p. 257.

107. *Ibid..*

108. *Ibid..*

109. *Ibid.*, p. 290; Eng., p. 273.

110. This reversal becomes obvious in the chapter "Die Logik von Frage und Antwort" (*ibid.*, pp. 351-60; Eng., pp. 333-41); see my "History of Art and Pragmatic History," § VII, included in this volume.

111. *Ibid.*, p. 280; Eng., p. 264.

112. *Ibid.*, p. 109; Eng., p. 102.

113. See *ibid.*, p. 110; Eng., p. 103.

114. This also follows from Formalist aesthetics and especially from Viktor Shklovsky's theory of "deautomatization"; cf. Victor Erlich's summary, *Russian Formalism*, p. 76: "As

the 'twisted, deliberately impeded form' interposes artificial obstacles between the perceiving subject and the object perceived, the chain of habitual association and of automatic responses is broken: thus, we become able to *see* things instead of merely *recognizing* them."

115. *Wahrheit und Methode*, p. 275; Eng., p. 258.

116. *Ibid.*, p. 280; Eng., p. 264.

117. In the 1927 article, "Über literarische Evolution," by Jurij Tynjanov (in *Die literarischen Kunstmittel und die Evolution in der Literatur*, pp. 37-60), this program is most pregnantly presented. It was only partially fulfilled—as Jurij Striedter informed me—in the treatment of problems of structural change in the history of literary genres, as for example in the volume *Russkaja proza*, Voprosy poètiki 8 (Leningrad, 1926), or J. Tynjanov, "Die Ode als rhetorische Gattung" (1922), now in *Texte der russischen Formalisten*, II, ed. J. Striedter (Munich, 1970).

118. J. Tynjanov, "Über literarische Evolution," p. 59.

119. "A work of art will appear as a positive value when it regroups the structure of the preceding period, it will appear as a negative value if it takes over the structure without changing it." (Jan Mukařovský, cited by R. Wellek, 1963, pp. 48, 49.)

120. See. V. Erlich, *Russian Formalism*, pp. 254-57, R. Wellek, 1963, pp. 48 ff., and J. Striedter, *Texte der russischen Formalisten*, I, Introduction, § X.

121. Hans Blumenberg, in *Poetik und Hermeneutik* 3 (see note 83), p. 692.

122. According to V. Erlich, *Russian Formalism*, p. 252, this concept meant three things to the Formalists: "on the level of the representation of reality, *Differenzqualität* stood for the 'divergence' from the actual, i.e., for creative deformation. On the level of language it meant a departure from current linguistic usage. Finally, on the place of literary dynamics, a . . . modification of the prevailing artistic norm."

123. For the first possibility the (antiromantic) reevaluation of Boileau and of the classical *contrainte* poetics by Gide and Valéry can be introduced; for the second, the belated discovery of Hölderlin's hymns or Novalis's concept of future poetry (on the latter see H. R. Jauss in *Romanische Forschungen* 77 [1965], pp. 174-83).

124. Thus, since the reception of the "minor romantic" Nerval, whose *Chimères* only attracted attention under the influence of Mallarmé, the canonized "major romantics" Lamartine, Vigny, Musset and a large part of the "rhetorical" lyrics of Victor Hugo have been increasingly forced into the background.

125. *Poetik und Hermeneutik* 2 (*Immanente Ästhetik—Ästhetische Reflexion*), ed. W. Iser (Munich, 1966), esp. pp. 395-418.

126. In *Zeugnisse—Theodor W. Adorno zum 60. Geburtstag* (Frankfurt a.M., 1963), pp. 50-64, and also in "General History and the Aesthetic Approach," *Poetik und Hermeneutik* 3. See also *History: The Last Things Before the Last* (New York, 1969), esp. chap. 6: "Ahasverus, or the Riddle of Time," pp. 139-63.

127. "First, in identifying history as a process in chronological time, we tacitly assume that our knowledge of the moment at which an event emerges from the flow of time will help us to account for its appearance. The date of the event is a value-laden fact. Accordingly, all events in the history of a people, a nation, or a civilization that take place at a given moment are supposed to occur then and there for reasons bound up, somehow, with that moment" (Kracauer, *History*, p. 141).

128. This concept goes back to H. Foccillon, *The Life of Forms in Art* (New York, 1948), and G. Kubler, *The Shape of Time: Remarks on the History of Things* (New Haven, 1962).

129. Kracauer, *History*, p. 53.

130. *Poetik und Hermeneutik* 3, p. 569. The formula of "the contemporaneity of the different," with which F. Sengle, "Aufgaben der heutigen Literaturgeschichtsschreibung," 1964, pp. 247 ff., refers to the same phenomenon, fails to grasp one dimension of the prob-

lem, which becomes evident in his belief that this difficulty of literary history can be solved be simply combining comparative methods and modern interpretation ("that is, carrying out comparative interpretation on a broader basis," p. 249).

131. In 1960 Roman Jakobson also made this claim in a lecture that now constitutes chap. 11, "Linguistique et poétique," of his book, *Essais de linguistique générale* (Paris, 1963). Cf. p. 212: "Synchronic description envisages not only the literary production of a given period, but also that part of the literary tradition which has remained alive or been resuscitated in the period in question. . . . Historical poetics, exactly like the history of language, if it wants to be truly comprehensive, ought to be conceived as a superstructure built upon a series of successive synchronic descriptions."

132. Jurij Tynjanov and Roman Jakobson, "Probleme der Literatur- und Sprachforschung" (1928), now in *Kursbuch* 5 (Frankfurt a.M., 1966), p. 75: "The history of the system itself represents another system. Pure synchrony now proves to be illusory: each synchronic system has its past and its future as inseparable structural elements of this system."

133. First in "Epochenschwelle und Rezeption," *Philosophische Rundschau* 6 (1958), pp. 101 ff., most recently in *Die Legitimatät der Neuzeit* (Frankfurt a.M., 1966); see esp. pp. 41 ff.

134. N.B. This was composed in 1967. (Tr.)

135. Lévi-Strauss himself testifies to this involuntarily but extremely impressively in his attempt to "interpret" with the help of his structural method a linguistic description of Baudelaire's poem "Les chats" provided by Roman Jakobson. See *L'Homme* 2 (1962), pp. 5-21; Eng. in *Structuralism*, ed. Jacques Ehrmann (Garden City, N.Y., 1971), a reprint of *Yale French Studies* nos. 36-37 (1966).

136. Now in *Gesellschaft— Literatur—Wissenschaft: Gesammelte Schriften 1938-1966,* eds. H. R. Jauss and C. Müller-Daehn (Munich, 1967), pp. 1-13, esp. pp. 2 and 4.

137. First in *Untersuchungen zur mittelalterlichen Tierdichtung*, see pp. 153, 180, 225, 271; further in *Archiv für das Studium der neueren Sprachen* 197 (1961), pp. 223-25.

138. Karl Mannheim, *Mensch und Gesellschaft in Zeitalter des Umbaus* (Darmstadt, 1958), pp. 212 ff.

139. In *Theorie und Realität*, ed. H. Albert (Tübingen, 1964), pp. 87-102.

140. *Ibid.*, p. 91.

141. *Ibid.*, p. 102.

142. Popper's example of the blind man does not distinguish between the two possibilities of a merely reactive behavior and an experimenting mode of action under specific hypotheses. If the second possibility characterizes reflected scientific behavior in distinction to the unreflected behavior in lived praxis, the researcher would be "creative" on his part, and thus to be placed above the "blind man" and more appropriately compared with the writer as a creator of new expectations.

143. G. Buck, *Lernen und Erfahrung*, pp. 70 ff. "[Negative experience] has its instructive effect not only by causing us to revise the context of our subsequent experience so that the new fits into the corrected unity of an objective meaning. . . . Not only is the object of the experience differently represented, but the experiencing consciousness itself reverses itself. The work of negative experience is one of becoming conscious of oneself. What one becomes conscious of are the motifs which have been guiding experience and which have remained unquestioned in this guiding function. Negative experience thus has primarily the character of self-experience, which frees one for a qualitatively new kind of experience." From these premises Buck developed the concept of a hermeneutics, which, as a "relationship of lived praxis that is guided by the highest interest of lived praxis— the agent's self-information," legitimizes the specific experience of the so-called humanities [*Geisteswissenschaften*] in contrast to the empiricism of the natural sciences. See his "Bildung durch

Wissenschaft," in *Wissenschaft, Bildung und pädagogische Wirklichkeit* (Heidenheim, 1969), p. 24.

144. Jurij Striedter has pointed out that in the diaries and examples from the prose of Leo Tolstoy to which Shklovsky referred in his first explanation of the procedure of "alienation," the purely aesthetic aspect was still bound up with an epistemological and ethical aspect. "Shklovsky was interested—in contrast to Tolstoy—above all in the artistic 'procedure' and not in the question of its ethical presuppositions and effects." (*Poetik und Hermeneutik* 2 [see note 125], pp. 288 ff.)

145. Flaubert, *Oeuvres*, I, p. 657: "thus, as early as this first mistake, as early as this first fall, she glorified adultery, its poetry, its voluptuousness. Voilà, gentlemen, what for me is much more dangerous, much more immoral than the fall itself!"

146. Erich Auerbach, *Mimesis: Dargestellte Wirklichkeit in der abendländischen Literatur* (Bern, 1946), p. 430; Eng., *Mimesis: The Representation of Reality in Western Literature*, trans. Willard R. Trask (Princeton, 1953), p. 485.

147. Flaubert, *Oeuvres*, I. p. 673.

148. *Ibid.*, p. 670.

149. *Ibid.*, p. 666.

150. Cf. *ibid.*, pp. 666-67.

151. *Ibid.*, p. 717.

152. "Die Schaubühne als eine moralische Anstalt betrachtet," in *Schillers Sämtliche Werke*, Säkularausgabe, XI, p. 99. See also R. Koselleck, *Kritik und Krise* (Freiburg and Munich, 1959), pp. 82 ff.

153. "Zur Systematik der künstlerischen Probleme," *Jahrbuch für Ästhetik* (1925), p. 440; for the application of this principle to works of art of the present, see M. Imdahl, *Poetik und Hermeneutik* 3, pp. 493-505, 663-64.

Chapter 2. History of Art and Pragmatic History

1. "Letter to André Lebey," Sept., 1906, *Oeuvres II* (Paris, 1960), p. 1543; also S. Kracauer, in *Die nicht mehr schönen Künste*, ed. H. R. Jauss (Munich, 1968), *Poetik und Hermeneutik*, III, p. 123.

2. Concerning the change of paradigm in the history of science, see Th. S. Kuhn, *The Structure of Scientific Revolutions*, (Chicago, 1962), and H. R. Jauss, "Paradigmawechsel in der Literaturwissenschaft," in *Linguistische Berichte*, I (1969), pp. 44-45.

3. P. Brockmeier, *Darstellungen der französischen Literaturgeschichte von Claude Fauchet bis Laharpe* (Berlin, 1963).

4. See H. R. Jauss, *Literaturgeschichte als Provokation* (Frankfurt, 1970), pp. 35 ff.

5. See H. R. Jauss, *Ästhetische Normen und geschichtliche Reflexion in der Querelle des Anciens et des Modernes* (Munich, 1964), pp. 23-33.

6. R. Koselleck, "Historia magistra vitae," in *Natur und Geschichte, Karl Löwith zum 70. Geburtstag* (Stuttgart, 1968), pp. 196-219.

7. See thesis quoted in note 5.

8. See *Nachahmung und Illusion*, ed. H. R. Jauss (Munich, 1964), *Poetik und Hermeneutik*, I, p. 191.

9. *Geschichte der Kunst des Altertums* (1764), ed. W. Senff (Weimar, 1964), p. 7.

10. *Ibid.*, p. 21.

11. *Über das Studium der griechischen Poesie*, ed. P. Hankamer (Godesberg, 1947), p. 153.

12. *Briefe zur Beförderung der Humanität*, 7th and 8th collections, in *Werke*, ed. Suphan (Berlin, 1883), XVIII, p. 57.

13. See H.-D. Weber, *Fr. Schlegels "Transzendentalpoesie" und das Verhältnis von Kritik und Dichtung im 18. Jahrhundert* (Munich, 1973), pp. 88-101.

14. This is the basic principle behind the history of modern poetry, with which Herder, in letters 81-107, along with Schiller and F. Schlegel (1796-1797), again takes up the questions of the *Querelle des Anciens et des Modernes*; see work quoted in note 4, pp. 72-74.

15. Voltaire, *Le siècle de Louis XIV*, Intr.

16. The fragment, dating from 1754, is quoted from *J. Winckelmanns sämtliche Werke*, ed. J. Eiselein (Donaueschingen), XII, pp. iii-xv; see also Fontius, *Winckelmann und die französische Aufklärung* (Berlin, 1968), *Sitz.-Ber. d. dt. Akad. d. Wsch. zu Berlin*, Cat. for language, literature and art, 1968, I, to whom I am obliged for the reference.

17. P. 7.

18. *Werke*, XVIII, p. 137.

19. In his presentation of modern poetry, 1796, Herder still holds fast to a "telos" of history, insofar as he asks, at the outset: "What is the law of this change? Does it change for the better or for the worse?" (p. 6), and at the end, concludes from a comparison of periods: *"tendimus in Arcadiam, tendimus!* To the land of simplicity, truth and morals goes our path" (p. 140). As regards the esthete (XXXII, p. 63) or *poetic philologist* (XXXII, p. 83) that one must be, in order to risk oneself on the ocean of historical observations, see Weber (note 13), p. 110.

20. Weber, *Fr. Schlegels "Transzendentalpoesie,"* p. 123.

21. *Ibid.*, p. 119.

22. *Werke*, I, pp. 441-44.

23. *Werke*, II, p. 112.

24. *Historik: Vorlesung über Enzyklopädie und Methodologie der Geschichte*, ed. R. Hübner (Munich, ^{5}1967), p. 35.

25. *Ibid.*, p. 34.

26. Droysen himself was caught up in the idea that in the history of art or literature "the sought-for, objective facts lie directly in front of us" (*ibid.*, p. 96).

27. See the critique of literary history by R. Barthes, in *Sur Racine* (Paris, 1960); Eng. *On Racine*, trans. Richard Howard (New York, 1964).

28. Jauss, "Literary History as a Challenge to Literary Theory" (Chapter 1 of this volume).

29. *Historik*, pp. 133, 167.

30. *Ibid.*, p. 91.

31. Droysen, *Historik*, § 16 (henceforth quoted only with page number or §).

32. Variant in manuscript print of 1858.

33. A. Thierry, *Sur les trois grandes méthodes historiques en usage depuis le seizième siècle* (1820); De Barante, *Préface de l'Histoire des Ducs de Bourgogne* (1824), and the anonymous article, "De la nouvelle école historique" (1828); quoted from K. Massmann, *Die Rezeption des historischen Romans von Sir Walter Scott in Frankreich von 1816 bis 1832*, Diss. Konstanz, 1969, esp. p. 118.

34. That there was here a "parallelism of intention . . . which justifies the assertion that the historical novel of the Scott type . . . was capable of fulfilling the programme of the eighteenth-century Scottish school of history more completely than it could itself" is also shown by E. Wolff, "Zwei Versionen des historischen Romans: Scotts 'Waverley' und Thackerays 'Henry Esmond,' " in *Lebende Antike, Symposium für R. Sühnel*, ed. H. Meller and H. -J. Zimmermann (Berlin, 1967), pp. 348-69 (esp. 357).

35. Ed. O. Vossler (Stuttgart, 1954), pp. 78-95 (henceforth quoted only with page numbers).

36. The beginnings of a new style are, according to K. Badt (see note 87), "often not tentative or imperfect, but—like Athene out of the head of Zeus—the new style stands com-

plete before us, perhaps a little coarse, but nevertheless fully and characteristically developed" (p. 139).

37. See Droysen, p. 285, and also A. C. Danto, *Analytical Philosophy of History* (Cambridge, 1965), who overlooks the fact that the difference between the "whole" of a work of art, and the never completed "whole of history" only exists so long as one does not consider the work of art in the historical dimension of its reception.

38. This preconception, which Danto seeks to explain as a "social inheritance" (pp. 224, 242), like his general attempt to establish a relative legitimacy for the historical, would be easier to grasp through Droysen's idea of analogies of historical experience. See *Historik*, p. 159: "Whatever is given in the nature of the thing, we have learnt from our experience and knowledge elsewhere of analogous situations—as the sculptor, restoring an old torso, has this basic analogy in the constant form of the human body."

39. The metric scheme alone is not enough to determine the generic form of a sonnet, as Danto, p. 256, obviously assumes.

40. See H. R. Jauss, "Littérature médiévale et théorie des genres," in *Poétique, revue de théorie et d'analyse littéraires* (1970), pp. 79-101 (esp. p. 92).

41. M. Heidegger, "Der Ursprung des Kunstwerks," in *Holzwege*, Frankfurt, 1950, p. 18 (Eng., "The Origin of the Work of Art," in *Poetry, Language, Thought*, trans. Albert Hofstadter [New York, 1971]); also the corresponding definition of *classical* in H.-G. Gadamer, *Wahrheit und Methode* (Tübingen, 1960), p. 272 (Eng., *Truth and Method*, no trans. [New York, 1975]): "a consciousness of permanence, of the unlosable meaning independent of all temporal circumstances . . . a kind of timeless present, which means contemporaneous for every present"; or E. R. Curtius, *Europäische Literatur und lateinisches Mittelalter* (Bern, 1948), p. 23 (Eng., *European Literature and the Latin Middle Ages*, [New York, 1953]): "The 'timeless present' which is an essential element of literature, means that the literature of the past can always remain effective in any present."

42. H.-G. Gadamer, pp. 261 ff.: *Die Rehabilitierung von Autorität und Tradition.*

43. W. Krauss, *Literaturgeschichte als geschichtlicher Auftrag*, in *Sinn und Form 2* (1950), p. 113.

44. P. 138.

45. In *Le Peintre de la vie moderne*, in *Oeuvres complètes* (Paris, 1951), pp. 873-76.

46. "Thesen über Tradition," in *Insel Almanach auf das Jahr 1966*, pp. 21-33.

47. See Adorno, p. 29: "(Here) one meets with the true theme of the recollection of tradition, which brings together all that has remained by the wayside, the neglected, the defeated, under the name of the out-of-date. There the living element of tradition seeks refuge, and not in the store of works that are to defy time"; and see especially S. Kracauer, whose philosophy of history in *History: The Last Things Before the Last* (New York, 1969) vindicates in many respects the demand "to undo the injurious work of tradition" (p. 7).

48. Gadamer, p. 261.

49. Concerning the term "*Konkretisation*" (materialization), which I have taken over from F. Vodička, see below.

50. *Wahrheit und Methode*, pp. 351-55.

51. "Edward Fuchs, der Sammler und Historiker," in *Angelus Novus* (Frankfurt, 1966), p. 304.

52. See the detailed critique by G. Hartman, "Toward Literary History," in *Daedalus* (Spring, 1970), pp. 355-83; also C. Segre, *I segni e la critica* (Turin, 1969), who also subjects the claims of semiological literary theory to well-argued criticism.

53. Northrop Frye, *Anatomy of Criticism* (New York, 1967), pp. 16 seq.

54. P. 348.

55. Paris, 1968 (*Mythologiques*, III), pp. 69-106.

56. "La structure, le mot, l'événement," in *Esprit* 35 (1967), pp. 801-21, esp. 808; spe-

204 OCR NOTES TO PP. 67-71

cial attention should be paid to this fundamental critique, which develops hermeneutic approaches to the problem of overcoming structural dogmatism.

57. *Sur Racine*, see esp. p. 17: "Les trois espaces extérieurs: mort, fuite, événement" and p. 54: "La faute (La théologie racinienne est une rédemption inversée: c'est l'homme qui rachète Dieu)", p. 55.

58. *Ibid.*, p. 156.

59. *Ibid.*

60. See statements of R. Picard and C. Lévi-Strauss, quoted by G. Schiwy, *Der französische Strukturalismus* (Hamburg, 1969), p. 67 and p. 71 respectively.

61. *Sur Racine*, p. 11: "In literature, which is an order of connotation, there is no *pure* question; a question is always nothing but its own scattered answer, which is split up in fragments, between which the meaning springs up and at the same time escapes." This new accentuation of the problem in itself implies what Barthes did not see—the answering character of the text, which is the prime connecting-point for its reception.

62. Hence the greater resistance of art to time—that "paradoxical nature" of the work, unexplained by R. Barthes: "it is a sign for history, and at the same time resistance against it" (p. 13).

63. *Die Appellstruktur der Texte: Unbestimmtheit als Wirkungsbedingung literarischer Prosa* (Konstanz, 1970), *Konstanzer Universitätsreden*, ed. G. Hess, vol. XXVIII.

64. This interaction has been described by H.-G. Gadamer as a "fusion of horizons": (*Horizontverschmelzung*), pp. 289 seq., 356. In my opinion, this description, with which I concur, does not necessarily give rise to the reversal of the relationship between question and answer which Gadamer (pp. 351-56) brings about in order to ensure the precedence of the "event of tradition" over understanding as "a productive procedure" (p. 280).

65. *Kritik und Wahrheit* (Frankfurt, 1967), p. 68.

66. *Ibid.*, p. 68.

67. *Ibid.*, p. 70.

68. *Ibid.*, pp. 88-91. In *Sur Racine*, the programmatic "literary history without individuals" is understood as a history of the literary institution; the mediation between production, communication, and reception remains quite open, and in the end R. Barthes has to confess that the result of this reduction is "simply history," and so no longer specific to the historicity of art (pp. 22-23).

69. Chapter 1 of this volume.

70. For my account of this, I am indebted to Jurij Striedter and the Research Group for the Structural Study of Language and Literature at the University of Constance, who have prepared a detailed presentation and a German edition of the most important texts of Prague Structuralism for the series *Theorie und Geschichte der Literatur und der Schönen Künste*, published by W. P. Fink, Munich, and have allowed me to quote from their translation of F. Vodička's book *Struktura vývoje* (since published: *Die Structure der literarischen Einbildung*, intro. by J. Striedter, Munich, 1976). The semiotic structuralism of Soviet literary study does not yet appear to be concerned with the problem of a structural history of literature so much as with structural analysis of literary genres. See K. Eimermacher, "Entwicklung, Charakter und Probleme des sowjetischen Strukturalismus in der Literaturwissenschaft," in *Sprache im technischen Zeitalter*, 30 (1969), pp. 126-57. Of prime importance are the writings of Jurij Lotman: *Lekcii po struktural' noj poetike* (Tartu, 1964), repr. Providence, Rhode Island, 1968.

71. In the collection of essays *Figures* (Paris, 1966), pp. 145-70.

72. "Structure et herméneutique," in *Esprit* 31 (1963), pp. 596-627; continued with: "La structure, le mot, l'événement," in *Esprit* 35 (1967), pp. 801-21.

73. P. 161.

74. *Ibid.*, pp. 162-64.

75. *Ibid.*, p. 167: "L'idée structuraliste, içi, c'est de suivre la littérature dans son évolution globale en pratiquant des coupes synchroniques à diverses étapes, et en comparant les tableaux entre eux. . . . C'est dans le changement continuel de fonction que se manifeste la vraie vie des éléments de l'oeuvre littéraire."

76. In *Quatre conférences sur la "Nouvelle Critique"* (Turin, Società editrice internazionale, 1968), p. 38.

77. *Ibid.*, p. 39.

78. *Ibid.*, p. 39: "Les grandes oeuvres rebelles sont ainsi trahies, elles sont — par le commentaire et la glose — exorcisées, rendues acceptables et versées au patrimoine commun. . . . Mais la compréhension critique ne vise pas à l'assimilation du dissemblable. Elle ne serait pas compréhension si elle ne comprenait pas la différence en tant que différence."

79. The most important writings of J. Mukařovský are to be found in "Chapters from Czech poetry," *Kapitoly z české poetiky* (Prague, 1948), 3 vols., and *Studie z estetiky* (Studies from Aesthetics) (Prague, 1966).

80. The book *Struktura vývoje* (Structure of Development), published in Prague in 1969, takes up two older works: *Konkretizace literárního díla* (Materialization of the Literary Work, 1941), and *Literární historie, její problemy a úkoly* (Literary History, Its Problems and Tasks, 1942); see note 70.

81. *Struktura vývoje*, p. 35.

82. P. 199.

83. P. 41.

84. P. 196.

85. P. 206.

86. This objection is raised by M. Wehrli in his address: *Literatur und Geschichte, Jahresbericht der Universität Zürich* (1969-1970), p. 6.

87. K. Badt, *Wissenschaftslehre der Kunstgeschichte* (p. 160). This was an unpublished work, which the author has kindly allowed me to quote from; it also proceeds from a consideration of Droysen's *Historik*, in order to establish a new methodological basis for the history of the fine arts (since published, Cologne, 1971).

88. *Ibid.*, p. 190.

89. Here I am following K. Kosík, *Die Dialektik des Konkreten* (Frankfurt, 1967), esp. the chapter: "Historismus und Historizismus," pp. 133-49.

90. *Ibid.*, p. 143.

91. *Ibid.*, p. 148.

92. *Ibid.*

Chapter 3. Theory of Genres and Medieval Literature

1. This was revived by the "Third International Congress of Modern Literary History," held in Lyon in May 1939 ("Travaux du 3e Congrès international d'Histoire littéraire moderne," *Helicon 2* [1940]), that was devoted to the genre problem that had been declared dead by Croce and that thereby provoked his scornful protest. Cf. G. Zacharias, "B. Croce und die literarischen Gattungen," dissertation, University of Hamburg, 1951. For further discussion cf. J. Pommier, "L'Idée de genre," *Publications de l'École Normale Supérieure*, Section des Lettres, II (Paris, 1945), pp. 47-81; René Wellek and Austin Warren, *Theory of Literature* (New York, 1942), ch. 17: "Literary Genres"; and W. Ruttkowski, *Die literarischen Gattungen* (Bern, 1968), useful for its bibliography.

2. H. Kuhn, "Gattungsprobleme der mittelhochdeutschen Literatur," in *Dichtung und Welt im Mittelalter*, 2nd ed. (Stuttgart, 1969), p. 45.

3. Cf. Kuhn, "Gattungsprobleme," p. 7: "But what does one do with the unsung maxim, rhymed discourse, the fable, with all the types that play, without boundaries, across

the didactic, the novelistic, the allegorical, from the smallest forms up to the great forms? Should the passion play function as tragedy, the *Fasnachtspiel* as comedy? Can the didactic and the religious literature of all forms constitute their own genres, since, as 'epic,' 'lyric' or 'dramatic,' they are only pseudotypes. And once again, prose of all kinds, literary and pragmatic, religious and scholarly and practical, with the most varied transitions into poetry: rhymed prefaces to *Lucidarius* and *Sachsenspiegel*, rhymed and prose chronicles world-historical as well as locally historical, the ritual literature?"

4. Croce's aesthetics were mediated in the United States through J. E. Spingarn, who counts among the ground-breakers of New Criticism; cf. Spingarn, "The New Criticism" (1910), in *The Achievement of American Criticism*, ed. C. A. Brown, (New York, 1954), pp. 525-46, and J. Hermand, "Probleme der heutigen Gattungsgeschichte," in *Jahrbuch für internationale Germanistik* 2 (1970), pp. 85-94.

5. On the founding of an historical aesthetics, cf. Peter Szondi, "Einleitung" to *Theorie des modernen Dramas* (Frankfurt a.M., 1956), and his "La Théorie des genres poétiques chez Friedrich Schlegel," *Critique* (March 1968), pp. 264-92.

6. Benedetto Croce, *Estetica*, 2nd ed. (Bari, 1902), p. 40.

7. *Ibid.*, pp. 40, 75.

8. The two names, *Erlebnisästhetik* and *Genieästhetik*, refer, respectively, to criticism represented by Dilthey's *Das Erlebnis und die Dichtung* (1907), and the late eighteenth-century theories of Hamann, Herder, and "Sturm und Drang." (Tr.)

9. Wolf-Dieter Stempel, "Pour une description des genres littéraires," in *Actes du XIIe Congrès international de linguistique Romane* (Bucharest, 1968), p. 565, on the fundamental condition of any theory of discourse: "Every act of linguistic communication is reducible to a generic and conventional norm, composed, on the level of the spoken language, of the social index and the situational index as a unity of behavior."

10. F. Sengle, *Die literarische Formenlehre* (Stuttgart, 1966), p. 19.

11. According to E. Coseriu, "Thesen zum Thema 'Sprache und Dichtung'," in *Beiträge zur Textlinguistik*, ed. Wolf-Dieter Stempel (Munich, 1971), pp. 183-88, esp. section II, 2; cf. Stempel: "Thus the genre, as it were, is at once of the system and of the utterance [*parole*], a status corresponding to that which Coseriu calls 'norm.' "

12. What Croce, *Estetica*, p. 78, called "the family atmosphere" (to indicate the similarity of expressions) and played against the concept of genre, thus receives a positive meaning.

13. Kant, *Kritik der ästhetischen Urteilskraft*, sec. 18. Here I am following the interpretation of Gerhard Buck, "Kants Lehre vom Exempel," *Archiv für Begriffsgeschichte* 11 (1967), p. 182, to which I owe this suggested solution of the genre problem.

14. With this formulation, J. G. Droysen in his *Historik*, ed. R. Hübner (Munich, 1967), pp. 9 ff., paraphrases the Aristotelian determination of mankind (*epidosis eis auto*) as opposed to the merely generic animals or plants (*De anima* II, 4.5). Droysen's formulation, which grounds his image of the continuity of progressive historical *labor*, is directed against the organic concept of development, and thus is also appropriate for the historicized concept of the literary genre.

15. Cf. Stempel, "Pour une description des genres littéraires."

16. Taking off from the theory of genre developed here, H. U. Gumbrecht, *Funktionswandel und Rezeption: Studien zum hyperbolischen Ausdruck in literarischen Texten des romanischen Mittelalters* (Munich, 1972), has investigated the limits of probability and the "literary tones" of various genres on the basis of a statistical study of hyperbolic expressions in twelfth- and thirteenth-century texts.

17. Juri Tynjanov, "Das literarische Faktum" (1924), in *Texte der russischen Formalisten*, Vol. I (Theorie und Geschichte der Literatur und der schönen Künste VI), ed. Juri Striedter (Munich, 1969), pp. 392-431; cf. Striedter, p. 1xii.

18. On the *gap*, cf. J. U. Fechner, "Zum Gap in der altprovenzalischen Lyrik," *German-*

ische-romanische Monatsschrift, 14 (new series; 1964), pp. 15-34; on the grotesque, cf. *Die nicht mehr schönen Künste* (Poetik und Hermeneutik, III), ed. H. R. Jauss (Munich, 1968), under *das Groteske*.

19. On Shaftesbury's *The Judgment of Hercules*, cf. Karl Viëtor, "Problem der literarischen Gattungsgeschichte," *Deutsche Vierteljahrschrift für Literaturwissenschaft und Geistesgeschichte* 9 (1931), 296-300.

20. André Jolles, *Einfache Formen: Legende, Sage, Mythe, Rätsel, Spiel, Kasus, Morabile, Märchen, Witz* (1930), 2nd ed. (Halle, 1956), p. 196.

21. Cf. *Chanson de geste und höfischer Roman* (Studia romanica IV) (Heidelberg, 1963), pp. 70 ff..

22. *Ibid.*, pp. 69-70.

23. References for the synchronic system correspond to the paragraphs of the outline:

1.1: Cf. Northrop Frye, *Anatomy of Criticism* (Princeton, N. J., 1957), pp. 248, 249, where he distinguishes a speaking poet and a listening audience (epic), a writing author and an unseen audience ([prose] fiction), the concealment of the author from his audience (drama), and the concealment of the poet's audience from the poet (lyric).

1.2: On the "signes du narrateur," cf. Roland Barthes, "Introduction à l'analyse structurale des récits," *Communications* 8 (1966), p. 19.

1.3: The opposition between "how-suspense" and "if-at-all-suspense" is developed by C. Lugowski, *Die Form der Individualität im Roman* (Berlin, 1932), pp. 41 ff.; on epic distance and the opposition between "passé du savoir" and "passé du recit" (future in the past), cf. H. R. Jauss, *Zeit und Erinnerung im Marcel Prousts "A la recherche du temps perdu"*, 2nd ed. (Heidelberg, 1970), pp. 18 ff.

2.1: On the etymology of *romanz* and *novela*, see Karl Vossler, *Die Dichtungsformen der Romanen* (Stuttgart, 1951), pp. 305, 306.

2.3: According to Erich Auerbach, *Mimesis: Dargestellte Wirklichkeit in der abendländischen Literatur*, 2nd ed. (Bern, 1959), chs. v, vi; Boccaccio, *Decameron*, Conclusione 3 (concerning the accusation that he had "troppa licenzia usata," and said to the women "cose non assai convenienti"): "La qual cosa io nego, per ciò chen niuna sì disonesta n'è, che, con onesti vocaboli dicendola, si disdica ad alcuno."

3.1: On the opposition between action and happening, which goes back to Hegel's aesthetics, see Jauss, *Chanson de geste und höfischer Roman*, p. 72; on Goethe's formulation (conversation with Eckermann on 25 January 1827) and its formerly unexhausted significance for the casuistry specific to the novella, see H.-J. Neuschäfer, *Boccaccio und der Beginn der Novellistik* (Theorie und Geschichte der Literatur und der Schönen Künste VIII) (Munich, 1969), pp. 76 ff.

3.2: The gradation of the protagonists in epic, romance, and novella corresponds to the three middle grades in Northrop Frye's classification according to the heroes' possibilities of action, cf. *Anatomy of Criticism*, pp. 33, 34; the scale can be differentiated according to the structural status of the types of action, as, for example, with Tzvetan Todorov's basic predicates (love, communication, help) or A. J. Greimas's *actants* (subject/object, giver/receiver, helper/opponent), cf. Barthes, "Introduction," pp. 15 ff.

3.3: On the structure of courtly adventures and their opposite world, see Erich Köhler, *Ideal und Wirklichkeit in der höfischen Epik* (Tübingen, 1956), chs. iii/iv; Boccaccio, *Decameron*, Concl. 18: "Conviene nella moltitudine delle cose diverse qualità di cose trovarsi."

4.1: On the degrees of reality, see below on Johannes de Garlandia's *Poetria*; on the various substrata of the saga (for the epic) and the fairy tale (for the romance) and their definition by Jakob Grimm, see Jauss, *Chanson de geste und höfischer Roman*, pp. 64 ff.; on the social character of the novella, see Erich Auerbach, *Zur Technik der Frührenaissancenovelle in Italien und Frankreich* (Heidelberg, 1921), p. 1.

4.2: The opposition between the ethics of action and the ethics of the event is developed by Jolles, *Einfach Formen*, p. 201.

4.3: On the relationship between epic and *mémoire collective*, see M. Bloch, *La société féodale*, Vol. I (Paris, 1949), pp. 147-63; on the social function of the romance, see J. Frappier, *Etude sur Yvain* . . . (Paris, 1969), pp. 185 ff.: the quote on the novella is taken from Auerbach, *Zur Technik der Frührenaissancenovelle*, p. 3.

24. My definition of the romance relies in many points on Paul Zumthor, "Le roman courtois: Essai de définition," in *Etudes litéraires* 4 (1971), pp. 75-90.

25. Juri Tynjanov and Roman Jakobson, "Probleme der Literatur- und Sprachforschung" (1928), in *Kursbuch* 5 (1966), pp. 74-76; cf. Jauss, Chapter 1 of this volume.

26. Cf. note 14; André Jolles, *Einfache Formen*, p. 7, intends the same principle when he speaks of "language as labor": "to establish the path which leads from language to literature . . . as we comparatively observe how one and the same phenomenon repeats itself in an enriched manner on another level, how a force governs the system as a whole, forming a structure and limiting the form, and elevating itself with each step."

27. Formulated linguistically, as the expansion of a semiotic system that fulfills itself between the unfolding and correction of the system; cf. Stempel, "Pour une description. . . ."

28. From Droysen, *Historik*, p. 198, referring to national peoples as "individual structures."

29. W. Kellermann, "Über die altfranzösischen Gedichte des uneingeschränkten Unsinns," in *Archiv für das Studium der neureren Sprachen* 205 (1968), pp. 1-22, who there summarizes the pertinent studies by A. M. Schmidt, Paul Zumthor, L. C. Porter and their reviewers.

30. W. Hempel, in a book review in *Romanische Forschungen* 73 (1961), p. 450, has called attention to this.

31. Kellermann, "Über die altfranzösischen Gedichte," p. 14.

32. The character of the fatras as "gloss" stems from P. Le Gentil, cf. Kellermann, *ibid.*, p. 4.

33. W. Kellermann, "Ein Schachspiel des französischen Mittelalters: die Resveries," *Mélanges* R. Lejeune, 1969, pp. 1331-46.

34. *Ibid.*, pp. 1335-36.

35. B. Goth, *Untersuchungen zur Gattungsgeschichte der Sottie* (Bochumer Arbeiten zur Sprach- und Literaturwissenschaft I) (Munich, 1967), pp. 37 ff..

36. Droysen, *Historik*, p. 209.

37. On this see Werner Krauss, *Studien zur deutschen und französischen Aufklärung* (Berlin, 1963), pp. 73, 74: "The attempt to explain the whole course of a literary period through the constant influence of basic economic relationships would not only call into question the meaning of literary history, but indeed destroy the existence of literature as an immanently coherent sphere of creativity. Literature would remain only an unorganic series of mere reflexes. The vulgar-materialist dissolution of literature into sociology misses the real essence of literary phenomena as much as the idealist explanation of the sovereignty of mental creativity does."

38. Krauss, "Die literarischen Gattungen," in *Essays zur französischen Literatur* (Berlin and Weimar, 1968), p. 13.

39. Erich Köhler, *Esprit und arkadische Freiheit: Aufsätze aus der Welt der Romania* (Frankfurt a.M. and Bonn, 1966), p. 86.

40. Krauss, "Die literarischen Gattungen," p. 9.

41. *Ibid.*, pp. 8, 9.

42. W. Mittenzwei, "Die Brecht-Lukács-Debatte," *Das Argument* (March 1968), pp. 12-43; also Karl Kosík, *Die Dialektik des Konkreten* (Frankfurt a.M., 1967); cf. *Texte der russischen Formalisten*, ed. Striedter, I, p. lxxviii.

43. Köhler, "Die Pastourellen des Trobadors Gavaudan," in *Esprit und arkadische Freiheit*, pp. 67-82.

44. Köhler, "Sirventes-Kanzone: 'genre bâtard' oder legitime Gattung?" in *Mélanges R. Lejeune*, p. 172: "While the *canzone* honors the ideal of individual fulfillment in *joi d'amor*, celebrating or also complaining of the happiness and pain of love, and the *sirventes* on the other hand denounces everything which opposes this ideal, it is the structural principle of the *sirventes-canzone* to *maintain* that ideal through the *representation* of *possible* fulfillments and *actual* hindrances."

45. Neuschäfer, *Boccaccio und der Beginn der Novellistik*.

46. *Ibid.*, p. 8.

47. As does W. Pabst, *Novellentheorie und Novellendichtung*, 2nd ed. (Heidelberg, 1967).

48. Viëtor, "Probleme der literarischen Gattungsgeschichte," p. 304.

49. Cf. H. Kuhn, "Gattungsprobleme der mittelhochdeutschen Literatur," pp. 46, 56 f., 61.

50. On this last aspect I can refer to my studies of the Renart-epigones: cf. *Untersuchungen zur mittelalterlichen Tierdichtung*, (Beihefte zur Zeitschrift für romanische Philologie C) (Tübingen, 1959), ch. V; also *Cultura neolatina* 21 (1961), pp. 214-19, and *Mélanges Delbouille*, 1964, Vol. II, pp. 291-312.

51. Benjamin, "Eduard Fuchs, der Sammler und Historiker," in *Angelus Novus* (Frankfurt a.M., 1966), p. 303.

52. I. Behrens, *Die Lehre von der Einteilung der Dichtkunst* (Beihefte zur Zeitschrift für romanischen Philologie XCII) (Halle, 1940); E. Faral, *Les arts poétiques du XIIe et du XIIIe siècles* (Paris, 1924); E. de Bruyne, *Etudes d'esthétique médiévale*, 3 vols. (Brugge, 1946), esp. II, 42.

53. According to Faral, *Les arts poétiques*, p. 82: "That which was a matter of style for the first critics became a matter of social dignity for the school of the twelfth and thirteenth centuries. It is the quality of the characters, and not that of the elocution, that furnishes the principle of classification"; and de Bruyne, *Etudes*, II, 41 ff..

54. Krauss, "Die literarischen Gattungen," p. 15.

55. E. R. Curtius, *Europäische Literatur und lateinisches Mittelalter*, 3rd ed. (Bern, 1961), "Exkurs V: Spätantike Literaturwissenschaft"; Eng. *European Literature and the Latin Middle Ages*, trans. Willard R. Trask (New York, 1953).

56. De Bruyne, *Etudes*, II, 18 ff..

57. Curtius, *European Literature*, ch. 17, sec. 5: "Die *Commedia* und die literarischen Gattungen."

58. For this essay the results of the *Grundriss der Romanischen Literaturen des Mittelalters* monographs on genres (to appear after Volume I) could not yet be evaluated. The significance of the *jongleur* repertories that have been handed down (e.g., that of Guiraut de Cabreira; cf. R. Lejeune, "La forme de 'l'ensehamen au jongleur' du troubadour Guiraut de Cabreira," in *Mélanges L. N. d'Olwer* (Barcelona, 1966), II, pp. 171-82), and of the generic groupings in the collected manuscripts for a historical systematics of literary genres, deserves a comprehensive investigation.

59. Cf. Jauss, *Untersuchungen zur mittelalterlichen Tierdichtung*, ch. IV A.

60. For the interpretation of this prologue, cf. R. Guiette, *Romania* 78 (1967), pp. 1-12.

61. Hugo Friedrich, *Epochen der italienischen Lyrik* (Frankfurt a.M., 1964), p. 90.

62. A. Jeanroy, "Les genres lyriques secondaires dans la poésie provençale du XIVe siècle," in *Mélanges Pope*, 1939, pp. 209-14; new definitions of the *escondig* (song of justification) and the *comjat* (song of farewell) are provided by Christian Fey, *Bild und Funktion der dompna in der Lyrik der Trobadors* (Heidelberg, Ph.D. dissertation, 1971).

63. Poirion, *Le poète et le prince: L'évolution du lyrisme courtois de Guillaume de Machaut à Charles d'Orléans* (Paris, 1965), pp. 313-316.

64. For a critique of these premises for E. R. Curtius's research into tradition (e.g., his *European Literature*, ch. 1), cf. W. Bulst, "Bedenken eines Philologen," in *Medium Aevum Vivum*, H. R. Jauss and W. Schaller, eds., Heidelberg, 1960, pp. 7-10, and Jauss, Chapter 1 of this volume.

65. J. Rychner, *La chanson de geste: Essai sur l'art épique des jongleurs* (Société de publications romanes et françaises LXXX) (Geneva, 1955); cf. "La technique littéraire des Chansons de geste," *Actes du Colloque de Liège*, September 1957 (Bibliothèque de la Faculté de philologie et de lettres de l'Université de Liège CL), ed. M. Delbouille (Paris, 1959); also the report of the Congrès de Poitiers (July 1959) of the Société Rencesvals, in *Bulletin bibliographique de la Société Rencesvals* 2 (1960), pp. 59-122.

66. Rychner, *La chanson de geste*, p. 48.

67. Rudolf Bultmann, *Die Geschichte der synoptischen Tradition*, 6th ed. (Göttingen, 1964), p. 4.

68. Cf. *ibid.*, p. vii.

69. A. Robert and A. Feuillet, *Introduction à la Bible* (Tournai, 1959), p. 150.

70. *Ibid.*, p. 150.

71. Robert and Feuillet; *Los géneros literarios de la Sagrada Escritura* (Congreso de ciencias eclesiásticas, Salamanca, 1954) (Barcelona, 1957); also, A. Lods, *Histoire de la littérature hébraïque et juive* (Paris, 1950); A. Benizen, *Introduction to the Old Testament*, 2nd ed. (Kopenhagen, 1952); H. C. Dodd, *The apostolic preaching and its developments*, 7th ed. (1957); K. Koch, *Was ist Formengeschichte? Neue Wege der Bibelexegese*, 2nd ed. (Neukirchen-Vluyn, 1967).

72. Robert and Feuillet, *Los géneros*, p. 123.

73. C. Kuhl and G. Bornkamm, "Formen und Gattungen," in *Religion in Geschichte und Gegenwart: Handwörterbuch für Theologie und Religionswissenschaft*, 3rd ed. (Tübingen, 1958), II, columns 996-1005.

74. Bultmann, *Die Geschichte*, p. 40.

75. *Ibid.*, pp. 40, 41.

76. Auerbach, *Literatursprache und Publikum in der lateinischen Spätantike und im Mittelalter* (Bern, 1958), p. 32; cf. Eng., *Literary Language and Its Public in Late Latin Antiquity and in the Middle Ages*, trans. Ralph Manheim, (Princeton, N. J., 1965), p. 37.

77. Cf. Bultmann, *Die Geschichte*, p. 4: "Just as the *locus in life* is not a unique historical event, but rather a typical situation or mode of behavior in the life of a community, the literary genre—or respectively, the *form* through which a particular piece is coordinated with a genre—is similarly a sociological concept and not an aesthetic one, however much such forms may be used in a later development as aesthetic means for an individualizing literature."

78. M. Waltz, "Zum Problem der Gattungsgeschichte im Mittelalter," in *Zeitschrift für romanische Philologie* 86 (1970), pp. 32 and 33, note 17, on the autonomy of courtly poetry, which sets in rather early: "The courtly forms also prefigure in other ways the stable genres of the later period: they live in a symbolic world (which they essentially carry with them) that is separated from the official religious one, and its socio-cultural function is less immediately comprehensible."

79. *Ibid.*, p. 35.

80. See the *Grundriss der Romanischen Literaturen des Mittelalters*, Vol. VI, C, pp. 160, 233 (forthcoming).

81. Roger Dragonetti, *Revue belge de philologie et d'histoire* 43 (1965), p. 118; cf. *GRLMA*, VI, C, p. 151.

82. Rainer Warning, "Ritus, Mythos and geistliches Spiel," in *Poetica* 3 (1970), pp. 83-114.

83. *Ibid.*, p. 102.

84. Summarized by Striedter, ed., *Texte der russischen Formalisten*, I, pp. lx-lxx.

85. *Ibid.*, p. lxvi.

86. *Ibid.*, p. lxv.

87. Juri Tynjanov provided the model of such an analysis of the history of a genre for the ode in "Die Ode als oratorisches Genre" (1922), in *Texte der russischen Formalisten*, II, ed. W.-D. Stempel (Munich, 1972), pp. 273-337; Boris Tomachevsky provides examples for the "penetration of the procedures of the vulgar genre into the higher genre" in "Thématique" (1925), in *Théorie de la littérature: Textes des formalistes russes*, ed. Tzvetan Todorov (Paris, 1965), pp. 263-307.

88. Cf. Köhler, "Zur Entstehung des altfranzösischen Prosaromans," in *Trobadorlyrik und höfischer Roman* (Berlin, 1962), pp. 213-23.

89. Tynjanov, "Die Ode als oratorisches Genre."

90. Jolles, *Einfache Formen.*

91. Jan Mukařovský, *Kapitel aus der Poetik* (Frankfurt, a.M., 1967), and *Kapitel aus der Ästhetik* (Frankfurt a.M., 1970); on these see Striedter, ed., *Texte der russischen Formalisten*, I, pp. lxi, lxxix; Jauss, Chapter 1 of this volume.

92. Concerning the "answering character" of the work of art, as well as the hermeneutic logic and tradition-forming function of the procedure of question and answer, I refer the reader to Chapter 1 of this volume.

Chapter 4. Goethe's and Valery's Faust: On the Hermeneutics of Question and Answer

1. Cyrus Hamlin, "Literary History and Tradition: The Importance of Goethe's *Weltliteratur* for Comparative Literature" (paper delivered at the Congress of the International Comparative Literature Association, Ottawa, 1973); Claus Träger, "Weltgeschichte—Nationaliteratur—Weltliteratur," in *Weimarer Beitrage*, Heft 7 (1974), p. 20; Manfred Gsteiger, "Pourquoi la littérature comparée?" in *Etudes de lettres*, III, 7 (1974), p. 14.

2. According to Roland Barthes; see my critique in Chapter 1 of this volume. For the following definition of myth I refer to André Jolles, *Einfache Formen*, 2nd ed. (Tübingen, 1958), p. 97, and *Terror und Spiel: Probleme der Mythenrezeption* (Poetik und Hermeneutik IV), ed. Manfred Fuhrmann (Munich, 1971), p. 201.

3. That all structural description in the field of communication acts cannot manage without the hermeneutic circle is also demonstrated by Umberto Eco, "Rhetoric and Ideology in Sue's *Les Mystères de Paris,*" in *International Social Science Journal* 19 (1967), p. 551.

4. Cf. "Au lecteur," in *Oeuvres* (Pléiade), ed. Jean Hytier (Paris, 1957-60), II, p. 275 (in the following this edition is cited with the act and scene numbers only); on this see *Les Cahiers*, edited in facsimile by the Centre Nationale de Recherche Scientifique (Paris, 1957-), XI (1925-26), p. 814 and XXIII (1940), p. 736.

5. According to the testimony of his daughter, Agathe Rouard-Valéry, in an interview with the newspaper *Les Spectacles*, 26 November 1970: "My father was very 'chauvinistic,' and he so to speak avenged the events by throwing himself into an obstinate labor, in order to use and channel the violence that was howling within him."

6. Harold Bloom, *The Anxiety of Influence: A Theory of Poetry* (New York, 1973), pp. 18-44.

7. On this see Sander L. Gilman, "Very Little Faust . . . Parodies of German Drama on the Mid-Nineteenth Century British Stage," *Arcadia* 8 (1973), pp. 18-44.

8. "Faust et le Cycle" (1965), now in *Les Critiques de notre temps et Valéry*, ed. Jean Bellemin-Noël (Paris, 1971), pp. 95-107.

9. Lucien Goldmann, "Rationalismus und Dialektik—Bemerkungen zu Valérys *Faust*," in *Festschrift zum 80. Geburtstage von Georg Lukács*, 1965, pp. 443-52.

10. Originally in *Die Legitimität der Neuzeit* (Frankfurt a.M., 1966), pp. 381, 421; then in the revised new edition, *Der Prozess der theoretischen Neugierde* (Frankfurt a.M., 1973), esp. pp. 189 and 241.

11. *Ibid.*, pp. 189, 190.

12. Cf. *ibid.*, p. 214.

13. Cf. *ibid.*, p. 252: "Kant now shows that absolutely no alternative presents itself, but rather that the drive of craving for knowledge itself, consistently pursued, ultimately, in taking hold of the totality of the conditions of objectivity, makes self-knowledge into a necessary theme."

14. Thus in "Schema zu 'Faust,' " cited from the commentary of Erich Trunz in *Goethes Faust*, 3rd ed. (Hamburg, 1954); in the following this edition is cited.

15. On this see my *Kleine Apologie der ästhetischen Erfahrung* (Konstanz, 1972), p. 8.

16. Cf. vv. 328, "A good man in his dark drive"; 1676, "Would a human mind, in its high striving"; 1742, "The striving of all my power"; 11936, "Whoever, always striving, makes the effort."

17. Odo Marquard, *Idealismus und Theodizee* (1965), now in *Schwierigkeiten mit der Geschichtsphilosophie* (Frankfurt a.M., 1973), pp. 52-65.

18. Bastet, "Faust et le Cycle," p. 97; this interpretation may also be supported by a passage in the *Cahiers* (1939-40), XXII, p. 589, entitled "Ego": "I was born, at twenty, exasperated by repetition—that is to say, against life. Awakening, dressing, eating, defecating, sleeping—and always those seasons, those stars. And history—known by heart—to the point of madness . . . this table repeats itself before my eyes for 39 years now. . . . All this passes for being 'poetic.' But for me, poetic is that which is opposed to this sad industry." Further on one also finds a phrase that is revealing for the reprise of the *affaire Marguérite*: "as soon as it was recognized, love appeared to me to be a repetition: all that 'certified sentiment' throughout the ages."

19. In *Cahiers* XXVIII, 921, Valéry calls his Faust a "Sisyphus of life."

20. II, 2; corresponding by, III, 2: "it is so easy to get rid of his soul, and to repurchase it, at a lower price, at the liquidation of the body."

21. Goldmann, "Rationalismus," p. 449.

22. "Despite the fact that the name of sensibility is currently applied only to phenomena of the senses, I believed it possible to annex other areas to this restricted sense; whence the term of generalized sensibility signifies that it concerns not only events produced by our senses, but all which presents itself under certain conditions of sponteneity and of response to a need, a lack, an excitement. In the customary usage the sensibility scarcely means anything but sensorial phenomena; I added phenomena of the intellectual order to it"—from the *Cours de Poétique au Collège de France*, cited by Karl A. Blüher, *Strategie des Geistes—Paul Valérys Faust* (Frankfurt a.M., 1960), p. 37.

23. Blüher, *Strategie des Geistes*, p. 36.

24. According to the formulation with which Valery concluded the explanation cited in note 22: "On the other hand, I insisted on the productive properties which seemed of such an importance that receptivity could be considered as a particular case of the general notion of the sensibility's production."

25. On this, Erika Lorenz, "Der Name *Lust* in Paul Valérys erstem Faust Fragment," in *Romanistiches Jahrbuch* 22 (1971), pp. 178-90. There are previous attempts at interpretation: "O unconscious *Lust*" from Rilke's poem "Imaginärer Lebenslauf" (E. von Richthofen); "yet all *Lust* wants eternity," from Nietzsche's *Zarathustra* (F. W. Müller); "He is to

eat dust, and with *Lust*" (Kurt Wais); or, lying much closer, "He demands the most beautiful stars from heaven, and from earth every highest *Lust*" from Goethe's *Prolog im Himmel* (Erika Lorenz). But they pay too little attention to the subtle play between Faust and *Lust*, and above all to the answering relationship in which Valéry's *Mon Faust* stands to Goethe, to render *Lust*'s connotations more precise.

26. *Schriften zum Theater* (Frankfurt a.M., 1963), VI, pp. 328-330.

27. Thus Trunz, *Goethes Faust*, p. 498. Here as in the whole essay, I could not by far, as a non-Germanist, work through the endless secondary literature, so that I presumably— or hopefully— overlap with the results of others' research.

28. Trunz, p. 514.

29. Karl Marx, *Ökonomisch-philosophische Manuskripte* (1844), cited from *Die Frühschriften*, ed. S. Landshut (Stuttgart, 1971), p. 234.

30. Here my interpretation touches on that of Wilfried Malch, *Die Einheit der Faust-Dichtung Goethes in der Spiegelung ihrer Teile . . .* , pp. 133-58, esp. p. 136, for whom only Helen would be the "revealing mirroring" of that "which could naturally be possible for such love." It seems to me that with this Malch, in the service of his thesis concerning Goethe's turn toward poetry of history, disguises the problem of guilt with Gretchen as well as with Philemon and Baucis, and thereby also disguises the problem of theodicy.

31. Here I can refer to my study "Racines und Goethes Iphigenie" (1973), now in *Rezeptionsästhetik als literaturwissenschaftliche Pragmatik*, ed. Rainer Warning (Munich, 1975).

32. "Goethe und Paul Valérys *Faust*," in *Mélanges de littérature comparée et de philologie, offerts à Mieczyslaw Brahmer* (Warsaw, 1967), p. 568.

33. Karl Löwith, *Paul Valéry— Grundzüge seines Denkens* (Göttingen, 1971).

34. Faust's utterance preceding the monologue—"For me perfumes are promises. Pure promises, nothing more. For nothing surpasses the promise in deliciousness. . . . Above all, nothing more" (II, 5)—at first still appears to be similar to Goethe's "Vorgefühl," but it obtains another meaning through the "pure," which refers to no "afterwards," and the later surpassing of the "nothing more" through the "full and pure knowledge."

35. In *Lust*'s words: "You yourself seem to be one of those moments marvelously full of all the powers that are opposed to death."

36. "What, then, are those exceptional visions which ascetics desire, compared to this prodigious thing which is to see whatever there is? The soul is a poverty."

37. Thus already in "Léonard et les philosophes," *Oeuvres*, I, 1261, and in *Cahiers* VII, 769: "Every philosophic system in which the human body does not play a fundamental role is inept, inapt."

38. Milton, *Paradise Lost* VIII, vv. 469-73, in *The Poetical Works of John Milton*, ed. Helen Darbishire (Oxford, 1952), II, p. 177:

> The Rib he formd and fashiond with his hands;
> Under his forming hands a Creature grew
> Manlike, but different sex, so lovly fair
> That what seems fair in all the World, seemd now
> Mean, or in her summd up, in her containd.

On this cf. Chrétien de Troyes, *Yvain*, ed. W. Foerster (Halle, 1906), vv. 1492-99.

> Onques mes si desmesurer
> An biauté ne se pot Nature;
> Que trespassee i a mesure.
> Ou ele espoir n'i ovra onques?
> Comant poïst avenir donques?
> Don fust so granz biautez venue?

Ja la fist Deus de sa main nue,
Por Nature feire muser.

(Never again, before or after, did Nature so surpass herself in beauty, for with this she stepped beyond all measure. Or perhaps she had nothing to do with it? How, then, could it happen? How did such great beauty arise? God himself created her with his mere hand, in order to astonish Nature.) The history of the *topos*, which here intersects with the competition between Nature and God, still needs investigation.

39. From *Cahiers* XXIV, p. 16.

40. *Oeuvres*, II, p. 1414.

41. Wais, "Goethe und Paul Valérys *Faust*," p. 558.

42. Wais, p. 578. Formulations such as "the never-satisfied Faustian striving toward the potential" (p. 574) or "never lingering, continually seeking the contradiction, meanwhile obtains a sharper definition through Valéry" (p. 571) betray the harmonization in itself that Kurt Wais presupposes (for Valéry the potential is not a goal to be sought; for Goethe the never-lingering is in no way the same thing as "seeking the contradiction").

43. For example, p. 562: "The concept of plenitude works as a doubled metaphor in the creative womb of Valéry's imagination, in the image of masculine epistemological power and feminine beauty, or mental clarity and warmth of soul. This has roots not merely in Valéry's antithetical mode of thought, but also in his life-history."

44. On this see the indispensable critique of Bloom's book by Geoffrey Hartman in *Diacritics* 3 (Spring 1973), pp. 26-32, now in his *The Fate of Reading* (Chicago, 1975).

45. E. von Richthofen, p. 130, calls attention to the fact that Valéry's drafts of the final acts have this sequence in the manuscript.

46. "In summation, the enchantment broken—here a scene of well-being—at least placing it after some error of Lust's—a minimal error but one which shatters the crystalline edifice—all harmonious" (*Cahiers* XXIV, 16).

47. Bastet, "Faust et le Cycle," p. 101.

48. Bastet, p. 101, on *Cahiers* XXIII, p. 894.

49. Bastet, p. 103: " '*Le Solitaire*,' it says in the unedited notes, '*is Suicide*.' "

50. Correspondingly, a fragment from the drafts of *Solitaire III* reads: "Solitaire (to Mephisto): 'When I think of the ridiculous temptations which you dared to propose to that Man-God! All your feeble-mindedness displayed itself that day" (*Oeuvres*, II, 1412).

51. On the Caligula motif, see Ned Bastet, p. 104.

52. Cf. Cahiers XXIV, 374-75: "Note, what I expect of myself, I expect of you—and I know that I cannot expect anything of myself which might be *already something of me*, ready to be imagined, foreseen, therefore of a finite me—that is to say, of an 'other.' For 'other' is an object which one can conceive only as finite."

Chapter 5. The Poetic Text Within the Change of Horizons of Reading

1. *Wahrheit und Methode* (Tübingen, 1960), pp. 290 ff. Available in English as *Truth and Method*, translation edited by Garrett Barden and John Cumming (New York, 1975).

2. *Ibid.*, p. 294.

3. *Einführung in die literarische Hermeneutik* (Frankfurt, 1975), p. 13.

4. R. Posner drew this conclusion from the debate: "Obviously, neither the prosody nor the semantics of the poem can be revealed through the mere description of the written text—to say nothing of the aesthetic code of the poem that above all makes use of these textual levels. Similarly to how one can get the prosodic indicators right only by beginning with their acoustic realization, one also can only describe the semantics adequately if one begins with a text that is already fully received and understood." See his "Strukturalismus

in der Gedichtsinterpretation," *Sprache im technischen Zeitalter* 29 (1969), pp. 27-58, esp. p. 47.

5. Now in *Essais de stylistique structurale* (Paris, 1971), pp. 307 ff.; cf. his "The Reader's Perception of Narrative," in *Interpretation of Narrative* (Toronto, 1978).

6. *Ibid.*, p. 29: "Instead of only looking for rules regulating narrative structures, I propose that we look for rules regulating actualization of such structures in the text, that is, regulating the very performance of literature as communication." On his "reader-reception modes," see *Semiotics of Poetry* (Bloomington, Indiana, 1978), pp. 115 ff.

7. In a still unpublished lecture on literary hermeneutics, Dubrovnik, 1978.

8. On this, see my *Ästhetische Erfahrung und literarische Hermeneutik* (Munich, 1979), p. 62 and chapter A 6. This book is forthcoming in the English translation of Michael Shaw from the University of Minnesota Press.

9. The Dubrovnik lecture (see note 7). *Wahrheit und Methode*, p. 291, touches on my qualification that in aesthetic perception understanding certainly implies interpretation, but does not at the same time have to articulate it as a theme. "Interpretation is not an act that occasionally and retrospectively attaches to understanding; rather, understanding is always interpretation, and interpretation therefore the explicit form of understanding."

10. *Das Problem der Relevanz* (Frankfurt, 1971).

11. *Essais de stylistique structurale*, p. 340.

12. *Der Akt des Lesens* (Munich, 1976).

13. "Analyse textuelle d'un conte d'Edgar Poe," in *Sémiotique narrative et textuelle*, ed. Claude Chabrol (Paris, 1973), pp. 29-54.

14. *Ibid.*, p. 30.

15. *Ibid.*, p. 32.

16. *Ibid.*, p. 51.

17. *Ibid.*, pp. 30 and 52.

18. *Ibid.*, p. 30.

19. *Immanente Ästhetik — Ästhetische Reflexion: Poetik und Hermeneutik II*, ed. Wolfgang Iser (Munich, 1966), pp. 461-84, esp. pp. 473 and 480: "For a concrete interpretation and for a judgment of the quality of the poem, it is not enough to provide its structural principle and to describe Apollinaire's poetic technique. A series of ambiguities is not yet a compelling whole. If this whole provokes an ever newer interpretation on the basis of the technique in which it is unfolded, then this interpretation is neither accidental in its details nor free from a fundamental orientation that is compellingly provided through the construction of the text. The first reading provides this compulsion through the suggestion of the rhythm. The interpretation must give itself over to this medium in which the poem moves" (Dieter Henrich). This interpretation is translated as "Group Interpretation of Apollinaire's 'Arbre,' " in *New Perspectives in German Literary Criticism*, ed. Richard E. Amacher and Victor Lange (Princeton, 1979), pp. 182-207.

20. On this, see my *Alterität und Modernität der mittelalterlichen Literatur* (Munich, 1977), esp. pp. 10 ff.

21. In the following, alliteration or phonetic recurrence is indicated through a raised hyphen.

22. According to the famous definition given in the *Projets de Préface* of 1859/60, in *Oeuvres*, ed. de la Pléiade (Paris, 1951), p. 1363.

23. *Fusées XVI*, in *Oeuvres*, p. 1187.

24. *Projets de Préface*, p. 1363.

25. With "world-anxiety" [*Weltangst*], I refer to W. Schultz, in *Aspekte der Angst*, 2nd ed., ed. H. von Ditfurth (Munich, 1977), pp. 14 ff. By it I understand that manifestation of anxiety that distinguishes itself from object-related fear, which probably began with the Christian religion, and which perhaps is to be related to the expectation of the

Last Judgment, in that it is the singularization of real anxieties into an indeterminate world-anxiety.

26. *Mon coeur mis à nu*, LXXXVII, in *Oeuvres*, p. 1225.

27. M. Milner, "Poétique de la chute," in *Regards sur Baudelaire* [Colloque de London, 1970], ed. W. Bush (Paris, 1974), pp. 86-107.

28. Here I rely upon C. Pawelka, who worked out this discovery in reference to its literarization in his Constance dissertation *Formen der Entwirklichung bei Franz Kafka* (1978).

29. I thank Karl Bertau for the reference that this figure of allegorical personification is nonetheless already to be found in the older German tradition with Heinrich Frauenlob, as, for example, in his *Marienleich*; cf. *Deutsche Vierteljahrsschrift* 40 (1966), p. 324.

30. Gaston Bachelard, *La terre et les reveries de la volonté*, cited by R. Galand, *Baudelaire: Poétique et poésie* (Paris, 1969), p. 335.

31. According to G. Durand, *Les structures anthropologiques de l'imaginaire*, cited in R. Galand, *Baudelaire*, p. 335.

32. To my knowledge, the history of Baudelaire's reception has not yet been worked on sufficiently. For advice I have drawn upon: C. Vergniol, "Cinquante ans après Baudelaire," in *La Revue de Paris* (1917), pp. 673-709; Henri Peyre, "La Fortune et l'influence de Baudelaire," in *Connaissance de Baudelaire* (Paris, 1951), pp. 155-78, and *Baudelaire devant ses contemporains*, ed. W. T. Bandy and C. Pichois (Paris, 1957). Of the (none too numerous) interpretations of our "Spleen" poem, the following were relevant to my investigation: Walter Benjamin, "Zentralpark" (1938/39?), in *Gesammelte Schriften* (Frankfurt, 1974), Vol. I, 2, pp. 655-90; R. B. Cherix, *Commentaire des Fleurs du mal* (Geneva, 1949), pp. 269-72; J. D. Hubert, *L'esthétique des Fleurs du mal* (Geneva, 1953), pp. 134-36; Gerhard Hess, *Die Landschaft in Baudelaires 'Fleurs du mal'* (Heidelberg, 1953), pp. 80-82; Sebastian Neumeister, in *Poetica* 3 (1970), pp. 439-54; K. A. Blüher, in *Sprachen der Lyrik* — Festschrift for Hugo Friedrich, ed. Erich Köhler (Frankfurt, 1975), pp. 22-45; and Laurent Jenny, in *Poétique* 28 (1976), pp. 440-49.

33. Cited in Bandy and Pichois, *Baudelaire devant ses contamporains*, p. 13.

34. Cited in the second edition (Paris, 1869), p. 14: "He points not to this side, but to the far side of romanticism—unexplored territory, a sort of prickly and fierce Kamtchatka."

35. *Ibid.*, p. 20: "No one has professed greater disgust for the turpitudes of the spirit and the ugliness of matter. He hates evil as a deviation from mathematics and from the norm, and in his quality of being a perfect gentleman, he scorns it as inconvenient, ridiculous, bourgeois, and—above all—improper."

36. From the *Notes et documents pour mon avocat*, cited in Vergniol, "Cinquante ans après Baudelaire," p. 684.

37. Walter Benjamin, "Zentralpark," in *Schriften I* (Frankfurt, 1955), p. 488; O. Sahlberg, *Baudelaire 1848: Gedichte der Revolution* (Berlin, 1977), p. 26; Wolfgang Fietkau, *Schwanengesang auf 1848* (Hamburg, 1978)—excellent for its precise uncovering of the historical context of *The 18th Brumaire of Louis Bonaparte*, "Napoléon le Petit" and Proudhon's writings; and D. Oehler, *Pariser Bilder 1 (1830-48)* (Frankfurt, 1979), p. 184.

38. Gautier, "Notice," p. 21. Joined to this, Heine is also quoted: "and it is not he who, like Heinrich Heine's philistines, is flabbergasted by the romantic efflorescence of new foliage, and swoons at the song of sparrows."

39. *Ibid.*, pp. 56 and 26: "Everything that distances man and, above all, woman from the state of nature appears to him as a happy invention."

40. *Ibid.*, p. 17: "the obscure fantasies that astonish the day, and everything that the soul, at the bottom of its deepest and last cavern, receives from the shadowy, the deformed, and the vaguely horrible."

41. *Oeuvres*, p. 458.

42. "Baudelaires Rückgriff auf die Allegorie," in *Formen und Funktionen der Allegorie* (Symposion Wolfenbüttel 1978), ed. W. Haug (Stuttgart, 1979), pp. 686-700.

43. On this, see F. Nies, in *Imago Linguae* — Festschrift for Fritz Paepcke (Munich, 1977).

44. See note 42.

45. From the evidence in P. Robert, *Dictionnaire alphabétique et analogique de la langue francaise* (Paris, 1964), S. V. *spleen*: "Our women were formerly ill with gout. . . . The English have *le splin*, or *la splin*, and die of humour" (Voltaire); "since this morning I have had *le spleen*, and such a *spleen* that everything I see when left alone disgusts me deeply. I hate the sun, and hold the rain in horror" (Vigny, *Stello*; here hatred toward nature appears as a symptom of the illness).

46. *Dictionnaire universel du XIXème siècle*: "Human societies, like individuals, have their periods of belief and disbelief . . . peoples become civilized, police themselves, then become refined and ennervated . . . the characteristic symptom of the decline of society is that immense *ennui* shared by all classes and individuals. *Spleen* is the new name, but the phenomenon is not new."

47. Gautier, "Notice," p. 30.

48. *Essais de psychologie contemporaine*, 9th ed. (Paris, 1895), p. 15.

49. *Ibid.*, pp. 18 ff.

50. "Not to forget the main thing, / We have seen everywhere, and without having searched for it, / From the top to the bottom of the fatal scale / The *ennuyeux* spectacle of immortal sin."

51. See my "Baudelaires Rückgriff," pp. 690 ff.

52. According to Hans Blumenberg, *Säkularisierung und Selbstbehauptung* (Frankfurt, 1974), p. 120: "As a willful style, secularization consciously seeks the relationship with the sacred as a provocation. It needs a large measure of the continued validity of the religious sphere of the original in order to achieve an effect, just as 'black theology' can unfold its blasphemous horror only there where the sacred world still exists."

53. Valéry himself testifies to this process of reception in "Situation de Baudelaire" (1924), *Oeuvres* (Pléiade) (Paris, 1957), I, p. 612.

54. "Far from them, see the dead years lean / On the balconies of Heaven, in outmoded dress / Smiling Regret rising from the depths of the waters."

55. *Ibid.*, p. 611.

56. Walter Benjamin, "Über einige Motive bei Baudelaire," in *Schriften* (Frankfurt, 1955), I, p. 458; in the following I rely primarily on "Zentralpark," in *Gesammelt Schriften* (Frankfurt, 1974), Vol. I/2, pp. 657-90.

57. *Gesammelte Schriften*, I/3, p. 1151.

58. H. Steinhagen, "Zu Walter Benjamins Begriff der Allegorie," cited in my "Baudelaires Rückgriff," p. 676; there Benjamin's rehabilitation of allegory in his whole work is extensively evaluated.

59. *Gesammelte Schriften*, I/2, p. 659.

60. *Ibid.*, p. 660.

61. *Ibid.*

62. *Ibid.*, p. 681: "The emblems return as commodities."

63. *Ibid.*, pp. 671 and 676.

64. *Ibid.*, p. 682.

65. In a footnote to "Der Flaneur," in *Charles Baudelaire: Ein Lyriker im Zeitalter des Hochkapitalismus* (Frankfurt, 1969), p. 59.

66. *Gesammelte Schriften*, I/2, p. 669: "If it is fantasy that brings the correspondences to memory, then it is thought that dedicates the allegories to it. Memory brings the two together." On this, see my *Ästhetische Erfahrung*, p. 126.

67. Gerhard Hess, pp. 68, 69.

68. *Ibid.*, pp. 69 and 72.

69. *Ibid.*, p. 81.

70. J. D. Hubert, pp. 134 ff.

71. *Ibid.*, p. 136: "Thus it seems that the first part of the poem represents an allegory of the private life of the poet tormented by the irritations of money and the pains of love, and that the second part symbolizes his situation within the century."

72. *Ibid.*, pp. 105 f.

73. Karl Blüher, p. 23.

74. *Ibid.*, p. 44.

75. *Ibid.*, p. 27.

76. Sebastian Neumeister, p. 441. The key to his interpretation is *Fusées* XXII, where Baudelaire clarifies the *idée poétique* in playing upon the movements of a ship ("which takes part in . . . the regularity and symmetry that are one of the primordial needs of the human mind, as much as complication and harmony are").

77. Thus, for example, the contradictory movement seen in lines 15-24, that on the one hand the disinterest grows to the level of the temporal conditions, while on the other hand the interest in the "I" declines to the level of the four perfect participles.

78. Laurent Jenny, p. 445, where the play of the grammatical person of the lyric subject is summarized as follows: "1. I am not MYSELF. 2. I am distinct from *THEM* in reference to death and the secret (they = desk, pyramid, vault). 3. I am *IT* and *IT* is a place of death (I = cemetery, old boudoir). 4. *IT* is *IT*; I am no longer of this world (it = *ennui*). 5. I see *YOU* become *IT* and this *YOU* is *MYSELF* (you = living matter, granite). 6. Beginning with my doubling, this *IT* sings (it = sphinx)."

79. *Ibid.*, p. 447.

80. *Ibid.*, p. 444.

81. One should also still refer to H. Mehnert, *Melancholie und Inspiration: Begriffs- und wissenschaftsgeschichtliche Untersuchungen zur poetischen 'Psychologie' Baudelaires, Flauberts und Mallarmés* (Heidelberg, 1978). It concerns an investigation, as rich in materials as it is in thoughts, into the iconography and the latent theory of inspiration in Baudelaire, to bring to light their derivation from older psychology, humoral pathology, and doctrines of temperaments. Mehnert's perspective also confirms that Baudelaire's spleen and ennui are no symptoms: "*Spleen* is thus perpetuated *ennui*, and signifies the loss of the *irritabilité* that is potentially stored in *ennui*" (p. 175). On our "Spleen" poem, Mehnert remarks: "The representation of the ossified *cellula memorativa*, the missing 'irritation' clothed in the ambivalent wrap of 'lycanthropia,' the encrusted heart and the whole space of inspiration (the connection between hearth and brain being broken) — these representations can be read out of the text as the 'psychological' substratum of the first fourteen lines" (p. 177). Unfortunately, the aesthetic transformation of this substratum did not interest Mehnert (lines 19-24 are bracketed altogether!), so that no consistent interpretation arises that allows itself to be entered into the history of the reception of our "Spleen" poem.

Index

Index

Cartesianism of, 130; and curiositas, 122-24; and link between things and thinking, 133; negates idealist notion of experience, 130-31; *plénitude* concept of, 130; *poésie pure* of, xvi; and rejection of symbolism, 125; role of Goethe for, 135, 138; significance of "Lust" for, 126-27. *See also Faust*, of Valéry

Verlaine, Paul, 177
Vidal, Raimon, 98
Viëtor, Karl, 94
Villena, Enrique de, 98
Villon, François, 99
Virgil, 96
Vita Nuova, 88
Viviani, 49
Vodička, Felix V., xvii, xviii, 72, 73
Volksbuch, 117, 118
Voltaire, François Marie Arouet, 47, 49, 116

Vossler, Karl, vii

Wais, Kurt, 129
Waltz, Matthias, 103
Warburg school: emphasis of, on tradition, 9
Warning, Rainer, xv, 104
Weber, H. -D., 50
Wellek, René, xxix, 30; and critique of I. A. Richards's theory, 22
"What is and Toward What End Does One Study Universal History?" 5-6
Wimsatt, W. K., xxviii
Winckelmann, Johann Joachim, 48, 49, 50
Wind, Edgar, 44
Work of art: in dialectical structuralism, 108; epistemological significance of, 31-32; historical essence of, 15; as self-mediating event, 31-32. *See also* Literary work
World literature (*Weltliteratur*): canon of, as formation of tradition, 111-12

Hans Robert Jauss is professor of literary criticism and romance philology at the University of Konstanz, West Germany, and is founder and co-editor of *Poetik and Hermeneutic.* He has taught at Columbia, Yale, and the Sorbonne. His writings include studies of medieval and modern French literature as well as theoretical works.

Timothy Bahti is assistant professor of comparative literature at Cornell University, an essayist, and a member of the editorial board of *Diacritics.*

Paul de Man, Sterling Professor of Comparative Literature at Yale University, is the author of *Blindness and Insight* and *Allegories of Reading.*